HQ734 .H869 2001

Holman, Thomas.

Premarital prediction of
  marital quality or
        c2001.

0 1341 0652674 9

2004 03 10

D1446274

Humber College Library
3199 Lakeshore Blvd. West
Toronto, ON   M8V 1K8

Premarital Prediction of Marital Quality or Breakup

Research, Theory, and Practice

Humber College Library

LONGITUDINAL RESEARCH IN THE SOCIAL AND BEHAVIORAL SCIENCES

An Interdisciplinary Series

Series Editors:

Howard B. Kaplan, *Texas A&M University, College Station, Texas*
Adele Eskeles Gottfried, *California State University, Northridge, California*
Allen W. Gottfried, *California State University, Fullerton, California*

A Continuation Order Plan is available for this series. A continuation order will bring delivery of each new volume immediately upon publication. Volumes are billed only upon actual shipment. For further information please contact the publisher.

Premarital Prediction of Marital Quality or Breakup

Research, Theory, and Practice

1 6020l

Thomas B. Holman

Brigham Young University
Provo, Utah

with
Paul James Birch
Jason S. Carroll
Cynthia Doxey
Jeffry H. Larson
Steven T. Linford

Kluwer Academic / Plenum Publishers
New York, Boston, Dordrecht, London, Moscow

Library of Congress Cataloging-in-Publication Data

On file

ISBN 0-306-46326-1

©2001 Kluwer Academic / Plenum Publishers, New York
233 Spring Street, New York, New York 10013

http://www.wkap.nl/

10 9 8 7 6 5 4 3 2 1

A C.I.P. record for this book is available from the Library of Congress

All rights reserved

No part of this book may be reproduced, stored in a retrieval system, or transmitted in any form
or by any means, electronic, mechanical, photocopying, microfilming, recording, or otherwise,
without written permission from the Publisher

Printed in the United States of America

*To Dean and Leatrice Holman, who prepared me
so well for marriage; to Linda, who has kept me despite
my self-inflicted premarital deficiencies;
and to Wilmer and Geneva Nicholls,
who prepared her for the task.*

Associates

Paul James Birch , Center for Family Preservation and Progress, Salt Lake City, Utah 84157

Kent R. Brooks, Religious Education Department, Ricks College, Rexburg, Idaho 83460

Jason S. Carroll, Department of Family Social Science, University of Minnesota, St. Paul, Minnesota 55108

Cynthia Doxey , Department of Church History and Doctrine, Brigham Young University, Provo, Utah 84602

Jeffry H. Larson , School of Family Life, Brigham Young University, Provo, Utah 84602

Steven T. Linford, Spanish Fork LDS Seminary, Spanish Fork, Utah 84660

David B. Meredith, Utah County Sheriff's Office, Spanish Fork, Utah 84660

Joseph A. Olsen, College of Family, Home, and Social Science, Brigham Young University, Provo, Utah 84602

Suzanne F. Olsen, School of Family Life, Brigham Young University, Provo, Utah 84602

Clifford Jay Rhoades, Ammon Senior Seminary, Idaho Falls, Idaho 83401

Robert F. Stahmann, School of Family Life, Brigham Young University, Provo, Utah 84602

Preface

This book should be of interest to scholars, researchers, students, and practitioners alike. Scholars, researchers, and students of personal relationship development will recognize in this book the first serious attempt in over 40 years to do a large-scale, longitudinal study of premarital factors that predict premarital breakup and marital quality; they should also appreciate our attempt to develop a theoretical rationale for predicted paths and to test those paths with the best available statistical tools. Practitioners—while generally not as interested in the intricacies of the statistical results—will find much that is useful to them as they help individuals and couples make decisions about their intimate relationships, their readiness for marriage, and how to increase the probability for marital success. Teachers, family life educators, premarital counselors, and clergy will find helpful our "principles for practice," particularly as described in Chapter 9, as they teach and counsel couples in any premarital situation.

My interest in the development of relationships from premarital to marital probably began when I got married in 1972 and started to notice all of the characteristics my wife and I brought from our respective families and how our "new beginning" as a married couple was in many ways the continuation of our premarital relationship, only more refined and more intense. My professional interest began when I did my doctoral dissertation in 1981 on premarital predictors of early marital satisfaction (the results of that study are reported in Chapter 8). While I have done research on other topics throughout my career, I have always returned to premarital relationship development as my main interest for my research and outreach efforts.

Collection of the premarital data began in 1989 when the PREParation for Marriage (PREP-M) Questionnaire became available for use by teachers, workshop leaders, clergy, premarital counselors, and researchers. At that time my cocreators of PREP-M (Dean Busby and Jeff Larson) and I knew we wanted to do a longitudinal study; the issue was simply when and how. An initial follow-up study was done with a small sample of those who had taken PREP-M and been married about one year (see Holman, Larson, & Harmer, 1994; Rhoades, 1994). Because the results were encouraging (see Chapter 8 for a full report of those results), I began planning a larger, longer-term follow-up. Funds were eventually obtained to begin the process of finding the sample members and getting them to participate in a follow-up.

I initially invited my doctoral student, Steve Linford, to participate in the research and write his dissertation from the data gathered. Steve was in charge of data collection, and another of my graduate students, Dave Meredith, entered all of the data. Dave was also invited to use the data and he wrote his master's thesis from it. After conceptualizing each chapter, I invited other faculty colleagues or graduate students to join as coauthors of various chapters and as joint coauthors of the entire book. I have a very strong bias that coauthored works are almost always better than single-authored works, and that one of the most important aspects of training and mentoring graduate students is to get them involved in the research and write-up—and to acknowledge their help by including their names on articles, chapters, or books to which they contribute, even if they were serving as paid graduate assistants for some or even all of the time.

Therefore, what evolved was a book with me as the "chief author" and with all of the others contributing to one or more of the chapters. Some contributed to their chapter(s) and also read all of the other chapters and made contributions, gave suggestions, and helped me integrate many ideas, eliminate overlaps, and edit the numerous voices to sound like one. Those who helped write one or more chapters and who helped with the whole book are listed on the title page as my coauthors. Those who chose only to contribute to their chapter have their names listed in the Contents and Associates pages, as well as at the beginning of their chapters, but not on the title page.

I express appreciation to the Family Studies Center, the Religious Studies Center, and the Department of Family Sciences for their financial support of this project. Special appreciation is given to JoNell Pabst, operations manager of the Marriage Study Consortium (which distributed and scored PREP-Ms), and Mark O. Jarvis, who both made essential contributions to the completion of this project.

                                                                          Thomas B. Holman

Contents

5. Individual Characteristics Influencing Marital Quality 105

Thomas B. Holman, Jeffry H. Larson, and Joseph A. Olsen

6. Social Contexts Influencing Marital Quality 119

Cynthia Doxey and Thomas B. Holman

Appendix A: PREParation for Marriage (PREP-M) 233

Thomas B. Holman, Dean M. Busby, and Jeffry H. Larson

Appendix B: The Relationship Quality Follow-Up Study 251

Thomas B. Holman and Steven T. Linford

Appendix C: A Century-End Comprehensive Review of Premarital Predictors of Marital Quality and Stability 263

Steven T. Linford and Jason S. Carroll

1

Premarital Factors and
Later Marital Quality
and Stability

Thomas B. Holman and Steven T. Linford

> *Most hypotheses have not been tested in ways that might refute the
> theory or elaborate on basic propositions. Examination of
> mediation, moderation, or intervening mechanisms, for example, is
> rare, as is research that links variables from different theories or
> disciplines. Instead much of this research has been atheoretical,
> tending to examine idiosyncratic groups of variables for their direct
> effects on marital outcome at some later time.... Consequently, the
> past 50 years have witnessed marital outcome, but not deeper in that
> the resulting findings have not advanced the field toward a more
> thorough explanation of marital development.*
>
> —Karney & Bradbury (1995, p. 22)

How is it that some marriages seem to be "happily-ever-after" marriages
(admittedly after a lot of blood, sweat, and tears), while others seem doomed to
unhappiness and divorce? Could we have predicted before marriage who would
end up happy, unhappy, or divorced? And even if we could have predicted, could
the couples heading for unhappiness have changed the future of their marriage by
changing their attitudes and actions in the present? Most premarital educational
and therapeutic interventions are based on the assumption that understanding and
improving premarital individual and couple interactional factors can influence both
the quality and the stability of the marital relationship. However, our understanding of the mate selection process and the aspects of it that are related to later

marital outcomes is very limited (Cate & Lloyd, 1992; Whyte, 1990). Thus, the central objective of this book is to clarify how premarital factors are related to premarital breakup and to later marital quality and stability.

The task of understanding and predicting the course of relationships from premarriage to premarital or marital breakup, or to intact marriages of varying degrees of quality, is complex. In this chapter we build a theoretical model of the development of premarital and marital relationships. We extend this model in Chapter 3 to include relationships that broke up—premaritally or maritally.

But before proceeding with this task, we wish to recognize and highlight the types of "real-life" situations that are represented in the statistical models we tested. What follows are four vignettes of couples, all of whom started out determined to live happily-ever-after. But after 8 years of marriage only two are still living that dream; one couple is divorced and another is in a stable but unhappy marriage. Could this have been predicted from the premarital qualitative data they gave us about their courtships? We invite the reader to try to predict which two are happily married, which couple is still married but unhappy, and which is divorced. In the epilogue we will reveal each couple's status.

Four Vignettes

Heidi and David[1]

Heidi is the fourth child of six. Her father was a dairy farmer who became an invalid early in Heidi's life. He eventually died and Heidi admits, "I basically don't remember my father." Her mother never remarried. Heidi remembers "sibling rivalries and fights," but she primarily remembers her childhood as "very happy" and her family as very close. Her high school years were not unhappy, but she has no longing to go back to those years.

David also came from a dairy farm family background. The second oldest in a family of four children, David learned to work long, hard hours. The small farming community he grew up in had been settled by his great-grandfather and bore his family name. David felt that this small-town life, surrounded by friends and relatives, helped him have "a pretty 'top of the world' opinion of things." "The town was named after the family, and when I was a little kid I always figured I was going to grow up and be President of the United States." He remembers his childhood as:

> Very happy, very happy. A few traumatic growing up moments, but nothing that had a long-range effect as far as putting a gloomy mood on my life or anything like that.

David was active in sports in his junior high and high school years and saw himself as a "model child" who liked being accepted by adults.

> But there were still a lot of times when I wanted to cut loose and just be one of the other kids type of thing and felt like I had this certain image that I had to keep up and that sometimes kind of clashed. Of course, there was always the adolescent sexual change that was a little bit bothersome because I felt like it was a subject that I couldn't talk about with my parents.... It was a bit of a frustrating period in that sense.

David remembers his parents as having a good marriage.

> They got along very well, I'm not sure of the word I'm looking for ... a peaceful existence, happy. As far as their relationship, I felt like it was very good, and it gave me a feeling of solidness and I think that is what I wanted when I got married.

The only thing he would want to do differently in his own marriage is to talk more openly about the sexual aspect—and not be a farmer. He felt his dad wasn't able to participate in school or athletic events with him because of the never-ending farm chores; and David did not want to miss out on some of the important events with his children that his father had missed with him.

Heidi and David met in Washington, D.C., where they were both in a semester-long internship program with their university. While there, they spent some time together with their large group of fellow students and had had just one date with each other. Heidi liked David right from the start.

> I was impressed from the very beginning. I thought he was a very capable person that just emulated a lot of qualities that I had always. So I guess that I was probably more interested in him in Washington, D.C. than [he was] in me. I was quite interested right from the beginning, but then when we left Washington and there was no contact, I didn't really expect to hear from him again or anything.

Their next encounter was a chance meeting on the university campus that led Heidi to invite David on a picnic that afternoon. Now David became interested.

> When I went up that weekend ... to see the other girl and that didn't work out and Heidi and I spent the afternoon up Willow Creek Canyon, I felt a very strong attachment and allowed things to develop then. I guess you could say that is when I really got hooked and started pursuing the matter.

After a few months of dating and seeing each other regularly, David popped the question. "I was looking," he says. "I found out I wasn't satisfied just to do the fun dates with different girls. I was starting to settle into a 'seek for a companion' pattern." Heidi, on the other hand, didn't expect things to move so quickly.

> He caught me off guard.... It is just that it took me by surprise. I always thought while I was dating him, there was never any question in my mind, that he would be a good father and a good husband and all those kinds of things. I was strongly physically attracted to him and that was a big part, too. But it did take me by surprise when the question actually came.

Heidi felt she needed to "take more time to see if that was what I really wanted." Eventually she decided it was, and they became engaged.

But the engagement was not without its ups and downs.

> David: There was one time when I thought she was going to break it off and I got very worried. I guess it was during Christmastime; I guess there was just a lot happening and I guess I had been taking her for granted a bit. Because we were engaged and I guess I'm kind of the merit-badge-type person, once you get one thing earned then that is out of the way and you move on to the next. I guess it was just a foregone conclusion that things were going to work out, and I had to learn that you have to always have that respect and that appreciation there ... I guess things had gotten too routine or I put her off too many times or whatever, and she got very emotional and laid the law [down] to me.

> Heidi: I had made these concessions and rearranged my schedule so that we could do this or that or another, and it seemed like just before we were to do it he would call and cancel it. The one that really got to me was when he canceled because he needed to run his sister's roommate [someplace], and when I got in touch with him what he had actually spent his time doing was running his sister's roommate out to a party!

But David shaped up, and as Heidi said, "I'd have to admit that the rest of our engagement was pretty smooth sailing."

Both Heidi and David felt that knowing each other's family was important. As Heidi said,

> I think we were fortunate in that my family was living right there so he saw me interact with all my brothers and sisters and my mother and whatnot. I remember that I went home with David at Thanksgiving time and that's the first time I really saw him interacting with his family members. I think you learn an awful lot about a person when you see how they treat their brothers and sisters and their mother. I remember thinking that I learned more about David in that weekend almost than before, and it all confirmed all of the positive feelings that I had, but at the same time it could have been a very negative experience, too.

Despite David's sister's interference on that one occasion, family and friend support was strong for their relationship. David's family, including his mother (his father was deceased by that time), siblings, and a number of cousins who had met Heidi, approved wholeheartedly of her. They felt she "fit right into the family." Heidi's family and others were equally supportive: "My mother loved David right from the start."

Linda and Steve

Like Heidi and David, Linda and Steve met at the university. They first met at a church-sponsored outing. Linda remembers that "he was very nice looking and just very clean looking." They then happened to meet in the hall on the way to class a few weeks later and talked. Steve remembers:

> I've always been rather shy around girls when I first meet them, so I didn't ask her out. We met accidentally again and it turned out to be at our apartment, where three other guys and I were living. We talked a bit longer and I asked her out then.

They were both very impressed with the other right from the start.

> Steve: Linda is a very nice person. She is vivacious and fun and she's pretty. And we got along very well. And as I mentioned before, I've always been a little shy and have not found it easy to meet a lot of girls, and I think that also had something to do with it. We talked easily and well together.

> Linda: I think [I was attracted to] his stability. Steve is a very gentle man, and is a very even tempered man. His nature is just very even tempered. And I just find him very gentle, and he represented to me a lot of the qualities that I thought I wanted in someone. So that's probably why I was attracted to Steve. He came from a nice, strong *family* background . His family is very strong, and he has a real devotion to them. He is very respectful to his parents and he is very tied to them.

The relationship developed very quickly, and they were engaged within 1-½ months after meeting. Although they made the decision to marry quickly, they decided to have a long engagement since, as Steve says, "We really didn't want to rush into things." Steve didn't recall the engagement as having any ups and downs, but Linda recalled some concerns she had during the engagement period.

> I was young, I had just turned 19. So I was really young. And I had gotten, not pressure, but outside influence about getting married and having a family. But we

had problems I think from the time we started dating. We're a lot different in some ways and maybe the same in some ways. Neither one of us is real good at communicating. I think I'm a little better now and Steve is a little better now than when we were dating. But neither one of us discussed feelings; we would get full of anger and neither one of us would talk. Also, Steve came from a very strict family background, and I came from a very wild background.

Linda's family background was indeed "wild" compared with Steve's. Linda was the oldest of two children. Linda's parents divorced when she was young, and Linda's mom went on to marry two other men. Each relationship was fraught with difficulties: "All three times she has married alcoholics and womanizers and that kind of thing." Linda's childhood was filled with emotional abuse from stepfathers and frequent family disruptions.

Steve, on the other hand, was the middle child of three children in a stable, affectionate family. "My parents were kind of rock-solid, stable people." He remembers his childhood as "carefree. It was a lot of fun."

Steve's parents were supportive of the marriage, but Linda's mother and stepfather were having serious problems and so she didn't want Linda to get married—ever. Despite Linda's occasional doubts, they proceeded to marry. Whatever doubts Linda had, she and Steve concluded they could work it out.

We assumed we could work it out. And I think we both wanted to get married. We felt we were doing the right thing. We were doing what we were supposed to do.

Jean and Bob

Bob was born in a small town that we will call Spring City, the youngest in a family of six children. Most of the children, now adults, worked in the family retail business. Bob remembers his childhood as happy, and his parents as being very involved in his life—attending sports events he was in, having family vacations, playing family games at home. His teenage years were what he called "stable." He had a few disagreements with his parents, but all of those were minor. He felt the biggest influence on his life was the respect he had for his parents.

So it was always, I guess, respect for them, knowing that I can't do anything to hurt them. That would be the last thing in the world I'd want to do. That was a big motivating force in my life.

Bob's mother died a few years after his marriage, but he remembers his parents' marriage as:

... always very happy. I never recall once ever hearing Dad raise his voice to Mom, or Mom raise her voice to Dad. [Their relationship] was always very touching, very tender.

Jean's father was born in the same small farming community Bob grew up in, but his employment took him to a large urban area on the West Coast of the United States. Jean was the youngest of a large family. Her memories of her early years are sparse. She does remember the atmosphere at her grammar school as being characterized by "a criminal element," but she neither felt threatened by, nor inclined to join in, the petty criminal behavior. Her high school years, however, are a source of many great memories.

They were great! They were the best [laughs]! They were really a lot of fun ....
I always had a lot of boyfriends, or boys that wanted to be friends, and a lot of girlfriends—I was a cheerleader and I was involved in a singing group. I was real involved. I had a great four years in high school.

Jean saw her parents' marriage as good, but not exceptional. "They never argued in front of the kids, ever. On the other hand, they weren't that affectionate in front of us either." She felt she was quite close to both parents, indeed, probably closer than most or all of her brothers and sisters. She was the only one of her siblings who could deal with her mother's bluntness and opinionatedness. "I can say, 'Mother, slack off a little....' My brothers and sisters just can't do that."

Even though Jean was not reared in the town of her father's birth, and had few occasions to visit it, it was in Spring City where she and Bob met.

Bob: We met here in Spring City actually, at a wedding reception of one of our good friends—one of my best friends married one of her best friends. The bride asked her to be at the book, and I was an usher.

Jean: My father was originally from Spring City, ... so while I sat at the book, some of my relatives would come through and I wouldn't know who they were but Bob would say, "Here comes your Aunt Maude and Uncle so-and-so." They'd come up to me and say, "Well, hello, how are you? I'll bet you don't know who I am." And I'd say, "Sure I do. You're...." And so we kind of had a good time. In fact, as we went through the line at the very end, we had gotten so well acquainted and joked all night, that as we walked through, Bob introduced me to the line as his fiancee; and I had a boyfriend back at [college]! One of my uncles took me aside and said, "You could do a lot worse!" And I said, "I don't even know this person!" But it was funny.

All joking aside, Bob's feelings for Jean developed very quickly. He explained it this way:

I've never been one for, you know, love at first sight, but really, sincerely, we really felt, we both commented on it, how comfortable and how, just at ease and how right we felt with each other.

They soon began seeing each other regularly and although no long-term commitments were made, they recognized that they "had a lot of the same values ... and interests." But it was not all smooth sailing. Jean graduated from college in December and went home some 800 miles away for Christmas. Their relationship was "pretty serious, but nothing earth-shattering yet, at that point." She still had the other boyfriend. She was also eager to look for a job, yet did not want to have a job that kept her a long distance from Bob, who was still at the university.

The old cliché "absence makes the heart grow fonder" was true in Jean and Bob's case. Jean quickly broke it off with the other boyfriend, and within a week of being home, called Bob and asked him to come out. He flew out the day after Christmas. At this point they both started thinking that a permanent relationship could evolve. They drove back to the university town ("That was the shortest 16 hours I've ever had!") and from then on, "we were together about every night, and things started to click...."

But there were still obstacles to marriage. Jean notes,

And it was really hard for me to decide whether I really wanted to make an effort to put out applications in the places I wanted to work or whether to come back to [the university town with Bob]. And that was really hard for me. I didn't want to be one of those dumb, you know, stereotypes, and it was just hard.

Jean decided to give the relationship a few months, so she took "a couple of short dumpy jobs." Then she went home with Bob for the first time, and the relationship almost ended.

Bob: I brought her home to Spring City ... to meet the family. So here's this girl that's been brought up in the [large urban] area, and she pretty much knows that if she marries me, she's going to be living here in Spring City. I had the [family] business to come back to. We came home Saturday night, and I showed her the town in about 5 minutes [laughs], and she was, I guess, really having some second thoughts.

Jean: I mean, it's 3 hours from nowhere! And his parents were quite a bit older. I thought they looked like grandparents ... 'cause he's the youngest and his dad was 50 when he was born. And so it was hard for me to think my children would probably not know their grandparents. That happened to me and I've regretted it all my life, or felt bad.

Bob: When I took her back [home] that night, she said, "I don't know if you want to come out and see me for a few days; let me think some things through." I was devastated! But I think I let her go for about a day, and I couldn't handle being away from her. We had a long talk, and she kind of aired her feelings about Spring City. I don't know, but as soon as the air was cleared, as soon as she got that off her shoulders, it was like it was okay again.

Jean: I guess I thought, "Well, I guess it really doesn't matter. I know I love this person, and I could really marry him." It wasn't really an issue of where we had to live anymore, I just realized that the few days not seeing him made me realize.

While Jean had some concerns about the small-town atmosphere and the age of Bob's parents, factors external to their relationship enhanced the movement toward marriage. They both felt lots of support from friends—not just support but enthusiastic support ("go for it!"). Family were also supportive. Bob said it this way about his parents:

They were supportive.... They always valued my judgment so they were always supportive of my decisions, or what I was thinking. I think it was an added plus [that they knew Jean's family].

From then on things went pretty smoothly until the marriage several months later, except for a few days of uncertainty about his employment when Jean's father offered Bob a job in his company out on the coast. But they decided to stay with Bob's family business, and they married the next June.

Becky and Josh

Becky is the youngest of three sisters. Her father was a dentist with a thriving practice; her mother worked part-time in the dental office. Becky remembers her parents' marriage as very close and loving, but with one feature she didn't like:

A good marriage. My mother waited hand and foot on my father. As I remember, my dad would come home from work and pick up a newspaper in the living room and my mother would say, "Leave your father alone. He's had a hard day at work; come help me with dinner"— which she still does. Their marriage—my father rules and reigns literally. A little more so than what I would have wanted.

Becky remembers family life as enjoyable and close.

We always went on a lot of trips, vacations together as a family. My father is a retired dentist and my mother would work with him, and we girls would go also and work for him and with him. So we did a lot together as a family. My mother is a very caring, loving person. We would always, at least once a week, go visit our grandparents, her parents. My father's were deceased. So I think we were a close family.

Her one major disagreement with her mother was over her mother redecorating Becky's room while she was away. The verbal fight they had was so unusual and traumatic that Becky still feels bad about it. She has always been very close to her mother, and loved her father, even if she didn't feel as close to him.

> I was very close to my mother and I was always trying to please my father. I loved him. I didn't feel really close, but I could just sit down and have a regular conversation. We can have good conversations together as long as we don't bring up a few things. Religion. He is not active [in our church], and that would cause conflict when you brought up religion. My mother is "ssssshhhh."

Josh, on the other hand, was the oldest of seven children in a family with very limited financial means. His father was a school teacher and his mother a home-maker.

He remembers his early childhood as being full of frequent family moves and living in a mobile home, small apartments, and even with his maternal grandmother while his father finished college. He remembers himself as very shy, which he attributes to his family's frequent moves and his lack of ability in sports. He saw his teenage years as fairly uneventful. "I was just a pretty good kid.... I had a pretty basic desire to want my parents to be proud of me."

Josh remembers his parents' marriage as a "happy marriage," but not without conflict. However, they seemed to handle their conflict fairly well.

> I don't recall ever seeing my parents really argue in a heated manner in front of us so that we could hear them, ever. They can talk fairly civilly, and you know they are not happy with each other, and now ... I recognize where my dad struggles with certain things because of differences of opinion about something. [But] it's a very happy marriage.

Becky and Josh met through one of Josh's sisters, with whom she was friends in high school. One Christmas, when Becky brought a gift to her friend, she met her friend's brother, Josh, who had just returned from 2 years abroad. They talked for a few minutes. Becky notes how they met:

> So from there, actually, his sister lined us up and she said, "Josh wants to go skiing," and she said to Josh, "Becky wants to go skiing," and so she kind of planned it, and I taught him how to ski and then from there it progresses.

They were both impressed with the other right from the start.

Josh: She was attractive and she was friendly, a very kind person, and I talked to her and we talked very easily. That was the most important thing right off. We felt very comfortable with each other, and we could communicate.

Becky: I thought he was very nice and understanding and interested in me for what I was. I didn't have to be a fake person or anything. I thought that was nice.

They began dating regularly after the Christmas holidays when both of them returned to the same university. Becky's good impression of Josh continued to grow:

He seemed to be interested in me, the real me, and I felt comfortable around him, and he still liked me and I was very attracted to that. He had the same values that I did and I liked the family situation that he came from. I noticed how his father interacted with his brothers and sisters and liked that and thought perhaps he would be the same way. So that interested me.

But internal and external factors were soon to intervene and temporarily sidetrack the budding relationship. Josh was increasingly interested in Becky and was tired of the game aspect of dating. So he decided to tell her exactly how he felt.

Josh: I think I kind of made a mistake in our relationship in that I decided, "I'm tired of this. I'm going to be really open with a girl." So we hadn't dated all that long and I was open with my feelings that this could be right and I wasn't trying to ask her to marry me, and I just said, "Do you feel the same way?"

Becky: I felt the same way he did, but I was getting scared thinking, what was I doing? So I said, "Wait." I was writing [to another young man] and so I was quite confused, and I wanted to cool things off and become a little more level-headed.

Josh thought there was more to it than another man or that she was feeling rushed.

She was only a freshman and she was in an apartment of girls and it happened that I had dated one of the girls that was in her apartment. This girl felt like she'd like to date me [still]. All these other girls in the apartment, they were good friends with her and they were into wanting to have a lot of fun and stuff and so between this one girl and the other girls, I think they started talking to her [Becky] and discouraging her and after about a month or two of dating I guess it finally got to her. To me it seemed like out of the cold blue she just— We were going to go skiing and she just said, "Forget it and get lost, and don't bother calling me again." To me it was like out of the clear blue and it just devastated me. I don't think I had ever felt so sorry about a girl before.

Josh continued to feel "totally desperate," and he needed to talk to someone. So he went to his clergyman and received the counsel to "play it cool." If it was to be, she would come around. They didn't see each other for a couple of months, but as the semester drew to a close, Becky let Josh know she would like to see him again. They began to see each other again occasionally. This time he kept his feelings to himself a little more, and within a few months they were engaged.

Other than the roommates who interfered, other significant others approved of the relationship. Becky's mother felt Becky was too young, but despite that misgiving, Becky's parents felt Josh would be a "good husband" and were support-I've of the relationship. Josh also felt nothing but support from both friends and parents.

During the engagement, Josh also worried a little about Becky's youth, about her family background, and her dependence on her family. But neither Josh nor Becky seriously considered ending the engagement. They married the next September.

Four couples, four courtships, four marriages. As we show later, two couples are happily married after 8 years, one couple struggles in a stable but unhappy marriage, and one couple is divorced.

These stories of real couples, real courtships, and real marriages bring us back to the questions posed in the first paragraph of this chapter. Is it possible to predict with any precision who will have a happy, stable marriage, who will have an unhappy but nevertheless stable marriage, or who will divorce? Moreover, can this knowledge be used to initiate change and growth in these or similar premarital couples?

The Conceptual Model

We begin by developing the conceptual model of premarital predictors that is tested in subsequent chapters. This involves several steps. After giving a brief history of the study of premarital prediction research, we provide a basic review of the quantitative and qualitative research on premarital predictors. This review looks at research relating to direct, simultaneous, and indirect premarital influences on marital outcomes, and also at possible gender differences.[2] We then build a theoretical case for which premarital factors should be important predictors and how they should relate to each other and the outcome variable of marital satisfaction. Finally, we present our general conceptual model that is the basis for the more specific conceptual and statistical models that follow in each of the later chapters. Each chapter begins with a more comprehensive and in-depth review of research on specific factors and of appropriate theoretical arguments for the specific factors under investigation in that chapter. Our purpose is to begin to paint a portrait with broad strokes in this overview; Chapters 3–8 will then add the detail to the picture. To finish this chapter we provide a brief overview of the chapters to follow.

A Review of the Research

Family science has a long history of attempting to predict marital quality or marital stability from premarital factors. Indeed, the preponderance of the earliest and most influential research about families cited the premarital prediction of later marital quality and stability as an important if not primary goal (Adams, 1946; Burgess & Cottrell, 1939; Burgess & Wallin, 1953; Terman & Oden, 1947). By the 1960s, Bowerman, in the influential *Handbook of Marriage and the Family* (1964), called for a theory of marital prediction. The interest in premarital prediction waned considerably in the 1970s and early 1980s, probably because of the need for theory development in this area and researchers' interest in studying alternatives to traditional marriage. In the late 1980s and 1990s, interest in strengthening marriages premaritally and maritally, and in preventing divorce, has increased. There has been a grass-roots and political interest in strengthening marriages (Popenoe, Elshtain, & Blankenhorn, 1996). Researchers have also shown renewed interest as evidenced by three recent extensive reviews of literature pertaining to the topic (Cate & Lloyd, 1992; Larson & Holman, 1994; Wamboldt & Reiss, 1989). Furthermore, a focus group on premarital research and education was recently organized within the National Council on Family Relations.

In all three of the reviews cited above, premarital predictors are organized under three general categories that correspond to family background factors, individual characteristics, and couple interactional processes. We conceptualize the research findings that we have presented in this book into the same broad domains with one exception: We conceptualize current social contexts, including social networks, as a separate domain (Duck, 1993).

Thus, at the most general level, we conceptualize a model of four broad premarital factors: family background factors, individual characteristics, couple interactional processes, and current social contexts as they relate to one aspect of marital quality—marital satisfaction. We will develop our conceptual model further by reviewing research that will help us hypothesize the strength of those direct relationships, the strength of each when taking the other factors into account, and the possible indirect relationships. Since three reviews of over 50 years of research have recently been completed by Wamboldt and Reiss (1989) using only the longitudinal studies, and by Cate and Lloyd (1992) and Larson and Holman (1994) using both longitudinal and cross-sectional research of premarital predictors of marital quality or stability, we will simply summarize their findings where appropriate. We also cite any important reviews or research not cited by these earlier reviews noted above or completed since they were published. Also, since we propose a model with indirect as well as direct relationships, we discuss any literature that demonstrates or hints at joint or indirect influences on marital quality. When we speak of direct relationships, we mean that a premarital factor has a direct, unhindered relationship with marital quality. An indirect relationship is when a premarital factor's relationship with marital quality goes through another premarital factor. A simultaneous, or joint, effect means two or more premarital factors are seen as simultaneously relating to marital quality, that is, both factors together predict marital quality better than either alone.

Family Background

Direct Effects. After reviewing 12 longitudinal studies of premarital predictors of marital quality, Wamboldt and Reiss (1989, p. 319) propose that "the research supports the hypothesis that family-of-origin experiences persist into later life and influence later development." However, they acknowledge that little is known about what actually persists and how it influences marital quality.

All three of the reviews cite research showing that the quality of the parents' marriage, including whether they divorced and the amount of conflict they had, the general family emotional environment, and the quality of the parent–child relationship, are all important factors. Amato and Keith's (1991) meta-analysis of 37 studies of parental divorce and adult children's outcomes, including marital quality, although not cited by any of the reviewers, makes an important contribution. They suggest that research shows that parental divorce has a small but significant relationship to children's marital quality.

A few researchers have used both partners' family background data to predict marital quality. Wilcoxon and Hovestadt (1985) found that the more similar the couple's family-of-origin experiences premaritally, the better was their marital adjustment, especially in the early years of marriage. Couillard (1990), however, found that similarity was related to high adjustment only if both members of the couple came from families with high levels of emotional health. Indeed, when the families of both individuals were low in emotional health, the lowest marital adjustment of the nine couple family-of-origin combinations resulted.

Holman, Larson, and Harmer (1994) compared husbands' family-of-origin characteristics with wives' marital satisfaction, and vice versa. They found that husbands' premarital perceptions of their home environment predicted both the husbands' and wives' marital satisfaction, but that wives' home environment did not predict either wives' or husbands' marital satisfaction.

Simultaneous Effects. Very few studies have attempted to test the direct effects of family-of-origin factors while simultaneously testing other premarital predictors of later marital quality. Whyte (1990), in his cross-sectional study of Detroit wives, is the only recent study of which we are aware that examines multiple influences. The wives' remembrance of family conflicts retained a fairly strong relationship to marital quality even when individual characteristics, couple characteristics, and social network influences were controlled. Bentler and Newcomb (1978), testing a model containing both family-of-origin structural variables and individual characteristics, found individual characteristics to be more predictive of marital success.

Indirect Effects. Only one study has attempted to demonstrate an indirect empirical link between family background and a marital outcome. Wamboldt and Reiss (1989, p. 328) suggest that "family-of-origin experience may influence current relationship satisfaction *because* prior family experience influences the consensus-building processes in the new relationship. In other words, the effect of origin family experience may be mediated by aspects of the couples' current interactional process."

A number of studies support the possibility of a link between family-of-origin factors and the other categories of predictors. For example, Amato (Amato, 1994; Amato & Keith, 1991) has shown that events and relationships in the family of origin are related to psychological well-being of adult offspring. Holman and Li (1997) have shown that early family relationships are related to the perceived support received for the current relationship. Doxey (1994), qualitative study of parents' effect on the adult-children's current marital quality, found that the adult-children's current support from parents for their marriages was generally a reflection of the long-term parent–child relationship, and that poor current relationships with parents negatively affected adult-children's marriages.

Clinical theory and clinical reports are replete with the idea that family-of-origin processes affect whom one chooses to marry and the quality of subsequent interpersonal (marital) relationships (e.g., Doherty & Baptiste, 1993; Framo, 1981; Benson, Larson, Wilson, & Demo, 1995). Using arguments from socialization theory and social constructivist theory, Wamboldt and Reiss (1989) provide an explanation for how socialization in the family of origin might influence subsequent intimate relationships, which in turn influence marital outcomes.

Gender Issues. Several of the longitudinal studies of premarital predictors of marital quality or stability discuss gender differences. Wamboldt and Reiss (1989) conclude that the studies show that women who continue to have a good relationship with their mothers after marriage do better in their own marriages. For men, greater closeness to mothers does not make much difference in the early years, but "closeness" predicts marital difficulties later in their marriages, and for both men and women, greater closeness to fathers improves their marriages. Wamboldt and Reiss's research further showed that greater levels of "expressiveness" in both the man's and woman's family of origin positively affected the woman's, but not the man's, later relationship quality. Conflict in the woman's family of origin was the only family background variable to affect the man's later relationship satisfaction. The findings of Holman et al (1994) (noted earlier) also suggest gender differences.

In light of the available research, we hypothesize that family-of-origin factors such as family demographics, family structure, and family processes are related to adult children's early marital quality. This relationship is maintained even when controlling for the influences of other factors. Furthermore, it is hypothesized that much of family-of-origin factors' contributions to marital quality are indirect through their influence on the other premarital factors of individual characteristics, couple interactional processes, and social network support.

These processes probably work differently for males and females. Both Wamboldt and Reiss (1989) and Holman et al. (1994) found that the spouse's family-of-origin characteristics had an effect on one's current marital satisfaction. Wamboldt and Reiss interpret their findings to mean that as "relationship architects," women's family-of-origin experiences and interpretations of their (male) spouses' families of origin were most important in both their own and their spouses' current relationship satisfaction. Holman et al. (1994), however, found that the higher the premarital evaluation of family of origin by the males, the higher were the females' and males' own marital satisfaction. The females' premarital evaluations of their origin families had almost no relationship to their own marital satisfaction or to the males' marital satisfaction. Given these findings, we will construct models that not only compare one's own family of origin to one's own marital satisfactions, but also will include the spouse's family-of-origin's relationship to one's own marital satisfaction.

Individual Characteristics

Individual characteristics are those features of each respondent that represent how the individual perceives him or herself. The aspects of the individual most frequently investigated are personality features, and attitudes, beliefs, and values associated with relationships.

Direct Effects. The research is consistent in demonstrating that some present personality attributes and beliefs premaritally affect later marital quality. The most commonly noted individual features include neuroticism, depression, impulsivity, and sociability or shyness (Cate & Lloyd, 1992; Larson & Holman, 1994). The healthier the personality feature, the greater is the marital satisfaction (Larson & Holman, 1994). Dysfunctional beliefs have also been shown to be negatively related to marital satisfaction (Kurdek, 1993). Conventional attitudes also seem to have some effect on marital outcomes, especially for men (Kelly & Conley, 1987; Whyte, 1990).

Simultaneous Effects. A few studies have tested the simultaneous effects of individual traits and other premarital predictors. As noted above, Bentler and Newcomb (1978) concluded that the personality variables were considerably more predictive of marital success than were family background variables. On the other hand, in Whyte's (1990) cross-sectional study of Detroit women, none of the personality traits were correlated with marital quality when other variables were included.

Indirect Effects. No studies were found that test the indirect effects of individual factors on later marital quality or stability, but there has been a great deal of theoretical speculation about this possibility. Kelly and Conley (1987, p. 36) speculate that findings that interpersonal processes like communication and conflict resolution are related to later marital quality actually are "the outgrowth of the personality characteristics of the partner." More recently, Duck (1993, p. ix) has argued that the way individuals "construe relationships ... affects the expectations and interaction patterns that the individuals bring to future relationships." Andersen (1993, p. 3) conceptualizes personality traits as "schemata," that is, as "knowledge structures that derive from prior experience and organize the processing of past and future information" He goes on to say that these personality variables, or self-schemata, "are more than summary cognitions of one's prior behavior. They actively determine the future of one's social relationships" (p.18). Communications research has shown that personality traits and communicational predispositions have substantial effects on people's relational behaviors.

Gender Issues. Larson and Holman (1994, p. 231), after reviewing all of the studies on how individual attributes affect marital quality and stability, conclude that there are "few apparent sex differences in personality effects on later marital outcomes." But they noted that none of the studies they reviewed specifically attempted to assess gender differences, so that final conclusions about such differences are premature. A related study by Holman and Li (1997) examined the relationship between numerous premarital factors and perceived readiness for marriage and found that females' perceptions of their physical attractiveness were positively related to their perceptions of the quality of the premarital couple's communication quality, which in turn was positively related to a sense of readiness to get married. Male's perceived physical attractiveness, however, was unrelated to communication quality, but was directly and negatively related to their readiness for marriage. While this study is not a test of our outcome variable of marital quality or stability, it indicates that there may be gender differences in how personality or individual factors influence other premarital or marital outcomes.

Given current research and theory, we hypothesize that individual factors, including personality features, individual beliefs and attitudes, and individually constructed ways of construing relationships, are directly related to early marital quality. We hypothesize that this relationship will be maintained even when controlling for the influence of other premarital factors. We also believe that these individual characteristics indirectly influence the marital criterion variable through the intervening influence of couple interactional processes. We further hypothesize that these individual factors will influence the intervening variables and marital criterion variable differentially by gender.

Social Context

Allan (1993) suggests that the approach to the study of personal relationships has evolved over the last 15 years from an emphasis on individual constructs to a focus on interactional and relational processes. In both instances the focus has been on discrete units, either the individual or dyad, and ignored the wider social contexts in which the individual and dyad are embedded. In research on marital quality, the same trend has occurred. In the 1980s and 1990s, most attempts to predict marital quality focused on dyadic interactional predictors (e.g., Filsinger & Thoma, 1988; Markman, 1981; Markman, Duncan, Storaasli, & Howes, 1987). More recently, however, there has been a renewed emphasis on the influence exerted on relationships by social, cultural, and contextual factors (e.g., Duck, 1993).

Among the three recent reviews of the literature, only Larson and Holman (1994) reviewed social context factors. They conceptualize such demographic factors as age at marriage, education, income, occupation, class, race, and gender as indicators of the sociocultural context of developing relationships, rather than as traits of the individual. We concur with this conceptualization. For example, we see race and gender as sociocultural designations that have meaning given them within a cultural setting, rather than having an innate meaning simply by virtue of race or sex. These variables, perhaps more than others, need to be seen as standing proxy for sociocultural meanings. Thus, while we briefly review the literature on these factors and use them in our analysis, we attempt to see beyond the proxy and understand how individuals see themselves or believe others see them because of their membership status in some group. For example, Whyte (1990, p. 206) found that blacks in his sample "had notably more brittle marriages than whites." The explanation, however, may be found in what it means to be black in a predominantly white culture, not in innate racial differences.

Direct Effects. Of these indicators of social context, only age at marriage is consistently and highly related to later marital quality (see Larson & Holman, 1994, and Whyte, 1990, for references and a more complete discussion). Since teenage marriages are considerably less stable than marriages contracted when persons are in their 20s, and marriages contracted in the mid to late 20s (after about age 25) may not experience any increase in stability (Burr, 1973; Vaillant, 1978), this relationship may be curvilinear. Other sociocultural indicators, such as premarital education, income, occupation, and race, continue to have some predictive ability, but usually drop out of the prediction when other premarital factors are entered into the equation (Whyte, 1990).

Social network support is another aspect of the social context that affects later marital outcomes. Support from family and friends for the relationship premaritally has long been seen as a predictor of later marital quality (Burgess & Wallin, 1953) and continues to have predictive power (Booth & Johnson, 1988; Cate, Huston, & Nesselroade, 1986; Kurdek, 1991; Whyte, 1990).

Simultaneous Effects. There is limited support for the social structural variables retaining much predictive power when other factors are taken into account. In Whyte's (1990) study, only age at marriage and race retained significant partial correlations to indicators of marital quality, and only age was significantly correlated with marital problems.

Parental support premaritally is related to marital quality, even when other factors are controlled. Whyte (1990) found premarital parental opposition to be positively related to marital problems, but unrelated to a marital quality measure.

Indirect Effects. No studies have specifically tested a model with premarital social contexts being related to marital quality through some intervening premarital variable. However, there is indirect support for such a relationship. If we assume that premarital relational factors are related to later marital quality (as we will demonstrate below), then research and theory on social contexts' relationship to premarital interactional and relational quality allows us to suggest such an indirect relationship. In an 18-month longitudinal study, Sprecher and Felmlee (1992) found perceived support from family and friends to be a positive predictor of subsequent premarital relationship quality. Holman and Li (1997), in a multivariate study of perceived readiness for marriage, found the contextual indicators of family and friend support to be the best predictor of marital readiness. Family and friend support is *directly* related to readiness for marriage, but also indirectly related through couple interactional processes. A recent qualitative study by Klein and Milardo (1993) showed that "third-party influences" affected relationship competence, including the management of interpersonal conflict. Indeed, the whole volume of which Klein and Milardo's chapter is a part (Duck, 1993) emphasizes that "forces creating and shaping relationships are not purely individual and dyadic" and that "competency in relating is in part assessed in terms of exterior societal criteria as well as those based on individual satisfaction or desire" (Duck, 1993, p. x). That is, people judge their relationships by reference to criteria current in society and that "third parties" are guardians of these criteria. By these third parties' moral commentary on relationships, they enforce these criteria and norms. Since marriage is a social contract, not merely an individual one, it must meet individual *and* social standards of assessment.

Gender Issues. No studies have specifically looked at gender differences in how social contexts relate to later marital quality.

We hypothesize that premarital social context factors, both structural variables and indicators of social network support, are related directly to marital quality. We further hypothesize that social context is also indirectly related to marital quality through the intervening factor of couple interactional processes.

Dyadic Interactional Processes

While the quality of the couple's premarital communication is the most obvious and the most studied couple interactional process, other premarital couple processes are also important for predicting later marital quality. Also included are social homogamy, interpersonal similarity, and interactional history.

Direct Effects. Homogamy, or social similarity, is generally viewed as a static structural quality of a relationship, but we view it as a socially constructed process that is a part of couple interaction. Lewis and Spanier (1979), in their comprehensive review of factors related to marital quality and stability, found some support for the relationship of premarital homogamy to later marital quality. Research since their review continues to show limited support for premarital social similarity being related to later marital quality (Antill, 1983; Birtchnell & Kennard, 1984; Kurdek, 1991).

Similarity of premarital attitudes, values, and beliefs is related to later marital quality (Fowers & Olson, 1986; Holman et al., 1994; Larsen & Olson, 1989). Research on gender-role similarity indicates that marital quality is greater not only when gender-role attitudes are similar, but also when both members of the couple emphasize either androgynous or traditional feminine role orientations.

Three aspects of couples' interactional history—length of acquaintance, premarital pregnancy, and premarital cohabitation—have an effect on later marital quality. Generally speaking, the longer the acquaintance, the better is the subsequent marital quality. Whyte (1990) found premarital pregnancy to be related to his measure of marital problems, but not to marital quality. From Larson and Holman's (1994) review of the literature, they conclude that cohabitation is related to lower subsequent marital quality.

A number of empirical studies have shown that premarital couple interactional processes are related to later marital quality. Several longitudinal studies show that the positivity or negativity of communication premaritally is related to later marital quality (Filsinger & Thoma, 1988; Markman, 1979, 1981; Smith, Vivian, & O'Leary, 1990). However, in a partial replication of Markman's earlier studies noted above, Markman et al. (1987) found only limited support for the relationship between premarital communication and later relationship quality. Kelly, Huston, and Cate (1985) found that premarital conflict was related to marital maladjustment for females, but not for males. There is also in the personal relationship literature substantial evidence that aspects of interactional processes are important antecedents of relationship quality (Dindia, 1994; Keeley & Hart, 1994; Planalp & Garvin-Doxas, 1994).

While most predictive studies look only at premarital couple communication and conflict, Wamboldt and Reiss (1989) suggest that the process of achieving consensus and a sense of a couple identity is also important. They found that couples who later constructed a shared view of the relationship ground rules had greater relationship quality.

Simultaneous Effects. Whyte (1990) found that the recalled level of feeling in love was related to both marital quality and problems, even when other premarital and marital factors are controlled. Markman et al. (1987) and Smith et al. (1990) found that introducing personality factors into the equation substantially reduced the predictive power of communication and conflict variables.

Indirect Effects. Interpersonal process variables are generally seen as the most contiguous to the marital quality variable; therefore, no indirect effects are indicated.

Gender Issues. While some have found gender differences (Filsinger & Thoma, 1988), others suggest that gender differences may be very small (Dindia, 1994). However, if as some claim (e.g., Wood, 1993), "talking" is the feminine mode of relationship maintenance, while "doing" is the masculine mode, we would anticipate that premarital communication indicators would be more related to marital quality for females than for males.

Given the above, we hypothesize that a number of features of premarital couple interactional processes, including homogamy, interpersonal similarity, communication, and consensus or agreement building, are directly related to subsequent marital quality, even when controlling for other premarital factors. We further hypothesize that the relationship should be stronger for women than for men.

A Review of the Theory

Bowerman (1964, p. 236) suggested more than 35 years ago that improvements in our ability to predict premaritally later marital outcomes depended more on theoretical development than on improved research techniques. The goal of this section of the chapter is to review theoretical strides made since Bowerman's suggestion and to provide a theoretical basis for the conceptual model studied in this book.

Bowerman's call for a theoretical basis for premarital prediction of marital quality did not go unheeded. Burr's (1973) groundbreaking book on family theory contains a chapter on "The Effects of Premarital Factors on Marriage," and referred specifically to Bowerman's call for theory. Burr synthesizes some theoretical propositions from the atheoretical prediction literature, reworks some of the few attempts that had been made to develop theory, and integrates these propositions (Burr, 1973, pp. 103–104). Burr demonstrates the usefulness of symbolic interactionism and reference group theory in explaining some of the previous findings in this area, particularly concerning individual characteristics, homogamy, and social networks. He hypothesizes direct relationships between the premarital factors and the marital outcomes but does not hypothesize any connections between the premarital factors themselves.

Lewis and Spanier (1979) reviewed the research about factors, including premarital ones, related to marital quality and stability, and did some ordering of the factors. They suggest that social exchange theory provides a framework for organizing all of the diverse findings. They view premarital factors as specific indicators of "resources." Like Burr, they conceptualize the premarital factors as having a direct relationship to marital quality, but do not order the premarital factors in regard to each other, nor do they connect the premarital "resources" to any marital factors except marital quality.

Burr, Leigh, Day, and Constantine (1979) critiqued Lewis and Spanier's approach and suggested that symbolic interaction theory provides a more elegant and parsimonious explanation of the findings regarding premarital predictors of later marital satisfaction. They suggested that the premarital factors were best conceptualized as indicators of the quality of role enactment, which they defined as "how well a person performs a role relative to the expectations for the role" (p. 58). Burr and his colleagues contributed three important pieces to the theorizing. First, they suggested that understanding the partner's quality of role enactment as well as ego's quality of role enactment was important for understanding self's marital satisfaction. This was the first time this had been suggested, and it had good theoretical grounding. Second, they added an idea not discussed in Lewis and Spanier concerning consensus about relevant role expectations, and suggest that consensus about how roles are to be performed is an important antecedent of marital satisfaction. Third, they clearly called for multivariate analyses and suggested that some factors are going to be more strongly related than others in a multivariate situation.

By the next decade, family systems theory and related theoretical perspectives, especially as conceptualized in family therapy theory, began to be used to explain how premarital factors influence marital factors. Hoopes's (1987) cogent review of assumptions of family systems theorists, researchers, and therapists demonstrates how much this perspective blends ideas from a family systems perspective, a family developmental perspective, and an ecological perspective.

Marks (1986) developed his theory of triangles, which comes in part out of his thinking about family systems, and more specifically out of family therapist-theorist Murray Bowen's ideas about triangles. While Bowen's ideas provided the foundation for Marks's theorizing, he deviated substantially from it. Instead of a triangle composed of three people in interaction with one another as with Bowen's theory, Marks conceptualizes each partner in a marriage as having three "corners" or points of reference (p. 3). The "inner corner" is the self corner, consisting of feelings, thoughts, impulses, and images. In this corner, people create a "marital paradigm" of notions about what marriage is and should be. It is formed primarily through observation of and interaction with parents. This marital paradigm profoundly influences whom we marry and how well we function in marriage. This corner then contains all of the remembered experience and meanings derived from experiences in the family of origin, and the personality characteristics that a person brings into a couple interaction. This inner corner is closely related to the partnership corner, so much so that they sometimes are indistinguishable. It is in this partnership corner where a person must coordinate the partner's space, movements, and general existence. The third corner consists of other important points of reference outside the self and the partner such as children, job, school, religion, kin, and so on. From Marks's point of view, all three corners must be understood if we are to understand the dynamics of marriage. Using qualitative data, Marks both induced the theory and found support for the ideas deduced from Bowen and others. Marks's systemic theory of triangles helps us see that issues from several levels of analysis need to be taken into account and that these levels are inevitably interconnected.

Wamboldt and Reiss (1989) combine family systems and a developmental approach in an attempt to clarify how some marriages succeed while others fail. After reviewing the major longitudinal studies of premarital-to-marital prediction, they conclude that three major categories of factors have emerged—background factors, personality characteristics, and interactional processes. They chose to limit their theorizing to the background factors and interactional processes. They suggest two complementary, but distinct, explanations for why family background factors continue to influence the ongoing marital relationship. One is the traditional socialization model that suggests that "individuals learn a repertoire of behaviors and cognitive and emotional schema" (p. 321) that they carry relatively unchanged into adult relationships, including marital relationships. The second explanation is a social constructivist model that takes a more developmental and systemic perspective, "and thereby acknowledges more possibility for change within the lifespan of individuals and between the generations" (p. 321). The key difference between the two perspectives is that while the socialization model assumes a great deal of continuity between what is learned in one generation (parent to child) and how one relates in the succeeding generation (adult child with his/her marital partner), the social constructivist model posits that it is not the family background per se that is important, but what one does in the present with that background. This latter model allows for change in interactional processes, especially in the case of marriage, since marriage is seen as the most important "second chance" for individuals to change how they relate intimately with others.

Cate and Lloyd (1992), in their book *Courtship*, also discuss premarital factors' influence on later marital outcomes. They take a developmental perspective when they say they believe that what happened in the courtship "sets the foundation for the later quality and stability of marriage," and that "courtship is, after all, the first (and perhaps most crucial) stage of the family life cycle" (p. 2).

Larson and Holman (1994) hold that an "ecosystemic perspective" is the most useful for organizing the research on the development of relationships from premarital to marital. This ecosystemic perspective "helps us understand a couple in the mate selection stage of the life course as a developing system that can and does respond to influences from within and without the system. The relationship develops at a number of levels, including the individual, couple, and contextual levels" (p. 229). They were the first to suggest the need to try to understand theoretically and empirically, the direct, indirect, and joint influences of the various classes of premarital factors related to later marital outcomes.

The most recent effort at making theoretical sense of this area is by Karney and Bradbury (1995). Their interest is in the longitudinal course of marriage, not just premarital to marital. They review a total of 115 longitudinal studies of marriage, including all of the premarital-to-marital studies we have reviewed. They note that any theoretical perspectives applied to "the longitudinal development of marriage" (p. 4) must account for changes over time. They review what they perceive as the four major theoretical perspectives used to explain variation in marital outcomes: social exchange theory, behavioral theory, attachment theory, and crisis theory. They do not include the interactionist perspectives, psychoanalytic views, and systems theory perspectives because, "despite their relevance to understanding marriage, [they] have not been as influential in shaping research" (p. 7) as the other four perspectives. Then after reviewing the findings of the 115 longitudinal studies, they create a model that integrates prior theory and research: a vulnerability–stress–adaptation model of marriage. For our purposes, the most important part of their model is the factor they call "vulnerability." They use attachment theory to suggest that "stable personality characteristics" developed premaritally, and ideas brought from the family of origin contribute to one's ability to deal with stressful events and how well couples adapt to difficulties in marriage. Interestingly, they do not discuss couple premarital interactional processes although they review many of the same studies we do regarding these factors.

Karney and Bradbury (1995) indicate that the theoretical perspectives they review do not specify the relationships among the variables thought to predict marital outcomes, but, like Larson and Holman (1994), they argue that much needs to be done if we are to understand marital development over time.

Our own theorizing is in line with much of what has been done recently. Our theory is most fundamentally a developmental theory and at its core makes assumptions consistent with a developmental perspective. Our own theory is developmental because most fundamentally our theorizing emphasizes the dimensions of time, change, and continuity (Klein & White, 1996). We assume, with family developmentalists, that developmental processes are inevitable, that all of the elements in and around the marital system change with time (Klein & White, 1996), and that the theory must encompass many levels of analysis (Klein & White, 1996; Rogers & White, 1993). Ours, then, is a theory of marital development, specifically of the development of the marital relationship from premarital to marital.

We also draw from the human development perspective, especially when looking at individual changes over time and the parent–child relationship. This perspective assumes, as Bretherton (1993, p. 280) says, that "parent and child operate as a co-developing two-person system embedded within also developing family and societal systems. Individual differences in the co-development of parent and child depend on the unique characteristics each brings to the initial relationship, as well as on the relationship patterns they co-create as each influences the other." From within this perspective we draw on two developmental perspectives that are most useful for conceptualizing the parent–child relationship: attachment theory and human ecology theory.

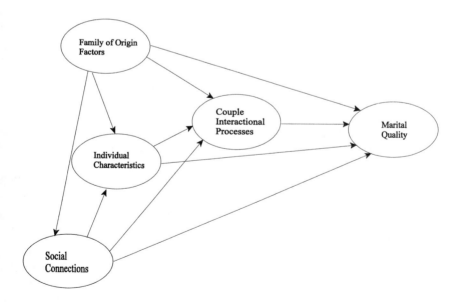

Figure 1.1. General model of premarital factors relationship to marital quality.

The General Conceptual Model

The path model in Figure 1.1 reflects graphically all of the theoretical reasoning and empirical findings about premarital factors that influence later marital outcomes, as discussed above. Figure 1.1 represents our general conceptual model and is the basis for the more specific conceptual models that follow in each of the data chapters.

Overview of Book Chapters

Chapter 2 presents the assumptions guiding this book and information on the sample and methods used in the study. We clarify where we stand in three areas. First, we explain our fundamental beliefs about marriage and family life. Second, we explain some of our fundamental assumptions about the research process and deal with the sticky philosophical issues of what is real, how we come to know what we think we know, and the best ways to generate knowledge. Third, we attend to the issue of the usefulness of the knowledge we have generated. We deal with the issue of change—how people change and if they really can. In other words, we must come to grips with the fundamental issue of free will and agency. Furthermore, once we explain our theory of change and agency, we then note the limits for change based on the type of knowledge we have produced.

In Chapter 2 we also describe our sample, both premaritally and maritally. We discuss how the data were collected and discuss each variable analyzed in the data chapters (except for Chapter 3 on breaking up, where different variables were used; those variables will be discussed in that chapter). Lastly, we discuss our analytic approaches and especially our use of structural equation modeling and LISREL 8.

Chapters 3–7 present findings from our study. In Chapter 3 we look at who broke up and why they believe they broke up. We also investigate how premarital factors help us understand the differences between those who broke up premaritally, those who divorced, those who married and are dissatisfied, and those who are married and are highly satisfied. Then, in Chapters 4–7, we take an in-depth look at the premarital factors of family-of-origin processes, individual characteristics, social contexts, and couple interactional processes as they relate to marital quality. Each chapter describes previous theoretical and empirical work as it relates to the premarital factor in question. We present the univariate, descriptive statistics for the variables under discussion, then offer the bivariate correlational analyses for examination. Finally, in each chapter we develop one or more multivariate models, statistically analyze each, and discuss the findings.

Chapter 8 also presents findings, but it is unique in that it uses samples not used in the other chapters. This chapter shows the results of four different longitudinal studies of premarital predictors. The first three studies use different samples than the one used in the rest of the chapters. The fourth study is from the sample discussed in the rest of this book. This last study brings together all we learned from the data analyses in Chapters 4–7 and tests a total model of premarital prediction of later marital quality.

Chapter 9 is a presentation of "principles for practice," based on our review of the research and the findings presented in this book. It includes summary tables and brief summary statements that should be particularly useful to family life educators, premarital counselors, clergy, and others who work with couples contemplating marriage. The chapter also contains recommendations for future research.

The epilogue informs the reader of the marital outcomes of the four couples introduced in Chapter 1 and how our model can be used to explain what happened to each couple. An invitation is also made to researchers and practitioners to use our premarital assessment questionnaire (the RELATionship Evaluation, or RELATE) and participate with us in studying and strengthening relationships.

Endnotes

1.   All names and other identifying information have been changed. All quotes are taken from a qualitative study of marriage done by the senior author in 1987. All of the couples married in 1979.

2.   A direct relation is when the premarital variable is seen as directly relating to the marital criterion variable. A simultaneous relationship is when the premarital variable under consideration is seen as having a direct relationship to the marital criterion variable, *simultaneously* with another premarital variable. For example, family of origin *and* individual traits both have direct and unique relationships with the marital criterion variable. An indirect relationship is when one premarital factor is seen as having an important relationship to the marital criterion variable *indirectly through* another premarital variable. For example, social contexts are related to couple interactional processes which in turn are related to marital satisfaction.

2

Assumptions and Methods

Thomas B. Holman and Steven T. Linford

> *At the beginning of our marriage, I was very unsure of myself and because of my unstable family background, I tended to feel that my instincts were wrong. I expressed disagreement but would usually go along with my husband. I sulked a lot and harbored a lot of resentment. After a baby and 2 years of marriage, I couldn't do it anymore and desperately wanted to divorce and escape. But some miracle we pulled through and have learned a lot about ourselves and each other. I feel I have come a long ways in exerting myself in expressing my opinions which means I sulk and pout less.*
>
> — Female respondent

> *Already many of our friends who were married around the same time are divorced. This is very sobering. Could it happen to us? Is it just luck? Why are we together and others aren't? I think the information the PREP-M gave us was very valuable. I know it's no guarantee, but it certainly helps you take your decision to marry more seriously and gives you some good tools to help make it work.*
>
> — Female respondent

Burr and Klein's (1994) introduction to their study of family stress and coping aptly summarizes the dilemmas of research, including research about relationship issues, in our postmodern era.

> Doing research in the social sciences in the 1990s is more complicated than it was a few decades ago. In the simpler era, we only worried about methodological

concerns such as clear hypotheses related to a theoretical idea, defensible design, sampling, measurement, and appropriate statistical analysis. In recent years, however, many more scholars have raised concerns about more fundamental issues that deal with philosophical assumptions, metatheoretical perspectives, and previously unrecognized biases such as insensitivity to gender differences. Now we also need to be concerned about such fundamental issues as the assumptions we make about reality, whether objectivity or certainty are possible or desirable, and whether we are searching for law-like statements about cause and effect. We also now realize the importance of clarity in stating the ultimate goals or objective of our research. (p. 8)

Our observation is that many, if not most, empirically oriented researchers simply ignore the dilemma and continue to publish empirical research as though unreflected positivism were still unquestioned in the scholarly and research community. Indeed, the fact that most empirical pieces can continue to be published with little or no reflection on underlying assumptions suggests that many reviewers, editors, publishers, and readers are still able to ignore the issue and not suffer overwhelming scholarly rebuff. Leaving out the entire "methods" section would be unthinkable, but leaving out the "assumptions" section is still apparently acceptable. While there are probably a number of reasons for this, what is important here is that we are persuaded by statements like Burr and Klein's, and by our reading of theoretical and philosophical literature, that we cannot with good conscience ignore some of the issues about assumptions.

We will therefore explicate our assumptions about marriage and family, the research process, and practice. We will not provide an extensive rationale for our assumptions, but will refer the readers to references that undergird our assumptions.

Although Tom Holman did the bulk of the writing of this section of the chapter, all of the authors have read it carefully and expressed their fundamental support for the assumptions. Indeed, I (Tom Holman) asked the various coauthors to help with the book based to some extent on my perceptions that their own assumptions were similar enough to mine to allow us to work together. Certainly we are not an "undifferentiated mass" of similar assumptions, but in general we were able to agree on the section that follows.

Assumptions

Assumptions about Marriage and Family

The very research questions we explored in this work make evident some of our assumptions about marriage. We were interested in studying factors that help us understand why heterosexual couples break up and, even more, why they stay together and how they maintain high-quality marital relationships. We were interested in premarital predictors of later relationship status and quality because we value marriage; we want to know more about these issues so we can strengthen marriages. We believe that stable, high-quality marriages are good for the individuals involved, the children who may come of their union, the communities they live in, and the society and civilization of which they are a part.

This does not mean that we do not acknowledge that there is a great deal of diversity in the ways people establish and maintain intimate relationships. We are simply saying that, all other things being equal, we believe adults, children, communities, and society are best served by long-term, stable, high quality heterosexual marriages. We understand that many family scholars and family practitioners do not share these views or values. Our purpose in sharing them is not to attempt to persuade others to share our views, but rather to help readers understand the questions asked, the methods used, and the findings presented within the context of the authors' assumptions about these things.

We believe there is a great deal of philosophical and empirical support for our position (see Abbott, 1981; Bellah, Madsen, Sullivan, Swidler, & Tipton, 1985, 1991; Elshtain, 1982; Etzioni, 1993, 1996; Popenoe et al., 1996). But arguing from a philosophical or empirical position never brings closure; many scholars and researchers could marshal philosophical and empirical counters to our position.

But we are dealing with assumptions here, not what logic or empirical observation "prove." Therefore, we acknowledge that our assumptions are built on more than logical arguments and empirical findings, although this kind of evidence adds to and grounds our assumptions. Most fundamentally, we simply believe these things about marriage and family based on alternative ways of knowing such as intuition, personal experience, and spiritual enlightenment (Burr & Klein, 1994; Madsen, 1966). We agree with Knapp's hermeneutic interpretation of so-called biases, or what hermeneutics calls "prejudices" or "preunderstandings" (Knapp, 1997, pp. 419–420). Rather than "getting in the way," these "preunderstandings are essential for understanding to proceed at all." They are what give meaning to what we do in science and why we do it.

Assumptions about the Research Process

We assume that empirical research is a legitimate way to increase understanding of relationship processes over time. We further believe that such research should be systematic, rigorous, and public. This is not a very controversial stand; many postmodern critics of empirical science agree that such science has its place (Guba & Lincoln, 1994; Slife and Williams, 1995; Knapp, 1997.)

However, we reject the implied determinism, or "efficient causality," of traditional empiricism and positivism. Instead we assume that humans are capable of free-will choices. We accept the argument, taken from the "final causation" perspective, that "even though one must necessarily be determined by one's goals and purposes (final causation), one may nevertheless have the free will ability to formulate those goals and purposes" (Slife & Williams, 1995, p. 217).

We are persuaded by postmodernist thinking that we are inextricably bound and constrained by the past. These assumptions, however, do not lead to the determinism of traditional empiricism and positivism. Instead, we acknowledge the postmodern view of time that is holistic, such that past, present, and future are always simultaneously involved in human action:

> The crucial point is that a postmodern view of time allows for the present (and future) to be constrained by the past and yet also admit possibility. The present is constrained by the past because no present is ever free of past context. For someone to make a meaningful choice in the present, the person must have some knowledge of the choice—the options available, their consequences, and so forth. This knowledge of the choice stems from the past. Indeed, without some past, the person would not even know that a choice was to be made. However, the present is not determined (necessitated) by the past, because the past itself is not determined or necessary. The past, according to many postmodernists, is "alive" and changeable, dependent on the possibilities of present and future contexts. Rather than lawful necessity being the rule of our nature, change and temporality provide better understandings. (Slife & Williams, 1995, p. 218)

However, some might think that a belief in free will, or the agency of humankind to make choices, is incompatible with the longitudinal, predictive, statistical models that are tested and presented in this book. We do not believe so. Free will has its own kind of predictability within the framework of final causality. Prediction is not based on past events that "cause" by necessity the outcomes of the present and future, but rather by the effect of freely chosen goals and intentions. These goals and intentions are responsible for thoughts and actions, and if these goals and intentions are deeply valued, people will maintain some consistency in these goals and choices, and they will therefore influence, in predictable ways, later thoughts and actions. As Slife and Williams (1995, p. 119) say, "This type of predictability is not the past 'pushing' the present behaviors and thoughts; according to teleologists, this is the 'future' in the present 'pulling' them."

Thus, the use of "traditional" data collection techniques, empirical models, and statistical methods is not inconsistent with our more postmodern view of humans. What is important is how we interpret or use the findings that come from our investigations. This leads to a discussion of our assumptions regarding practice.

Assumptions about Practice

It is ill-conceived to think that the results and products of scientific inquiry can have no meaning beyond their implications for theory. While some talk of the distinction between "pure science" and "applied science," we think the distinction is false. It is based on the traditional split between object and observer of traditional empirical and positivist science to which we do not subscribe. Scientific results are always practical or applied, in some way or another. If they were not, our societies would not have supported science and its resultant technology to the extent they have.

Like most social scientists, we approach our research not simply out of "scientific curiosity," but because we hope to learn something that will ultimately be helpful—in this instance, helpful to couples considering marriage. The issue, then, is not whether our findings should or could have practical value, but rather how best to understand our findings, neither understating them nor overstating them, so that they are available and understandable to practitioners who help couples establish and maintain stable, long-lasting, high-quality marriages, as well as to the couples themselves.

Our approach, like our approach to research, stems from some of our basic assumptions about humankind and its capacity to change. As noted above, we believe people have the ability to make choices and that these choices influence thoughts and behaviors in the future. But, unlike many postmodernists, we believe that generalization is possible, desirable, and even inevitable. We agree with Burr and Klein (1994, p. 26) when they say, "It is the body of shared and continually evolving abstract generalizations that are socially constructed that is the most valuable payoff in the scientific method." We are persuaded by Burr's (Burr, Jensen, & Brady, 1977; Burr & Klein, 1994; Burr, Mead, & Rollins, 1973) argument for the usefulness of *general principles*. General principles are general statements that usually have an *if–then* quality to them, the *if* part connoting the part of the process where intervention is most likely to make a difference and create change, and the *then* part connoting the outcome that will result in a fairly predictable way, given variation in the *if* part (Burr & Klein, 1994, p. 26). However, we disagree with Burr that the covariational results of complex statistical analyses do not provide a basis for intervention. We believe we will demonstrate that results from such statistical analyses can produce useful general principles.

Having thus established our assumptions about marriage and families, about the research process, and about practice, we proceed with a discussion of the methods. We describe the sample characteristics, the measures used, the procedure for gathering both the premarital and the marital data, and the primary analytic techniques used. This discussion of methods applies primarily to the models tested in Chapters 4–7 and the last study in Chapter 8. Differences in the sample characteristics, measures used, and analytic procedures in Chapter 3 and the first three studies in Chapter 8 are discussed in those chapters.

Methods

Sample

The sample used in Chapters 4–7, and in the last study in Chapter 8, included 376 couples (752 individuals) who took the PREP-M (PREParation for Marriage) Questionnaire (Holman, Busby, & Larson, 1989) between 1989 and 1993, who were either seriously dating or engaged to be married, who provided tracking information, and who subsequently completed a follow-up questionnaire in early 1997. Table 2.1 contains the premarital and marital demographic characteristics of the sample.

Measures

The PREParation for Marriage Questionnaire (PREP-M) was developed in 1989 from a revision of the Marital Inventories (Yorgason, Burr, & Baker, 1980). The PREP-M is a 204-item questionnaire designed to measure important background and family-of-origin characteristics, personality variables, social context factors, and interactional processes of premarital couples (see a copy of the PREP-M in Appendix A). Since its development in 1989, approximately 13,000 respondents have taken the PREP-M.

The follow-up survey included items directly from the PREP-M, revised items from the PREP-M, as well as newly created items (see a copy of the follow-up survey in Appendix B). Items focused on marital status, marital quality, and marital stability. The criterion variable for this study was marital satisfaction.

Chapters 4–8 are tests of the premarital predictors of later marital quality (satisfaction). Below are listed the latent variables and their indicators used in those chapters. Chapter 3 on premarital and marital breakup does not use structural equation modeling and therefore does not use the latent variables noted below. In that chapter we describe the items and scales used. No further explanation of the latent variables used in Chapters 4–8 is given in those chapters, since all of them are described here below.

The hypothesized predictor and the criterion variables (used in Chapters 4–8) include 16 latent variables: family of origin (4), individual characteristics (4), social support (2), couple interactional processes (5), and marital satisfaction (1). The latent variables, along with their indicators, are found in Table 2.2. The items' coded designations are in parentheses so that readers can find the full item in Appendix A or B.

Following is a description and elaboration of the measures we used for the various constructs included in Table 2.2 and used in the analyses reported in Chapters 4–7 (and Study # 4 of Chapter 8). The measures are grouped according to the five conceptual elements of the conceptual model in Figure 1.1.

Table 2.1. Sample Characteristics

	Premarital		Marital	
	Males	Females	Males	Females
Mean age	22.57	20.86		
Age at marriage			23.98	22.15
Years married:			4.96	4.96
Length of engagement:				
Less than 1 month	2	0		
1 to 3 months	57	48		
3 to 6 months	128	135		
6 to 12 months	93	93		
1 to 2 years	34	44		
More than 2 years	12	10		
Yearly income				
None	16	40	6	84
Under $5,000	167	256	6	40
$5,000–$14,999	155	60	19	38
$15,000–$24,999	26	14	58	54
$25,000–$49,999	11	4	206	132
$50,000 or more	1	0	80	28
Race				
African American	1	1		
Asian	3	2		
Caucasian	357	361		
American Indian	1	0		
Latino	8	6		
Mixed/biracial	2	3		
Other	3	3		
Religious affiliation				
Catholic	45	43	42	43
Protestant	32	37	27	31
Latter-day Saint	286	289	289	292
Islamic	1			
Eastern religion	1	1		
Other	2	3	9	7
None	9	2	8	3
% of respondents who are students	72.6%	82.9%		

Table 2.1. (continued)

Completed education				
Some high school	2	2	1	0
High school	17	11	5	2
Some college/tech	261	271	47	59
Associate's degree	35	41	16	13
Bachelor's degree	57	47	139	247
Master's degree	4	4		
Grad/ professional (uncompleted)			65	22
Grad/ professional (completed)			102	32
Respondents' fathers' education level:				
Elementary school	3	3		
Some high school	10	6		
High school	50	29		
Some college/tech	75	58		
Associate's degree	15	16		
Bachelor's degree	98	106		
Master's degree	65	89		
Doctorate degree	22	39		
Professional	38	26		
Respondents' mothers' education level:				
Elementary school	2	1		
Some high school	7	8		
High school	79	58		
Some college/tech	121	139		
Associate's degree	47	21		
Bachelor's degree	94	115		
Master's degree	20	29		
Doctorate degree	2	1		
Professional	4	1		

Family-of-Origin Factors

Family Structure. Family structure was measured by two items that asked the marital status of the father and the mother while the respondent was growing up. Responses included married (first marriage), divorced or separated and not remarried, husband or wife deceased and spouse not remarried, remarried after a divorce, and remarried after the death of a spouse.

Parent's Marital Quality. Two items asked about the satisfaction of father or mother in their marriage in the home where the respondent grew up. Five responses ranged from 0 = Very Dissatisfied to 4 = Very Satisfied.

Parent–Child Relationship Quality. Quality of relationship between the respondent and his/her parents was measured by three indicators: father/respondent relationship, mother/respondent relationship, and respondent's satisfaction with the family environment.

Table 2.2. Latent Variables and Indicators for Measurement Models

Latent variables	Indicators[a]
I. Family of Origin	
1. Family Structure	Father's family structure (V77)
	Mother's family structure (V79)
2. Parent's Marriage Quality	Father's satisfaction in marriage (V52)
	Mother's satisfaction in marriage (V53)
3. Family's Sociodemographic Background	Father's education (V109)
	Mother's education (V110)
	Father's occupation (V112)
	Father's income (V115)
4. Parent–Child Relationship Quality	Father/respondent relationship (V54–V56)
	Mother/respondent relationship (V61–V63)
	Respondent's satisfaction with family environment (V47–V50)
II. Individual Characteristics	
1. Emotional Health	Respondent feels sad and blue (V126)
	Respondent feels hopeless (V136)
	Respondent feels depressed (V145)
2. Impulsivity	Respondent acts impulsively (V118)
	Respondent has trouble controlling temper (V128)
3. Self-Esteem	Respondent feels he/she has a number of good qualities (V120)
	Respondent feels useless (V124)
	Respondent has a positive attitude toward self (V130)
	Respondent feels he/she is no good (V134)
	Respondent feels he/she is a person of worth (V139)
	Respondent inclined to feel like a failure (V143)
4. Values and Attitudes about the Importance of Marriage	Expect marriage to give more personal satisfaction (V17)
III. Social Support	
1. Social Network Approval	Male's parents' approval of marriage (V190)
	Female's parents' approval of marriage (V192)
	Friends' approval of marriage (V193)
2. Network Connection	Fused parent/child relationship, support of future in-laws (V127, V137, V146, V195, V199)

Table 2.2. (continued)

3. Sociocultural Characteristics	Age at marriage (EL2) Education (V108) Income (V114)
IV. Couple Interactional Processes	
1. Similarity on Values and Personality	Actual similarity of religious beliefs (V3, V14, V25) similarity of morals (V11, V22, V32), similarity of sexual attitudes (V5, V16, V27), similarity of family planning (V4, V7, V15, V19), and similarity of attitude of importance of family (V10, V17, V21, V28, V31) Perceived similarity of emotional health and self-esteem (V126 ,V136, V145, V120, V124, V130, V134, V139, V143) Perceptual accuracy on personality (same items as directly above)
2. Relationship-Enhancing Communication	Empathic/open communication (V121, V131, V140, V125, V135)

The indicator father/respondent relationship was measured by a scale consisting of three items designed to measure frequency of father's demonstration of physical affection, participation in enjoyable activities, and shared communication. Respondents chose from response categories ranging from 0 = Never to 4 = Very Often. The indicator mother/ respondent relationship was a scale consisting of three items that were identical to the father/respondent relationship except for the word *mother*. The third indicator was a scale indicating the respondent's perceptions of parental discipline. The scale contained four items measuring the frequency of father and mother being consistent in discipline and explaining why they were disciplining. The fourth indicator, also a scale representing the respondent's satisfaction with the family environment, was composed of four items that measure respondent's satisfaction in varying aspects of the home environment. The response categories ranged from 0 = Very Dissatisfied to 4 = Very Satisfied.

Individual Characteristics

Emotional Health. The latent variable emotional health in the individual characteristics category was measured by three indicators or items. The items measured the frequency of the respondent feeling sad and blue, hopeless, and depressed. The response categories ranged from 0 = Never to 4 = Very Often.

Impulsivity. The second construct or latent variable in the individual characteristics category was impulsivity, measured by two indicators. Respondents were asked how often they have difficulties because of impulsive acts and how often they have trouble controlling their temper. The response categories ranged from 0 = Never to 4 = Very Often.

Self-Esteem. Self-esteem was the third latent variable of individual characteristics. It was measured by a single scale composed of six items. Respondents rated (1) if they felt they had a number of good qualities, (2) if they felt useless, (3) if they had a positive attitude towards themselves, (4) if they thought they were no good at all, (5) if they felt they were a person of worth, and (6) if they were inclined to feel like a failure. Response categories ranged from 0 = Never to 4 = Very Often.

Expectation of Marriage. Expectation of marriage was measured with the following single attitudinal item: I expect marriage to give me more real personal satisfaction than just about anything else I am involved in. The five response categories ranged from 0 = Disagree Strongly to 4 = Agree Strongly.

Social Connections

Social Network Approval. Social network approval consisted of items asking respondent's perceptions about both sets of parents' approval of the premarital relationship, and of friends' approval of the relationship. Parental approval was measured by two indicators: (1) male's parents' approval of the marriage, and (2) female's parents' approval of the marriage. Friend support was measured by a single indicator: "Our friends approve of our marriage." Responses ranged from 0 = Disagree Strongly to 4 = Agree Strongly.

Network Connection. Attachment to parents was measured by a scale consisting of three items. The items were designed to measure independence from parents, parents who "run" respondents' lives, and respondents' emotional involvement in their families. The indicators had response categories ranging from 0 = Never to 4 = Very Often.

Respondents also responded to two items about how much they liked their future in-laws. The five response categories range from 0 = I dislike her/him very much to 4 = I like her/him very much.

Sociocultural Characteristics. A single indicator measured age at marriage. Age at marriage was assessed retrospectively on the follow-up survey by a single item that allows respondents to fill in the years and months of marriage. Education was measured by one indicator. The indicator assessed the level of education attained by the respondent. The response categories of the education variable range from 0 = Elementary school to 8 = Professional (M.D., J.D., D.D.S.). Income was measured with a single item indicator. The nine response categories ranked from 0 = None to 8 = $70,000 or more.

Couple Interactional Processes

Similarity on Values and Personality Characteristics. There were five latent variables in the category of couple interactional processes. The first latent variable is similarity on values and personality characteristics. Four scales were the indicators of this latent variable. The first indicator is a scale that measures the actual similarity between the couple on the issues of religious beliefs, morals, sexual attitudes, family planning, and importance of family. Personality characteristics, actual and perceived similarity, and perceptual accuracy were computed using the items from the aforementioned emotional health and self-esteem items. An explanation of the difference between actual similarity, perceived similarity, and perceptual accuracy is given in Chapter 7.

Relationship-Enhancing Communication. Relationship-enhancing communication was assessed by (1) the degree to which the respondent understands what his/her partner is trying to say, (2) the respondent's understanding of partner's feelings, (3) the respondent's ability to listen to the partner in an understanding way, (4) sitting down with partner and talking things over, and (5) talking over pleasant things that happen during the day. Relationship-enhancing communication is assessed by two scales. The first was based on the respondent's perceptions of his/her own communication on the five items measuring relationship-enhancing communication. The second scale was his/her perceptions of the partner on those same items. The response categories for the indicators ranged from 0 = Never to 4 = Very Often.

Relationship-Diminishing Communication. Relationship-diminishing communication was assessed by two scales. The first was based on the respondent's perceptions of his/her own communication on six items measuring relationship-diminishing communication. The second scale was his/her perceptions of the partner on those same items. The response categories for the indicators ranged from 0 = Never to 4 = Very Often.

Consensus on Relationship Issues. The latent variable, consensus on relationship issues, in the category of couple interactional processes, was measured by the participant's response to an item that asks, "Most people have some areas where they agree and others where they disagree. How much agreement do you and your partner have in the following areas?" The areas listed were leisure activities, handling finances, religious matters, demonstrations of affection/intimacy, ways of dealing with parents or in-laws, amount of time spent together, and number of children to have. The response categories ranged from 1 = Always disagree to 4 = Always agree.

Couple Identity Formation Processes. This latent variable consisted of three single item indicators: (1) How often have I thought our relationship might be in trouble? (2) How often have I thought seriously about breaking off our relationship? and (3) How often have my partner and I discussed terminating our relationship? The response categories ranged from 0 = Never to 4 = More than six times.

Marital Quality

Marital Satisfaction. The aspect of marital quality addressed in this study was marital satisfaction, "an individual's affective response varying in the amount of gratification with something" (Burr, Leigh, Day, & Constantine, 1979, p. 68). Marital satisfaction was measured using a scale composed of six items designed to assess the level of satisfaction in certain aspects of the relationship (i.e., physical intimacy, love, conflict resolution, relationship equity, quality of communication, and overall satisfaction). Respondents rated their satisfaction by choosing one of five response choices ranging from 0 = Very Dissatisfied to 4 = Very Satisfied.

Procedures

The PREP-M questionnaire was administered primarily in therapy or counseling sessions, or in a classroom setting. Most of the respondents returned their completed questionnaire to their clergy, counselor, or teacher, who sent it to a central location where the instrument was scored, the data stored, and a printout of the results was computed and returned to the respondents. Each respondent gave permission for his/her results to be used in research.

In the summer of 1996, a list was compiled of all couples who were either seriously dating or engaged at the time they completed the PREP-M, who had completed the questionnaire between 1989 and 1993, and who had given consent to participate in a follow-up study. In addition to their consent, each individual provided the name, telephone number, and address of a contact person who would know of their current residence. In the fall of 1996, research assistants telephoned the contact persons and obtained the subjects current addresses. Two different cover letters were prepared for the respondents. One cover letter was specifically written to the premarital couples who we knew had subsequently married each other (based on information provided by the contact persons). The other cover letter was written to those who we were unsure whether or not they had married the individual with whom they had taken the PREP-M. Using the Dillman (1978) method we made four mailings. The first mailing consisted of a cover letter, survey(s), and a return envelope(s). The second mailing, 1 week after the first, was a postcard reminder sent to everyone. The third mailing, 3 weeks after the first, included another cover letter and a replacement survey(s), sent only to the nonrespondents. The fourth mailing, sent 7 weeks after the first mailing, was similar to the third mailing, with the exception that it was sent by certified mail to emphasize its importance. In all, follow-up surveys were sent to 2176 individuals; 1016 individuals returned the follow-up survey. Of still married couples, both members of 376 couples returned the questionnaires, a response rate of 47%.

Analysis

The primary statistical method used in Chapters 4–7 and in last study in Chapter 8, is linear structural equation analysis (LISREL 8). LISREL 8 worked well for this project because the constructs (latent variables) are generally measured by multiple indicators. The statistical program (1) uses the indicators (items and scales) to measure the hypothesized latent variables, (2) conducts a confirmatory factor analysis of the indicators of the latent variables, and (3) computes coefficients for the structural paths between the latent variables. Separate structural models for males and females were tested.

The first step in the analysis process was to test the measurement model. The testing of the measurement models involved specifying the degree to which the observed variables (indicators) defined a construct or latent variable through the use of confirmatory factor analysis. It "reflects the extent to which observed variables are assessing the latent variables in terms of reliability and validity" (Schumacker & Lomax, 1996, p. 64). The relationships between observed variables and the latent variable (lambdas) are viewed as "factor loadings" and interpreted as validity coefficients. A significant lambda coefficient has a *t*-value equal to or greater than 1.96. In addition to the lambda coefficients, LISREL also computes squared multiple correlations for the observed variables which serve as measures of reliability. A squared multiple correlation greater than .10 is considered adequate, with correlations over .20 considered strong.

The next step was to test the structural model. Structural equation models are often diagramed by a path model in which the hypothesized factors are viewed as latent variables. The term *latent variables* is used because these variables are not directly observed or measured; they are inferred. Thus, they must be indirectly measured through the use of observable or *indicator variables*. In testing the structural model, coefficients are calculated that show the relationships between the latent exogenous variables and the latent endogenous variable(s). Coefficients above .10 with a *t*-value greater than 1.96 are considered to be substantively and statistically significant. Also, we computed the squared multiple correlations, or the R^2, which explains the amount of variance in the dependent latent variable that is explained by the independent variable(s).

LISREL 8 provides a number of fit indices that test the fit between the data and the theoretical model. One such method is the chi-square test. A non-significant chi-square (p-value $> .01$) is evidence that the theoretical model fits the data. In addition, if the critical N exceeds the N in the sample, it is hypothesized that the model also fits. Another statistical method that provides evidence of "fit" is the goodness-of-fit index (GFI) and the adjusted goodness-of-fit index (AGFI). The closer the index scores to 1.0, the better is the fit. A score of .90 or above indicates a good fit. The models used in this study all had strong goodness-of-fit indices and adjusted goodness-of-fit indices.

The Strengths and Weaknesses of the Study

In the most recent comprehensive review of the literature on premarital prediction of marital quality, Larson and Holman (1994) note the shortcomings of the research and make recommendations for the future. They recommend six things. First, they note that, too often, researchers have relied on data collected for other purposes. These studies usually do not contain many variables that measure factors critical to premarital prediction. The consequence is that we end up knowing more about demographic factors than family or relationship process variables. That is why Larson and Holman recommend that more research be done with samples specifically designed to test the relationship between the multiple demographic, attitudinal, behavioral, and process variables, and marital quality. Second, they recommend that special emphasis be paid to the use of valid, reliable, multidimensional family process variables. Third, they note that most samples are small, use only one partner, and are atypical in some way. Most samples are of white, middle-class, college students. Larson and Holman call for larger samples, samples consisting of both partners, and less homogeneous samples. Fourth, most studies in the past have been cross-sectional, the premarital data being collected during the marriage at the same time the quality of the marriage is assessed. There need to be more true longitudinal designs where the premarital data are actually collected premaritally and the marital data collected during the marriage. Fifth, since very few studies take into account sex or gender differences, Larson and Holman (1994) suggest that efforts be made to analyze the partners separately by sex. Sixth, most published research has been about one or at most two domains, such as the family of origin, individual traits, social network support, or relationship characteristics and processes. Larson and Holman recommend the testing of multivariate, multidomain models.

This research addresses almost all of the issues raised by Larson and Holman. The premarital data were gathered specifically to study premarital predictors of marital quality. The instrument used—the PREP-M—was developed on the basis of the best research and theory available at the time; its aim was to assess all of the areas previous research had shown to be important. An attempt was made to assess family and relationship processes as well as they can be assessed with paper-and-pencil questionnaires. Our sample size is the largest, since Burgess and Wallin's, of the truly longitudinal studies designed to predict marital quality from premarital factors. Burgess and Wallin's study, published in 1953, actually used data gathered premaritally in the late 1930s and maritally in the early 1940s. Thus, ours is the first large-scale premarital prediction of later marital quality study attempted in over 50 years! Our sample includes only "matched" couples, that is, both members of the couple completed both the premarital questionnaire and the follow-up questionnaire. All of our analyses are performed separately on the wives and husbands. Lastly, our study investigates indicators of all of the important domains noted in Chapter 1 in the review of the literature—individually, in pairs, and together simultaneously. Furthermore, we examine indirect as well as direct effects.

Our most apparent Achilles heel is the composition of our sample. Like many before it, it is largely made up of white, middle-class college students. Some readers might also be concerned with the large percentage of respondents who are members of the Church of Jesus Christ of Latter-day Saints, or Mormons. Therefore, a brief comment about Mormons seems in order. Recent research with Mormon samples that has looked at marriage and family differences in Mormons versus non-Mormons has generally found relatively few differences (Heaton, Goodman, & Holman, 1992; Holman, 1996). Most of the differences between Mormons and non-Mormons are in some selected attitudes and values rather than in actual behavior, although they do differ in a few behaviors. For example, because of Mormonism's clear emphasis on the importance of marriage, and family life, and premarital sexual abstinence, Mormons are more likely to see marriage and family, as well as premarital sexual abstinence as important, and are less likely to have cohabited outside of marriage. But they do not differ significantly from non-Mormons in most areas in how they actually behave in marriage and family relationships. Their marital satisfaction is the same, their contentment with marital and family roles is similar to that of non-Mormons, and their relationships with their children are similar (Heaton et al., 1992). Indeed, the current president of the LDS Church, Gordon B. Hinckley, recently expressed concern about Mormon families' drift toward the mainstream: "I lift a warning voice to our people. We have moved too far toward the mainstream [in our families]" (Hinckley, 1997, p. 69).

However, studies of highly religious Mormons do show them to be more different from non-Mormons than just a normal cross section of Mormons. Holman (1996), in his study of Mormon mate-selection processes, suggests that highly religious American Mormon young adults follow much the same course as other American young adults in mate selection. However, they seem to add unique "twists" to the process, such as attempting to maintain premarital sexual abstinence, and moving through the mate selection process more rapidly than other Americans.

In the analyses for this book we found no difference in the perceived marital quality based on religious affiliation or religiosity. The reader should, however, take into account the composition of the sample when generalizing to another population. The more divergent the population being considered is from our sample, the less confidence they can have in making generalizations. Until more research is done, good theory can help one decide where their population is most likely to differ from our sample. As we will again note at the end of this book, while the data collection techniques, the samples, and analytic procedures used here move this area of research forward immensely, much still remains to be done to assess adequately the premarital prediction of marital quality.

3

Breaking Up before and after Marriage

David B. Meredith and Thomas B. Holman

From a serious premarital relationship:

She acted as if I were a dream come true, then called me on the phone one day and was very rude and gave no explanation. She wouldn't tell me what was going on. It's been difficult to trust or be close to anyone since.

— Male respondent

During an engagement:

With time, I realized this wasn't the person for me. He wasn't setting any goals, or at least striving for them. He was used to having things handed to him with minimal work on his part. It was a tough, painful thing to do to break my engagement.

— Female respondent

In marriage:

My wife and I were temporarily separated (one month) during the third year of marriage. My wife wanted a divorce, but we were asked to reconcile. Our relationship is much better today, though far from perfect.

— Male respondent

From a divorce:

He no longer loves me—I still love him.

— Female respondent

Holmes and Rahe (1967) rate divorce and marital separation as the second and third most stressful life events, respectively. Only the death of a spouse is considered more traumatic. Despite its trauma, divorce rates reveal a 50% failure rate for first marriages, and an even higher failure rate for further marital unions (Ganong & Coleman, 1989; Martin & Bumpass, 1989). For this reason, marital dissolution has been studied extensively (e.g., Raschke, 1987; Whyte, 1990).

Breakups of intimate relationships other than marital relationships, however, have seldom been studied. For every thousand divorces in the United States, untold thousands of premarital relationships fail (Whyte, 1990).

Our primary purpose in this chapter was to help the reader better understand premarital breakups. Also, since a few of our respondents were divorced or maritally separated when we administered our follow-up survey, we also briefly discuss marital breakups, although divorce or legal separation was not our primary interest. We chose to approach this task in two ways. The first was by simply asking the respondents why they thought they broke up. We did this primarily to replicate and extend one aspect of what we believe is the best study of premarital breakup in the literature—Hill, Rubin, and Peplau's 1976 study. Albrecht, Bahr, and Goodman (1983) followed the same procedure in their study of marital disruption; therefore, we also asked our divorced or separated respondents why they thought their marriages broke up.

Our second approach to understanding breakups was to compare the premarital breakup group and the divorced and separated group to our respondents who were still married to the person with whom they had completed the PREP-M premaritally. Here again our interest was to replicate and extend what we believed to be the landmark research in this area—the research of Fowers and Olson (1986), Holman et al. (1994), and Larsen and Olson (1989). In all three of these studies, premarital data from the breakup groups were compared to the premarital data of those who were still married. The married group was divided into two subgroups: married with high satisfaction and married with low satisfaction.

Given our interests and the previous research, we addressed three questions in this chapter. First, what factors did couples perceive as having contributed to their premarital breakup? Second, what were the factors that divorced or separated couples perceived as having contributed to their marital breakup? Third, can premarital factors predict which of four relationship conditions—broken up premaritally, divorced or separated, married with low satisfaction, and married with high satisfaction—individuals fall into?

We begin our answer to all three of these research questions by noting and briefly reviewing the landmark study or studies that provided the framework for our research. After reviewing the studies relating to each research question, we describe how we operationalized the variable to answer the research question, and then we present our findings with respect to that research question. A general discussion follows the presentation of our findings relative to all three research questions. We begin with the perceptions of the reasons for a premarital breakup.

Perceptions of Factors Involved in Premarital Breakups

In their landmark study of premarital breakups, Hill et al. (1976) tracked 231 premarital couples. By the end of the 2-year study period, 103 couples had broken up. Most (95%) of the members of the 231 couples in the sample were or had been college students at the time of the initial questionnaire. Ninety-seven percent were white. Their average ages were not reported. The couples had been dating for a median period of about 8 months.

We were particularly interested in replicating and extending three aspects of the Hill et al. study. First, what factors did the couple members perceive as contributing to the breakup? Second, who precipitated the breakup? Third, how did those who broke up before marriage differ from those who were still together? We discuss the first two of these questions in this section, but leave the third question until after we have discussed divorced couples, at which time we compare the premarital breakup group with three other groups—divorced/separated, married with low satisfaction, and married with high satisfaction.

On the first question, Hill et al. (1976) found that the three most frequently mentioned factors contributing to breakup were "becoming bored with the relationship," "differences in interests," and "desire for more independence." They found a fairly high correlation between the women's reports and the men's reports of reasons for the breakup, especially on what they called "nondyadic factors," i.e., factors that were not aspects of the relationship itself. Hill et al. also reported that each person was more likely to see him- or herself as the one breaking up, rather than the partner or by mutual agreement. By combining men's and women's reports, they conclude the women broke off the relationship 51% of the time, the men 42%, and that it was mutual in only 7% of the cases.

Our Study of Premarital Breakup Factors

Our sample consisted of 272 individuals who indicated that they broke up premaritally with their partner. Of these, 43 (86 individuals) matched as couples. Like the study of Hill et al, the majority of our sample (88% of the women and

77% of the men) were in college when they completed the premarital assessment. Average ages were 20 for the women and 22 for the men. At the time of the initial assessment, they had been dating for a median period of 6 months to 1 year.

Included in our "Follow-Up Questionnaire" was a list of 19 potential factors influencing the decision to break up premaritally (see Appendix B, Section C), and a single item asking who precipitated the breakup. Thirteen of these factor items were taken from Hill et al. (1976). Each item required the subject to indicate if he or she considered it to be "one of the most important factors," "a contributing factor," or "not a factor," in the decision to break up. We examined only those items perceived as "one of the most important factors" for breakup, a decision more conservative than the approach by Hill et al. (1976). Table 3.1 is a summary of our findings for premarital breakups.

Individuals in Premarital Breakups

We first looked at the factors listed as important by 272 of our respondents. In the next section, we compare data only for people whose former partner also responded. The most common factors listed as highly important by women were (in order): "breakdown in communication," "differences in background," and "decrease in mutual feelings of love." For men, the top three factors were: "decrease in mutual feelings of love," "breakdown in communication," and "living too far apart." The items least frequently nominated by men were "physical abuse" and "pressure from man's parents." In comparison, women were least likely to link "physical abuse," "substance abuse," and "differences in religious attitudes and practices" for their premarital breakup.

In no instance did men report an item significantly more often than women. In contrast, women listed "differences in background," "women's desire to be more independent," and "pressure from man's parents" significantly more often than did men. Although just failing significance at $p = .05$, "finances" and "breakdown in communication" were also cited more often by women. The trend is clear: Women reported more causes for breakup than did men (Table 3.1).

Hill et al. (1976, p. 161) found that "women rated more problems as important than did men," a finding confirmed in the present study. Men listed an average of 2.12 serious factors leading to breakup, whereas women listed a mean of 3.07 factors ($t = -2.852$, $p = .007$).

There was some disagreement between the sexes as to who ended the relationship. Women reported themselves as the initiator of the breakup 26 times, the male 6 times, and a mutual breakup 9 times. Men, however, reported that they chose to breakup 17 times, that it was the female's choice 11 times, and that it was mutual 13 times.

Table 3.1. Self-Reported Major Factors Contributing to the Ending of a Premarital Relationship (Percentage Reporting)

		Women's reports	Men's reports	t-test
1.	Becoming bored with the relationship	09.3	07.1	0.37
2.	Differences in interests	23.3	11.6	1.53
3.	Differences in backgrounds	34.9	11.6**	3.57
4.	Differences in intelligence	07.0	07.0	0.00
5.	Conflicting sexual attitudes	09.3	09.3	0.00
6.	Conflicting marriage ideas	25.6	20.9	0.53
7.	Woman's desire to be more independent	16.3	02.3*	2.22
8.	Man's desire to be more independent	04.7	09.3	1.00
9.	Living too far apart	25.6	26.2	0.00
10.	Woman's interest in someone else	25.6	20.9	0.81
11.	Man's interest in someone else	11.6	14.0	-0.37
12.	Pressure from woman's parents	07.0	04.7	0.44
13.	Pressure from man's parents	11.6	00.0*	2.35
14.	Substance abuse (i.e. alcohol, drugs)	02.3	02.3	0.00
15.	Differences in religious attitudes and practices	02.3	02.3	0.00
16.	Finances	14.0	02.3	1.95 ($p < .06$)
17.	Decrease in mutual feelings of love	32.6	33.3	0.00
18.	Breakdown in communication	41.9	28.6	1.96 ($p < .06$)
19.	Physical abuse	02.3	00.0	1.00

Note. Data for those couples for which both man's and woman's reports were available ($N = 43$). Percentages are those citing factor as "one of the most important factors." Significance tests based on paired sample T-tests. *$p < .05$. **$p < .001$.

Couples in Premarital Breakups

Forty-three former couples returned follow-up data. This matching allowed us to consider couple agreement and differences in premarital breakups.

Only 4 of the 19 possible premarital factors on the Follow-Up Questionnaire yielded significant partner correlations. These areas of significant agreement were "woman's interest in someone else" $r = .62$), a "breakdown in communication" $r = .52$), "differences in background" $r = .50$), and "man's desire to be more independent" $r = .31$). On average, couples list one factor in common as a highly significant precipitate, which translates into about 27% couple agreement. Extrapolating these results, 50% of the factors marked by men, and 36.5% of those listed by women were in agreement with their partner. The most commonly nominated factors for couples were: "breakdown in communication," "decrease in mutual feelings of love," and "living too far apart."

Finally, we agree with the prior finding of Hill et al (1976) that women initiate breakup more frequently than do men. Couple agreement, however, was mixed concerning the perception of breakup $r = .30, p = .05$). To make sense of the discrepancy, combined scores were tallied (as was done in the research of Hill et al) giving an estimated 45% breakups initiated by women, 28% by men, and 27% mutually decided.

Premarital Subject Comments

The Follow-Up Questionnaire asked for comments, and left space for such comments, on each page of the questionnaire. While we received comments on most pages of the questionnaire, the pages about premarital and marital breakups had many more, and more detailed, comments than any of the others. We believe it is useful to share a few of those comments with the reader. Our participants' comments provide a vivid image of factors they feel culminated in the breakup. For example, concerning finances and future goals one woman noted:

He wanted to live off of my income ... have me put him through school ... he had *no* desire to achieve anything on his own merits. He also assumed a lot about our relationship without ever asking me how I truly felt. He lacked ambition and a desire to assume responsibility.

Pressure from parents, differing backgrounds, and distance can break a relationship apart:

We came from very different economic condition—my parents were very bothered by this and didn't hesitate to tell me this. We dated seriously for 2-½ years when he left to go to another city for college. With the other differences mounting, the distance made it worse.

In a similar relationship:

We were very in love and we had a lot of differences in what we valued and how we wanted to live our lives. Also his upbringing and attitude toward women was not the same as mine. It took me a long time to realize these things because I loved him so much.

Lastly, the relief of getting out of an abusive relationship:

My boyfriend at the time we took the [PREP-M questionnaire] had different morals than I did. He slept with many of my friends and did many things I felt were illegal and unethical. I had to be away from him for 6 months before I had the strength and courage to combat his manipulation and get out of the relationship. He soon after got a girl pregnant and married her but is now with his second wife and has had many extramarital affairs. I made the mistake of strongly encouraging him to accept my religion, which he did on the surface. I was very naive and codependent. I felt I could "help" him. Except for the 2 years of emotional turmoil, I escaped the relationship unscathed, which I am thankful for, since several girls' lives have been destroyed by him. I now believe he had a mental illness and an addiction to sex and drugs. I feel that the PREP-M was accurate at predicting our incompatibility. He didn't like the results because he "loved" me, but it was right on target and fortunately I've grown up a lot since then. Thanks.

Perceptions of Factors Involved in Divorce or Separation

The 1983 book by Albrecht et al., *Divorce and Remarriage: Problems, Adaptations, and Adjustments*, reported results from 500 "ever-divorced" individuals.

While tabulating "problems in marriage," Albrecht et al. reported, "In our survey, each respondent was asked to identify the major reasons why he or she felt that the marriage had failed. Respondents could list as many reasons as they desired" (p. 99). The four most important reasons listed were (in order of most to least important): infidelity, loss of love for each other, emotional problems, and financial problems. Albrecht et al. did not consider gender differences in their study.

Our Study of Divorce or Separation Factors

Using the findings of Albrecht et al. as a guide, our interest was in identifying those factors our respondents who were divorced or separated listed as involved in the marital disruption. Only 28 of our 1016 respondents were divorced or separated. While our sample is small, we find the results instructive and hope they add to our knowledge of perceptions about divorce and separation.

We received data from 25 husbands and wives who divorced and 3 who had separated from the person with whom they took the PREP-M. Fourteen of these individuals matched as couples. The average length of marriage for all 28 individuals was 3.82 years, with a mean of 1.69 years since separation or divorce. Women's age at marriage averaged 21.26 years, whereas men were about 2 years older at 23.85 years of age.

A list of 14 factors influencing divorce and separation was included in the Follow-Up Questionnaire (see Appendix B, Section D). Twelve of these items were taken from the Albrecht et al. (1983) research on reported reasons for divorce. As with the premarital breakup couples, we looked only at those items considered to be the most decisive ones. Table 3.2 shows our results for divorced and separated individuals.

Divorced or Separated Individuals

Table 3.2 shows discrepant perceptions of the key causes for divorce and separation between the sexes. For women, the most frequently listed factors were "communication problems" and "religious difference." They also frequently mentioned "control/power problems." For men, "communication problems" ranked foremost, with "infidelity," "emotional problems," and "control/power problems" equally marked second.

Given our small sample, one possible divorce and separation factor yielded a significant gender effect. "Differences in religious attitudes and practices" was cited as a major factor by significantly more women than men, a factor pointed to by over 50% of women.

Unlike the premarital couples, there was no significant difference in the number of factors reported by men and women. Men averaged 2.91 factors, whereas women had a mean of 3.00 factors ($F = 0.019, p = .891$).

Divorced or Separated Couples

From our sample of divorced or separated individuals, 14 respondents matched with a former spouse, enabling a limited consideration of couple agreement and difference. Our initial search found no significant correlation between partners' report on any of the 14 possible factors.

Given our small sample size, this is not surprising. "Sexual problems" ranked closest to significance $r = .73$), but failed to reach conventional levels of significance with a p-value of .06.

Nevertheless, couples generally agreed on two (1.86) of the factors precip-
itating divorce or separation, resulting in about a 44% couple agreement. From this
we see about 70% of the factors marked by men, and 58% of those listed by women
were in agreement with their partner. The most commonly nominated factors for
divorced or separated couples were "communication problems," "differ-ences in
religious attitudes and practices," and that they "no longer loved each other."
(Couple data are not shown in Table 3.2.)

Premarital Prediction of Relationship Status

As we noted above, earlier research (Fowers & Olson, 1986; Holman et al.,
1994; Larsen & Olson, 1989) has demonstrated that premarital factors can predict,
with some accuracy, relationship conditions; that is, whether a person ended up in

Table 3.2. Self-Reported Major Factors Contributing to the Ending of a
Relationship (Divorced or Separated Individuals) (Percentage Reporting)

		Women's reports (N = 16)	Men's reports (N = 12)	F
1.	Infidelity	18.8	33.3	1.02
2.	No longer loved each other	25.0	25.0	0.02
3.	Emotional problems	31.3	33.3	0.07
4.	Financial problems	06.3	00.0	0.68
5.	Physical abuse	12.5	00.0	1.45
6.	Alcohol	06.3	00.0	0.68
7.	Sexual problems	25.0	25.0	0.02
8.	Problems with in-laws	00.0	16.7	1.48
9.	Neglect of children	00.0	00.0	—
10.	Communication problems	56.3	83.3	1.91
11.	Married too young	18.8	16.7	0.00
12.	Job conflicts	00.0	08.3	1.48
13.	Differences in religious attitudes and practices	56.3	16.7*	4.24
14.	Control/power problems	43.8	33.3	0.72

Note. Data are for all individuals only (N = 28). Percentages are those citing factor as "one of the most
important factors." Significance tests based on multiple One-Way ANOVA (Factor = Gender). * $p < .05$.

one of four groups: premarital breakup, divorced/separated, married with low satisfaction, married with high satisfaction. In this part of the chapter, we replicate and extend these findings. Also, we look more carefully at what kinds of factors premaritally differentiate between the groups.

Both the Fowers and Olson and the Larsen and Olson articles looked only at similarity between couple responses on 11 or 12 scales. From their work we can conclude that highly satisfied married individuals have greater premarital similarity on a variety of issues, than do married individuals with low satisfaction, divorced/separated individuals, or individuals who had broken up premaritally. Both studies also showed that what they call "individual scores" also differentiate the groups, but the authors did not describe what "individual scores" were.

Holman et al. (1994), however, found that similarity scores did not adequately differentiate between married-satisfied, married-dissatisfied, and canceled/delayed, but that measures of individual "readiness" (such as emotional health, self-esteem, ability to communicate, etc.) and individuals' perceptions of their partners' "readiness" did differentiate the groups. The quality of the home environment also differentiated between the married-satisfied and the married-dissatisfied for the males. In comparison, "couple readiness" (how much the couple had formed a couple identity, support from family and friends, and so on) differentiated between married-satisfied, and married-dissatisfied, and canceled/delayed, but only for the females.

This research suggested that aspects of all four of the premarital conceptual areas identified in Chapter 1—family-of-origin quality, individual characteristics, social contexts, and couple interactional processes—may be useful in differentiating among the four groups we are investigating. In Chapter 1 we reviewed the relationship between aspects of these four conceptual areas and marital quality. Here we review what we currently understand about premarital correlates of relationship stability, bridging premarital and marital breakups. Factors are placed into one of four categories: family-of-origin background factors, individual characteristics, social contextual factors, and couple interactional processes.

Family-of-Origin Background Factors

As reported in Chapter 1, Wamboldt and Reiss (1989, p. 319) proposed that "family-of-origin experiences persist into later life and influence later development." Conceptually, we classify family-of-origin background factors as those experiences, processes, and structures from one's family of origin that impact later intimate relationships. However, there is a notable dearth of research on the relationship between family background and relationship breakup. The most reliable findings have shown that parental divorce increased the likelihood of divorce for the children (Glenn & Kramer, 1987; Greenberg & Nay, 1982;

McLanahan & Bumpass, 1988); a finding summarized by White (1990) and by
Larson and Holman (1994). Burgess and Wallin (1953) reported that an
overattachment to mothers by sons, and daughters to fathers was related to
premarital breakup. Similarly, Vaillant (1978) and Kelly and Conley (1987)
supported the idea that an enmeshed mother–son relationship is related to later
divorce.

Individual Characteristics

Individual characteristics have received notable attention in research on
predictors of premarital instability. Simpson (1987) reported that the ability to
remain differentiated during social interaction, rather than compromising one's
actions to appear socially desirable, was related to premarital stability. In 1953,
Burgess and Wallin reported that personality difficulties resulted in a greater
likelihood of premarital relationship failure.

A host of personality and health factors have been linked with marital breakup.
Physical illness, especially when disrupting a couple's sexual relationship, stresses
marital relationships, thereby making them less stable (Booth, Johnson, White, &
Edwards, 1986; Doherty & Campbell, 1988; Ell & Northen, 1990). Mental illness
was predictive of marital instability (Kelly & Conley, 1987; Vaillant, 1978).
Similarly, impulsivity was negatively related to couple permanence (Kelly &
Conley, 1987), whereas extroversion had a positive influence (Bentler &
Newcomb, 1978). Dysfunctional beliefs in a marital relationship created instability
(Baucom & Epstein, 1990; Eidelson & Epstein, 1982; Larson, 1988, 1992),
whereas conventionality stabilized marriage (Bentler & Newcomb, 1978; Kelly &
Conley, 1987; Whyte, 1990). Holman et al. (1994) reported that their composite
personality strengths measure (which includes measures of emotional health,
impulse control, and self-esteem) was positively related to marital stability in early
marriage.

Social Contextual Factors

Relationships are embedded in their larger contexts, and these larger contexts
influence the quality and stability of relationships. We argued in Chapter 1 that we
think of concepts like age, race, gender, education, and income as "socially
constructed" concepts, rather than as traits possessed by, or characteristic of,
individuals. In a sense, our sociocultural environment "tells" us when we can
marry based on what is "right" for our age, race, education, gender, and so on.
(See Chapter 6 for an in-depth review of this issue.)

Generally speaking, these socially constructed factors have been found to have
some influence on the stability of both premarital and marital relationships (Surra,

1990; White, 1990). As a complete review of this literature is beyond the scope of this chapter, we give only a brief review of the social contextual factors that affect *marital* stability, discussing only the major findings. In addition, we mention *marital* stability literature only as it relates to our review of *premarital* stability. We begin by considering the broader cultural predictors of stability.

Of all social contextual forces, age is one of the strongest predictors of both premarital and marital breakups. Specifically, marriage at a young age is highly related to marital instability and divorce (Booth & Edwards, 1985; Glenn & Supancic, 1984; Martin & Bumpass, 1989; Sweet & Bumpass, 1988). Referring to Martin and Bumpass's 1989 research, White (1990, p. 906) remarks that "age at marriage is the strongest predictor of divorce in the first five years of marriage." Premaritally, highly discrepant age is predictive of breakup (Hill et al., 1976).

Race and education also have some impact on relationship stability. Glenn and Supancic (1984) and Whyte (1990) found that African Americans have significantly less stable marriages. White (1990, p. 907), in her review of research in the 1980s, concluded that "black Americans are more likely than white Americans to divorce, and this difference is strong and consistent. The racial differential cannot be explained by controlling socioeconomic status and background factors." For married couples, well-educated husbands have more stable marriages (Whyte, 1990), whereas wives with graduate degrees have higher separation rates (Houseknecht & Spanier, 1980).

Gender also plays a roll in breaking up. Earlier in this chapter we reviewed the findings of Hill et al. (1976) showing that females were more likely to initiate a premarital breakup. Our own findings reported earlier in this chapter confirm those findings. Our findings suggest that wives are more likely to initiate a marital breakup as well.

We also have "closer-in" social factors that influence the quality and stability of our relationships. These are often conceptualized as "social networks," "social support," or "alternative attractions."

Social support from family and friends has a stabilizing influence on relationships, a finding identical in both premarital and marital relationships (Booth & Johnson, 1988; Burgess & Wallin, 1953; Cate, Huston, & Nesselroade, 1986; Felmlee, Sprecher, & Bassin, 1990; Kurdek, 1991). Support from family and social connections, along with age, prove to be two of the best predictors of couple permanence. In contrast, the effects of sociodemographic variables are generally small, and factor out of multivariate prediction models (Whyte, 1990).

Alternative attractions have long been considered an important factor in marital dissolution (e.g., Levinger, 1979, 1983). For premarital relationships, several studies have found that high quality of the best alternative dating partner, whether real or imagined, and ease with which an alternative can be found, are predictive of couple breakup (Simpson, 1987; Attridge, Berscheid, & Simpson, 1995; Felmlee et al., 1990; Rusbult, 1983; Sacher & Fine, 1996; Simpson, 1987).

Couple Interactional Processes

A couple's communication skills, social homogamy, interpersonal similarity, and interactional history all fall under the rubric of couple interactional processes. This dimension contains some of the strongest premarital predictors of couple breakup.

Interpersonal similarity of attitudes, values, and beliefs are related to marital stability (Fowers & Olson, 1986; Holman et al., 1994; Larsen & Olson, 1989). Further, couples who stay together in marriage after 4 years have more similar personalities than those who separate or divorce (Bentler & Newcomb, 1978). Similarity in physical attractiveness is also related to premarital couple permanence (Hill et al., 1976). Premaritally, similarity in educational aspirations and intelligence correlate with couple permanence (Hill et al., 1976). Similar findings are reported in studies of premarital social homogamy (i.e., similar race, religion, SES), whereas "cultural divergence" predicts couple breakup (Burgess & Wallin, 1953).

Additional factors that predict premarital couple permanence are a long duration of the relationship (Attridge et al., 1995; Felmlee et al., 1990; Sacher & Fine, 1996; Simpson, 1987), increased time spent together (Attridge et al., 1995; Felmlee et al., 1990), and greater diversity of activities performed together (Attridge et al., 1995). Burgess and Wallin (1953) and Hill et al. (1976) found that prolonged separations are related to premarital breakup. Premarital relationships with a high degree of satisfaction relative to "costs" tend to remain stable (Attridge et al., 1995; Rusbult, 1983; Sacher & Fine, 1996; Simpson, 1987). In contrast, less exclusive, more distant, and less committed relationships fail with greater frequency (Attridge et al., 1995; Burgess & Wallin, 1953; Hill et al., 1976; Simpson, 1987).

A couple's premarital sexual history influences both their premarital and marital relationship. For premarital couples, sexual experience is predictive of greater couple longevity (Simpson, 1987). However, greater premarital sexual intercourse is related to the probability of divorce (Kelly & Conley, 1987). Further, Janus and Janus (1993) report that divorced men and women had higher incidence of premarital sexual experience compared with still married individuals. Linked with this is Simpson's (1987) finding that more liberal orientations to sexual relations predicts premarital couple breakup.

White (1990, p. 906), summarizing divorce factors from the 1980s, concluded, "Several excellent studies provide unassailable documentation of the fact that premarital childbearing increases the risk of divorce in subsequent marriage, but that, by itself, a premarital conception does not" (see Billy, Landale, & McLaughlin, 1986; Martin & Bumpass, 1989; Morgan & Rindfuss, 1984; Teachman, 1983; Wineberg, 1988).

In the same review, White (1990, p. 906) also listed cohabitation as a factor predictive of divorce, explaining that "the kinds of people who choose to flout convention by cohabiting are the same kinds of people who flout normative marital behavior, have lower commitment to marriage as an institution, and disregard the stigma of divorce" (see Bennett, Blanc, & Bloom, 1988; Booth & Johnson, 1988; White, 1987).

Last, we found little support for the idea that premarital communication "problems" are a significant factor in relationship dissolution. Although premarital dyadic communication is linked to marital *quality* (Filsinger & Thoma, 1988; Markman, 1979, 1981; Smith et al., 1990), there is no reported link between premarital communication and marital *stability*. For premarital couples, only Attridge et al. (1995) list communication, specifically greater self-disclosure to one's partner, as predictive of couple permanence.

Results

We split the subjects into four groups and performed multiple One-Way ANOVAs on relevant premarital factors. The orthogonal contrasts method of multiple comparisons was used to identify significantly differing groups. The four groups of individuals were: premarital breakups ($N = 86$), divorced and separated individuals ($N = 28$), those married at the time of the follow-up study with low marital satisfaction ($N = 129$), and highly satisfied married individuals at the time of the follow-up study ($N = 89$).

We have already described in depth the premarital and divorced/separated individuals; however, use of married individuals involved a discriminating process. Included in the Follow-Up Questionnaire was a scale of seven items probing the quality of one's ongoing marriage (see Appendix B, Section E, Subsection F). After we dropped one item (F.5), the other six questions factored into one component, and alpha reliability tests showed good internal consistency for this scale ($\alpha = .86$). From this, we created a multi-item satisfaction variable.

To adequately separate the highly satisfied married individuals from the unsatisfied married individuals, we eliminated all cases plus or minus one standard deviation from the mean of the composite satisfaction scale. In other words, our married individuals all reported their satisfaction levels for their marriage within the outer tails of the sample distribution.

An exploratory probe for gender differences not only yielded few significant differences, but, with the reduced sample sizes, tended to "wash out" some of the important group effects. Further, understanding eight groups simultaneously in one table proved to add only confusion, and made results difficult to judge. Therefore, no gender effects are reported.

Factors examined were original items and scales reported by the individuals on the PREP-M. The decision as to which items to include in this comparison was based on the availability of relevant questions and scales prescribed by the review of literature. All of the variables used are described fully in Chapter 2.

Background Factors

Table 3.3 illustrates our *F*-value, *p*-value, and mean scores for each of the items or scales considered in the analysis. The superscripts of the mean scores show significant differences between groups. Corresponding letters are placed under group names. See the notes in Table 3.3 for help in explaining the numeric coding.

Background variables were divided into four principle areas. Family socio-demographic background included four single-item variables that evaluated the education level of parents (two items), father's primary occupation, and family income. Family structure consisted of two single items that detailed whether an individual's parents were currently in their first marriage. Parent's marital quality consisted of two questions on how well satisfied one's parents were in their marriage. Last, parent–child relationship quality consists of three multi-item scales looking at the individual's relationship with parents, and satisfaction with the home environment.

All of the values in Table 3.3 are scored in a positive direction. We begin our report of significant findings with the right-hand side of the table where the married with high satisfaction group differs from the three other groups. There we compare the married with low satisfaction with each of the two groups to the left of it, and we note the significant differences between the divorced/separated group and the premarital breakup group. Married individuals who are highly satisfied have the highest reported mean scores in 9 of the 11 areas, and 6 of these are significantly different from at least one of the other groups. The married with high satisfaction group had significantly higher mean scores than the married with low satisfaction group on 6 of the 11 comparisons: father's education, father's marital satisfaction, mother's marital satisfaction, relationship with father, relationship with mother, and satisfaction with home environment. The married with high satisfaction group had significantly higher mean scores on father's education, relationship with mother, and satisfaction with home environment than did the divorced or separated group. Additionally, the married with high satisfaction group had significantly higher mean scores than did the premarital breakup group in father's education level, relationship with father, relationship with mother, and satisfaction with home environment.

The married with low satisfaction group did not differ from the divorced/separated group on any background items. They differed significantly from the premarital breakup group on only 1 of 11 family-of-origin comparisons. The married with low satisfaction group had significantly lower satisfaction with their home environment than did the premarital breakup group. The divorced/separated group differed on only one background item from the premarital breakup group; they had a significantly lower mean on father's education than did the premarital breakup group.

Table 3.3. Background Factors

	F-value/p-value	Premarital breakups (N = 86) (a)	Divorced or separated (N = 28) (b)	Married (low sat.) (N = 129) (c)	Married (high sat.) (N = 89) (d)
Family Sociodemographic Background[*]					
Father's Education Level	5.417/0.001	4.90 [b]	3.96 [a, d]	4.63 [d]	5.36 [b, c]
Mother's Education Level	1.186/0.315	3.74	3.29	3.59	3.78
Father's Primary Occupation	1.208/0.307	0.23	0.11	0.16	0.21
Father's Current Income	0.006/0.999	6.03	6.07	6.06	6.05
Family Structure[**]					
Marital Status of Father	1.623/0.184	0.81	0.86	0.81	0.91
Marital Status of Mother	0.769/0.512	0.86	0.82	0.81	0.88

Table 3.3. (continued)

Parent's Marital Quality[†]					
Father's Satisfaction	2.736/0.044	2.98	2.89	2.80 [d]	3.27 [c]
Mother's Satisfaction	3.675/0.013	2.93	2.89	2.70 [d]	3.25 [c]
Parent–Child Relationship Quality					
Relationship with Father	8.411/0.000	2.48 [d]	2.54	2.34 [d]	2.83 [a, c]
Relationship with Mother	10.043/0.000	2.83 [d]	2.85 [d]	2.68 [d]	3.13 [a, b, c]
Satisfaction with Family Environment	11.762/0.000	2.79 [c, d]	2.77 [d]	2.56 [a, d]	3.14 [a, b, c]

Note. Data represent group means. Alphabetic superscripts indicate statistical significance at the .05 level using the a priori contrasts orthogonal method for multiple comparisons in SPSS.

* Education Level based on a nine-point scale from 0 to 8. Higher scores indicate more advanced degrees. Father's Primary Occupation based on a dummy scale. 1 indicates professional occupation, whereas 0 represents all others. Father's Current Income based on a nine point scale from 0 to 8. Higher scores indicate greater financial resources.

** Family Structure items are based on dummy scaling. 1 indicates parent is currently in a first marriage, whereas 0 represents all other marital statuses.

† All other scales based on five-point Likert scaling, with means between 0 and 4. Higher scores indicate greater levels of reported satisfaction.

Individual Characteristics

As in the previous table, Table 3.4 illustrates the F-value, p-value, and mean scores for each of the items considered. The notes in Table 3.4 help explain the numeric coding. Values are all coded in a positive direction. From the original PREP-M questionnaire, three composite scales were used to compare individual characteristics—emotional health, impulsivity, and self-esteem. Attitudes and beliefs consisted of six multi-item scales probing religiosity, moral behavior, sexual abstinence, conservative attitudes toward family planning, importance of family living, and need for autonomy in a relationship.

Married with high satisfaction individuals reported the highest mean levels for all three personality scales. This group had significantly higher emotional stability premaritally than did the premarital breakup group, and significantly higher impulse control and self-esteem than did the married with low satisfaction group. Of the six attitude areas, the highly satisfied married group had the highest mean scores in all except the need for autonomy. Highly satisfied married individuals showed the lowest need for autonomy in a relationship, whereas premarital breakup individuals showed the greatest need. Further, sexual attitudes followed a steplike progression, premarital breakup individuals being the most liberal, and highly satisfied married individuals being the most conservative.

Social Contextual Factors

Social contextual factors are included in Table 3.5, and follow the same format as with the other tables already described. Values are all coded in a positive direction. The notes in Table 3.5 help interpretation of the table and scores.

As mentioned, social contextual factors include influences outside the dyad and contextual factors specific to the time and place of the relationship. Four items asked about social location, three of these probed support from significant others for the relationship, and the fourth was a five-item scale measuring the concurrent relationship with one's parents and potential in-laws. This last scale is meant to uncover the amount of differentiation from one's family of origin and support for future kin relationships.

Although our sample age range was only 18 to 30, some small, but statistically significant differences showed up. The married-low satisfaction group was significantly older when they answered the premarital questionnaire than were the premarital breakup group and the married-high satisfaction group. Also, the married-low satisfaction group had achieved a slightly higher educational level and income level than did the married-high satisfaction group. The divorced/separated had the highest premarital income level of the four groups, significantly higher premaritally than the married-high satisfaction group.

Table 3.4. Individual Characteristics and Attitudes

	F-value/p-value	Premarital breakups (N = 86) (a)	Divorced or separated (N = 28) (b)	Married (low sat.) (N = 129) (c)	Married (high sat.) (N = 89) (d)
Individual Characteristics					
Emotional Stability	3.597/0.014	2.86 [b, d]	3.10 [a]	2.98	3.12 [a]
Maturity/Control	3.205/0.023	2.62 [d]	2.71	2.60 [d]	2.82 [a, c]
Self-Esteem	3.869/0.010	3.28 [d]	3.32	3.27 [d]	3.49 [a, c]
Attitudes and Beliefs					
Religious Beliefs Important	4.605/0.004	3.43 [d]	3.30 [d]	3.58	3.78 [a, b]
Moral Behavior Important	1.971/0.118	3.34 [d]	3.48	3.47	3.56 [a]
Conservative Sexual Attitudes	0.831/0.477	3.25	3.36	3.41	3.49
Conservative Family Planning	0.595/0.619	2.28	2.14	2.21	2.30
Family Is Important	5.625/0.001	3.37 [d]	3.35 [d]	3.39 [d]	3.61 [a,b, c]
Need for Autonomy	5.888/0.001	2.13 [b, c, d]	1.85 [a]	1.90 [a]	1.75 [a]

Note. Data represent group means. Alphabetic superscripts indicate statistical significance at the .05 level using the a priori contrasts orthogonal method for multiple comparisons in SPSS. Scales based on five point Likert scaling, with means between 0 and 4. Higher scores indicate a more positive response to the item/scale.

Table 3.5. Social Contextual Factors

	F-value/p-value	Premarital breakups (N = 86) (a)	Divorced or separated (N = 28) (b)	Married (low sat.) (N = 129) (c)	Married (high sat.) (N = 89) (d)
Age (in years)	03.425/ .017	21.21 [c]	21.39	22.04 [a, d]	21.56 [c]
Support from Man's Parents	08.468/ .000	2.87 [c, d]	3.18	3.33 [a]	3.51 [a]
Support from Woman's Parents	18.878/ .000	2.51 [c, d]	2.79 [c, d]	3.20 [a, b, d]	3.45 [a, b, c]
Support from Friends	14.666/ .000	2.93 [b, c, d]	3.29 [a, d]	3.42 [a, d]	3.62 [a, b, c]
Parent and In-law Relationship*	07.951/ .000	2.88 [d]	2.71 [c, d]	2.96 [b, d]	3.13 [a, b, c]

Note. Data represent group means. Alphabetic superscripts indicate statistical significance at the .05 level using the a priori contrasts method for multiple comparisons in SPSS. Scales based on five point Likert scaling, with means between 0 and 4. Higher scores indicate a more positive response to the item/scale.

* Parent and In-law Relationship is a composite measure of differentiation from parents and support from future in-laws.

The highest mean values for all support items were reported by those who later were highly satisfied married people. Also, the three items measuring support from significant others all increase in a steplike fashion between groups, premarital breakups having the least support and married-high satisfaction the most.

The married-high satisfaction group receives significantly more premarital social support for their relationship than do any of the other groups in all four areas, except for support from the man's parents, in which they are significantly different from only the premarital breakup group. Individuals in the married-low satisfaction group also enjoy a greater level of support than do the divorced or separated in two areas, and in all four than the premarital breakup group.

Couple Interactional Processes

Table 3.6 illustrates our F-value, p-value, and mean scores for each of the items considered. We separated the couple interactional processes into six principle areas: premarital relationship history, similarity, communication behaviors, perceived partner communication behaviors, couple agreement, and premarital dyadic crystallization. Since not all of the items included in Table 3.6 are positively coded, interpretation is more item specific (see Table 3.6 for specifics).

Two items measured the perceived similarity in a couple's mental abilities and the individual's education level. The married-high satisfaction group had the most perceived similarity in mental ability (significantly so, compared with the premarital breakup group), and the least education level similarity (especially compared with the married-low satisfaction group).

Additionally, a couple similarity/discrepancy score was composed by merging each of the attitudinal and belief variables mentioned in Table 3.4. This we did by summing the absolute differences of male and female scores for each scale. Since our other analyses use only individuals, an altered sample was prepared. The sample size for each group is in the notes in Table 3.6. Although no significant differences are found between groups, it is noteworthy that married-high-satisfaction couples have the least discrepancy in their attitudes, and premarital breakup couples hold the most disparate attitudes and beliefs.

Communication behaviors involve two multi-item scales, one looking at the degree of relationship-enhancing communication behaviors, and the other at the degree of relationship-diminishing communication behaviors. Highly satisfied married individuals reported the most relationship-enhancing and least diminishing communication. Indeed, they were higher on premarital relationship-enhancing communication than were any of the other groups. The married-low satisfaction group also had significantly more relationship-enhancing communication behaviors than did the premarital breakup group. Those who broke up premaritally showed the least relationship-enhancing and most relationship-diminishing communication of all of the groups.

Table 3.6. Couple Interactional Processes

	F-value/p-value	Premarital breakups (N = 86) (a)	Divorced or separated (N = 28) (b)	Married (low sat.) (N = 129) (c)	Married (high sat.) (N = 89) (d)
Similarity in Mental Abilities	01.457/.226	2.89 [d]	3.07	3.05	3.15 [a]
Education Level*	02.627/.050	3.48	3.29	3.53 [d]	3.24 [c]
Discrepancy in Attitudes and Beliefs**	01.500/.217	2.95	2.56	2.85	2.48
Communication Skills					
Relationship-Enhancing	21.663/.000	3.17 [c, d]	3.25 [d]	3.32 [a, d]	3.67 [a, b, c]
Relationship-Diminishing	11.513/.000	1.41 [d]	1.24 [d]	1.31 [d]	1.04 [a, b, c]
Perceived Partner's Communication Skills					
Relationship-Enhancing	11.352/.000	2.71 [c, d]	2.74 [d]	2.87 [a, d]	3.12 [a, b, c]
Relationship-Diminishing	16.187/.000	1.31 [b, c, d]	1.06 [a, d]	1.11 [a, d]	0.81 [a, b, c]
Couple Consensus					
Consensus on Various Issues***	15.621/.000	2.73 [b, c, d]	2.97 [a, d]	3.03 [a, d]	3.23 [a, b, c]

Table 3.6. (continued)

Relationship Identification Formation

Perceived Rel. Difficulties	07.507/.000	2.15 [b, c, d]	1.64 [a]	1.59 [a]	1.30 [a]
Thoughts of Terminating Rel.	06.979/.000	1.49 [b, c, d]	0.64 [a]	0.99 [a]	.80 [a]
Discussing Breakup	07.989/.000	1.20 [b, c, d]	0.43 [a, c]	0.82 [a, b, d]	.55 [a, c]
Satisfaction with Rel.	17.437/.000	3.22 [b, c, d]	3.50 [a, d]	3.66 [a, d]	3.88 [a, b, c]

Note. Data represent group means. Alphabetic superscripts indicate statistical significance at the .05 level using the a priori contrasts method for multiple comparisons in SPSS. Scales based on five-point Likert scaling, with means between 0 and 4. Higher scores indicate a more positive response to the item/scale.

* Education Level based on a nine point scale from 0 to 8. Higher scores indicate more advanced degrees.

** Discrepancy Scores based on a composite measure of couple differences on all variables listed under the same heading in Table 3.4. Since couples rather than individuals were used, the *N* for each group should read from left to right: 36, 7, 49, 61 for this analysis. Lower score indicates more similarity in couple's attitudes and beliefs.

*** Issues include: leisure activities, finances, religious matters, affection, dealing with in-laws, time spent together, and number of children to have.

Similarly, each individual was asked an identical set of questions on the PREP-M to evaluate his or her partner's relationship-enhancing and relationship-diminishing communication behaviors. The results are roughly parallel to those reported by individuals concerning their own communication behaviors. Highly satisfied married individuals reported that their partners had the most relationship-enhancing and least relationship-diminishing communication behaviors. Those who broke up premaritally reported that their partners manifested the least relationship-enhancing behaviors and the most relationship-diminishing communication behaviors.

A single multi-item scale asked the amount of couple consensus on various issues. The issues ranged from leisure activities and finances, to in-laws and number of children to have. Here too, the highly satisfied married group scored highest on couple agreement, and the premarital group scored lowest. Indeed, the married-high satisfaction group had achieved significantly more premarital consensus (agreement) than did all three other groups, and the premarital breakup group had significantly less consensus than did any of the other groups. The final area evaluated couple identity formation process. The premarital breakup group had significantly higher mean values (lower identity formation) for each of these items than did all three other groups. The last item asked general satisfaction with one's relationship. Of all the groups, the highly satisfied married group had significantly higher premarital satisfaction, and the premarital breakup group significantly lower. Further, satisfaction decreases steplike toward the premarital breakup group.

Each group was contrasted on 42 comparisons across the four conceptual areas. The married-high satisfaction group had premarital scores that differed significantly from the married-low satisfaction group 55% of the time, from the divorced/separated group 36% of the time, and from the premarital breakup group 57% of the time. The married-low satisfaction group had premarital means that were significantly different from the divorced/separated just 10% of the time, and from the premarital breakup group 33% of the time. The divorced/separated group differed in a statistically significant manner from the premarital breakup group 23% of the time.

Discriminant Analysis

To explore our observation that highly satisfied married individuals differed from all other groups combined, we entered all of the previously described analyses into a discriminant analysis. From these hypothesized groups (highly satisfied married individuals versus all others), the analysis was able to predict group membership accurately 85% of the time. Further, "relationship-enhancing communication" proved to be the most powerful predictor of group discrimination, with 64% of the cases accurately classified.

Discussion

Why do some couples break up before marriage? Why do some marry and then end the marriage with a divorce? Are couples who stayed married different from those who broke up either premaritally or maritally? Why do some couples stay in an unsatisfying marriage, while others opt out of their marriage? While there have been a few groundbreaking studies on premarital breakup, marital breakup, and differences between premarital breakup, divorced/separated, married-low satisfaction, and married-high satisfaction groups, our study adds uniquely to understanding these groups by obtaining (1) people's perceptions after the fact as to why they broke up, (2) premarital data collected before the breakups that allow us to predict whether couples would breakup, and (3) a comparison of those who broke up premaritally, who divorced or separated, who are married but are very dissatisfied, and who are married and are very satisfied with marriage.

Perceptions of Reasons for Premarital and Marital Breakups

We can conclude a number of things from the personal perceptions of why partners thought their relationships ended. First, no single factor dominated in either premarital or marital breakup. On average our respondents saw two to three factors contributing to premarital breakup and three factors contributing to marital breakup.

Second, no single *class* of factors alone accounted for breakups. The ecosystemic, developmental perspective taken in this book suggests that factors from a number of contexts that the couples are more or less connected to influence a process like breaking up. These contexts include the individual, the couple system, the family they were embedded in, and other systems in their social context. While they mostly saw factors in their interpersonal relationship as contributing to their breakups, individual personality or values characteristics, past and current relationships with parents, and support or lack thereof in their social networks and social contexts were all seen as contributing to breaking up.

Third, men and women had some agreement about the breakups, but there were some differences in their perceptions of the breakup. Women perceived significantly more factors to be involved in the breakups than did their male partners. Furthermore, the premarital couples had only 27% agreement on breakup factors. However, the divorced men and women each saw the same number of factors as important (about three) and had much higher agreement on what those factors were than did the premarital couples.

Women and men disagreed on who broke off the premarital relationship, women saying they did considerably more often than did the men. Women said they initiated breakups 27 times; men said women did only 11 times. We suspect that the reason for this difference has something to do with the desire of individuals to think they were in control of the situation and that they chose the course of action, rather than having it thrust on them by someone else.

Fourth, there is some congruence between the perceptions expressed several years after the fact, and their evaluations of their relationships before the breakups actually occurred. Poor communication quality was indicated before the breakup actually occurred and communication problems were seen as a major factor in the breakup several years after it actually occurred. Both in the evaluations of the relationships before the breakups and in perceptions several years after the breakups, a number of personal, interpersonal, family background, and contextual factors figured into the breakups.

Fifth, our research is consistent with the two major studies of perceptions—the Hill et al (1976) study of perceptions of premarital breakup and the Albrecht et al (1983) study of perceptions of marital breakup. Even though our samples are small, the congruence between our findings and theirs gives us greater confidence in our findings. Moreover, their data were probably collected in the early 1970s and early 1980s respectively, while ours were collected in the mid-1990s. Thus, the congruence we see indicates that despite rapid social change in some areas in that period of 15 to 20 years, the course of failed relationships has stayed much the same.

Premarital Predictors of Relationship Breakup and Quality

Our interest was also to learn if the premarital data provided by the couples could predict which of four relationship categories—premarital breakup, divorced/separated, married-low satisfaction, or married-high satisfaction—existed several years later. The most general conclusion we can reach from our findings is that self-report data from couples before they are married can differentiate the relationship status and quality several years later. Several more specific conclusions can be made.

The most obvious conclusion is that the married-high marital satisfaction group is the most different group. This group almost always had higher levels of the premarital predictors generally thought to be related to later relationship quality than did the other groups. In other words, they almost always had higher levels of the premarital factors that theory and research suggest are more likely to lead to higher marital quality. The discriminant analysis confirmed that the married-high satisfaction group was uniquely different among the groups.

Like Fowers and Olson (1986), Larsen and Olson (1989), and Holman et al. (1994), we generally found that the means increased (or decreased) in a stepwise manner from the premarital breakup group to the married-high satisfaction group. The married-high satisfaction group was most different premaritally from the people who ended up breaking up premaritally or who married and were low on satisfaction and least different from the divorced/separated group.

The premarital breakup group was also quite different from other groups, having significant differences on 57% of the comparisons with the married-high satisfaction group, 33% of the comparisons with the married-low satisfaction group, and 23% of the comparisons with the divorced/separated group.

Two of the groups, married-low satisfaction and divorced/separated, were almost indistinguishable. While the married-low satisfaction group usually had slightly higher means, they were significantly different on only 4 (10%) of the comparisons. There were no significant differences between these two groups on the 11 family-of-origin comparisons and on the 9 individual characteristics comparisons, and on only 1 of the 12 couple interactional comparisons. However, there were significant differences on 3 of 4 social context comparisons and those differences are instructive. Premaritally, those who eventually married and 6 years later had unsatisfying marital relationships reported significantly higher support from the woman's parents and from friends for the premarital relationship, and reported a closer and healthier relationship with their parents and their future in-laws. A logical conclusion is that this higher level of network support continued after the marriage for the low-satisfaction group, and thus, with network support (or pressure), they are either trying to work it out in the marriage or feeling pressure to stay in the marriage no matter the cost to personal satisfaction, or at least not feeling any support from the social network to move toward marital dissolution.

Given that these social network differences are the only differences of real import between the divorced/separated and married-low satisfaction groups, we conclude that social network support or pressure is a pivotal factor in whether marriage partners decide to stay in an unhappy marriage or leave the marriage. Furthermore, the premarital breakup group had the lowest social network support premaritally for their relationships, and it was significantly different from both married groups in three of the four social network comparisons. Interestingly, the premarital breakup group members had somewhat better relationships with their parents and would-be in-laws than did those who would later marry and then divorce or separate, although not at a statistically significant level. This hints that with little network support, and yet healthier relationships with parents and partner's parents, the breakup group members had the ability to break up a relationship that almost certainly would have been unhappy as a marriage.

To continue in this train of thought, it is clear that those who broke up premaritally were wise to do so. They were much more similar premaritally to the divorced/separated group and the married-low satisfaction group than to the married-high satisfaction group. Indeed, in most cases, their means were the lowest (or highest in negative situations) of the four groups.

But this led us to ask, why did they break up premaritally while other couples quite similar to them went ahead and married, only to be very unhappy in marriage or ended up divorced/separated? A close look at our data leads us to suggest a complex answer. First, although the differences are not statistically significant, the premarital breakup group came from families with a slightly better socioeconomic base, with a more stable and higher quality parental marriage, and no worse and often better parent–child relationships and family environment than those of the divorced/separated group or the married-low satisfaction group. Second, as we have noted, the premarital breakup group more likely had their social network "warning" them that the impending marriage was fraught with problems. Thus, what we may be seeing is young people with a more secure family and friend relations base, from which to make the often emotionally wrenching decision to call off an intimate relationship, than that of those who went ahead and married when sirens should have been going off all around them, warning them of impending problems. Third, the premarital breakup group's premarital individual characteristics paint an interesting picture of how these people thought. They had the least emotional stability of the four groups, but were no more immature (or impulsive), and had no lower self-esteem than did the other breakup groups, especially the married-low satisfaction people. Moreover, they expressed a significantly greater need for autonomy than did any of the other groups. It is conceivable that what we are seeing is the difference between what attachment scholars note are two kinds of "insecure" individuals (Bartholomew, 1993; Koski & Shaver, 1997). The two types are "dismissing" individuals who tend to form negative models of others and who are comfortable without close intimate relationships—possibly the premarital breakup group—and "preoccupied" individuals who tend to form negative models of themselves, be highly dependent, and are afraid others do not value them—possibly the divorced/separated and married-low satisfied group members.

Fourth, the premarital breakup group members were significantly more likely than were the other groups to see their partners as engaging in relationship-diminishing communication behaviors (this fits with our interpretation of them as insecure, "dismissing" individuals who have formed negative models of others), significantly less likely to have achieved consensus with their partners on important relationship issues, and more likely not to have solidified their sense of a couple identity.

Thus, we suggest that individuals who break up a relationship that has the makings of a poor-quality marriage tend to have at least a marginally adequate resource base from the family of origin, to have a personality and attitudes that value autonomy and independence, and to recognize that the interactional processes in the relationship are not good.

However, their "wisdom" in breaking off the particular relationship does not necessarily bode well for their future relationships. If the differences between the premarital breakup group and the other groups were simply in the couple interactional arena, then we could speculate that not only were they wise to break off that relationship, but also that they could look forward to a stable, high-quality marriage with another person with whom they developed high-quality premarital interactional processes. But given that they had significantly poorer parent–child relationships and emotional stability, lower impulse control, and self-esteem, attitudes not supportive of long-term, high-quality marital relationship, and continuing less unhealthy relationships with their parents and other adults, than those of the married-high satisfaction group, we can speculate that whenever they do marry, they are headed toward the divorced/separated or married-low satisfaction groups.

Implications for Practice

These results, both the ex post facto perceptions of those who broke up, and the a priori data from the individuals, lead us to make the following recommendations for practitioners.

1. Since knowledge of the premarital relationship can foreshadow the status and quality of the future relationship, assessments need to be done that will help couples understand the strengths and weakness of their relationships. There are a number of good paper-and-pencil assessment tools available to practitioners, including the RELATIONSHIP Evaluation (RELATE), which is the updated and expanded version of the PREP-M, the instrument used to gather the premarital data for this book. More information is given about its use as an assessment tool for practitioners and researchers in Chapter 9. Other comprehensive instruments that have good reliability and validity, and provide good feedback for the couple and practitioner, are discussed in Larson, Holman, Klein, Busby, Stahmann, and Peterson's (1995) review of comprehensive premarital assessment instruments.

2. Interventions need to help couples make hard decisions about whether to marry, since premarital couples who end up divorced/separated or married with low satisfaction do not look much different from couples who break up premaritally.

3. Interventions need to continue with individuals who break up premaritally, since without change, their prognosis for forming a stable, high-quality marital relationship is not good.

4. Interventions need to address four major areas—family-of-origin relationships and statuses, individual personality characteristics and values, ongoing social network support, and couple interactional processes.

5.   As nonmarital relationships simulate legal marital relationships involving
     shared domicile, sexual interaction, shared financial and other resources,
     long-term cohabitation, and even childbearing and child rearing, there is
     a greater need to help couples recognize that many of the same issues that
     create marital problems and dissolution are going to affect them. The
     issues for premarital, nonmarital, and marital relationships appear to have
     their genesis in the same sets of factors—family of origin, individual
     characteristics and values, social network support, and couple inter-
     actional processes.

Implications for Research and Theory

Our research points to a number of things that could be done to advance
human researchers' understanding of relationship structural and quality outcomes,
and practitioners ability to intervene to strengthen premarital and marital
relationships.

1.   There is a need for larger, more representative longitudinal comparative
     studies. The studies, including ours, done to compare premarital breakup,
     divorce/separation, married-low quality, and married-high quality have
     used small samples of mostly White, young adult, college-attending,
     never previously married individuals.
2.   Our results demonstrate better than any previous findings that while less
     successful relationships (premarital breakup, divorced/separated, married-
     low satisfaction) are more similar to each other than they are to the
     married-high satisfaction group, there are also differences between the
     less-successful groups. Research needs to be done and theories developed
     that help us understand these differences and how to intervene effectively
     to help couples develop stable, high quality relationships.
3.   It would seem especially important to be able to distinguish between those
     who broke up premaritally, but whose prognosis for future success in
     relationships was high, and those who are so similar to individuals who
     later dissolve the marriage or endure an unsatisfactory marriage, that their
     prognosis for a successful relationship is low.
4.   Our data hint at the importance of social networks in distinguishing
     between divorced/separated individuals and married-low satisfied
     individuals. Greater understanding is needed on how parents, in-laws,
     other family members, and friends can influence not only marital stability,
     but also marital quality.

5. Our research needs to be guided by theory, especially theories that will help us better understand both continuity and change from premarital to marital.

The goal of this chapter was primarily to help readers understand why couples break up and how practitioners can plan interventions to strengthen premarital relationships. We attempted to improve the reader's understanding by using ex post facto perceptions of breakups, and a priori predictors of not only breakups, but also, for comparison purposes, marital satisfaction at two levels.

The chapters that now follow attempt to help the reader better understand those who have stayed married. Each chapter takes one of the four conceptual areas from the theoretical model in Chapter 1 (Figure 1.1) and investigates and analyzes it in detail. Recommendations for practice, research, and theory are also included in each data chapter on the issues investigated in that chapter. Then a final data chapter (Chapter 8) presents findings from four other previously unpublished longitudinal studies of premarital predictors of marital quality, and the findings of a test of a final (total) model based on the data set used in the other data chapters in this book. Principles for practice are developed based on the findings of all of the data chapters (Chapters 3–8), and implications for research and theory development are discussed in Chapter 9.

4

Family-of-Origin Structures and Processes and Adult Children's Marital Quality

Thomas B. Holman and Paul James Birch

> *My husband comes from a broken home. His mother remarried a man who already had two sons; his father remarried three more times. [My husband] has told me that he never wants to put our children [when we have some] through all the confusion he had to go through. My parents have been married 37 years and still going. My father's parents have been married 64 years and still going.*
>
> —Female respondent

> *I have written a lot about his parents because I do feel the way he was raised contributed to many of our problems. He was forced to participate in school and church activities which would make his parents look good and really couldn't make choices for himself. He realized how wrong his parents were when we married and he saw my parents as well as others.*
>
> —Female respondent

> *My husband and I come from very different backgrounds, and he has taught me a great deal about commitment. I come from divorced parents, and his are still together; his parents' example is good for us.*
>
> —Female respondent

That parents influence their children is attested in comments like these from our respondents and in folk wisdom with such clichés as "The acorn doesn't fall far from the tree," "A chip off the old block," and "Like father, like son." The idea that the basis for marriage is our relationships with our parents is fascinating enough to the general public to have recently received attention in Reader's Digest (Brothers, 1997). But the influence of the family of origin on mate choice and marital quality has also been worthy of scholarly debate in philosophical, religious, and literary writings (see Adler, 1952), as well as the social and behavioral sciences.

In the social sciences, the work and writings of Sigmund Freud had a foundational influence in the development of the idea that parents could have an effect on their children's later, even adult, well-being. Freud's idea was that the mother–child relationship was "unique, without parallel, established unalterably for a whole lifetime as the first and strongest love-object and as the prototype of all later love relationships—for both sexes" (Freud, 1940/1949, p. 45). This perspective influenced most early research on mate selection (e.g., Strauss, 1946) and marital quality. In addition, many influential marital therapy theorists (e.g., Boszormenyi-Nagy, Framo, and Bowen) were trained in the psychoanalytic tradition, of which Freud was the founder. Given Freud's influence, it is not surprising that family-of-origin factors have been some of the most frequently used variables in predicting marital quality, especially in the earliest longitudinal research (Adams, 1946; Burgess & Wallin, 1953; Kelly & Conley, 1987; Terman & Oden, 1947; Vaillant, 1978). One of the problems with these early longitudinal studies was that they tended to group family-of-origin variables into one large factor, mixing structural variables and a multitude of process variables about the parents' marital relationship, the child's childhood happiness, and parent–child relationships. Burgess and Wallin, the most authoritative of these early studies, concluded from their own and earlier research that "a young person has a better than average chance of marital success if he has been reared in a home of education and culture where the parents are happily mated, where they have close affectionate relations with their children, and where discipline is kindly but firm and physical punishment rare" (1953, p. 513). From this finding, they concluded that aspects of the general fiber of the home environment, the quality of the parents' marriage, and the parent–child relationship are important.

After reviewing these and other more recent longitudinal studies, Wamboldt and Reiss (1989) conclude that family background factors are the weakest predictors (i.e., family of origin, individual characteristics, and interpersonal processor), but that they are by no means trivial. Wamboldt and Reiss then add, "Viewed as a whole, this research does support the hypothesis that residues from one's family-of-origin experience persist into later life and influence later development. Unfortunately, what actually persists and precisely how later marital development is influenced remain unknown" (1989, p. 319).

Purpose

The general model presented in Chapter 1 posits that the family of origin has a direct as well as an indirect influence on later marital quality. This chapter examines one of the variables from the general model (in this case, family of origin), and decomposes it into its basic components, and examines their relationships to marital quality in detail. Through this process we can begin to elucidate and articulate the factors and processes that "actually [persist] and precisely how later martial development is influenced" (Wamboldt & Reiss, 1989, p. 319).

Family-of-Origin Factors Related to Marital Quality

We distilled four distinct categories of findings from the literature on family-of-origin factors that are related to later marital quality. We thus see the category of "Family of Origin" from the general model as being composed of the more specific categories of family structure, parents' marital quality, family environment, and parent–child relationship. We first review the empirical research on the relationship between each of these factors and marital quality. On the basis of this review, we then offer a model of how family of origin variables relate to marital quality by building an empirical and theoretical case for which variables to include and offer an ordering of the variables in terms of their relative contributions to marital quality. Finally, we conduct an empirical test of the model and offer implications of our findings.

Family Structure

Most of the research on the influence of family structure on adult children's outcomes has investigated the relationship between parents' divorce and adult children's divorce. That research shows conclusively that parents' divorce is related to adult children's proneness to divorce, and that this relationship, while reduced, is still present even when various controls are introduced (Amato, 1996; Amato & Keith, 1991; Glenn & Kramer, 1987; McLanahan & Bumpass, 1988; Mueller & Pope, 1977; Pope & Mueller, 1976). In her review of the determinants of divorce in the 1980s, White (1990) cites a growing literature that shows a positive relationship between parental divorce and children's divorce, with no contradictory findings. Lowered marital quality almost certainly precedes the dissolution of the marriage, although not necessarily always (Lewis & Spanier, 1979). Thus, if this were the only literature available, we could deduce a relationship between parents' divorce and adult children's marital *quality* based on the relationship between parents' divorce and adult children's marital *stability*.

Indeed, the empirical evidence of a relationship between parents' divorce and adult children's marital quality is sparse. Wamboldt and Reiss's (1989) small sample study found no significant relationships between parents' divorce and adult children's marital adjustment, even though the correlations are in the range that larger samples have reported. However, in a meta-analysis of 37 studies of parental divorce and adult well-being, Amato and Keith (1991) conclude that parental divorce is related negatively to adult children's marital quality.

Family Environment

Family environment includes the events, processes, people, interactions, and perceptions that were part of the family in which the respondent grew up. This variable taps the *general* environment surrounding the person, as opposed to the *specific* relationship between the child and the parents. From an ecological and family systems point of view, we would expect the family "environment," "atmosphere," or "climate" to influence adult children's well-being and social competence.

Several of the early studies contained measures of the family of origin's social background, but the fact that they were often grouped with other family variables makes it difficult to assess their separate effect. Terman and Oden (1947), including the "educational and occupational achievement" of parents in their study, evidently found the bivariate correlation of these items to be unrelated to the marital happiness of their intellectually gifted sample. Burgess and Wallin (1953), on the other hand, found that higher education and higher income of fathers was related to later marital success of their children.

More recent studies continue to find small but often statistically significant correlations between some aspect of the parents' social background and the adult child's marital quality. Skolnick's (1981) longitudinal study of marital satisfaction in midlife found that fathers' education was significantly related to midlife men's marital satisfaction, but not to women's. On the other hand, fathers' occupation was related to women's marital satisfaction, but not to men's. A measure of fathers' socioeconomic status was related to both men's and women's marital satisfaction.

Whyte's (1990) cross-sectional study of Detroit women married between 1925 and 1984 found wives' subjective class origin to be positively related to a measure of marital quality and negatively related to a measure of marital problems at the bivariate level. But when included in a multivariate model that included other premarital as well as marital variables, wives' class origin failed to maintain a statistically significant relationship with marital quality and marital problems. Other family social context items, such as parents' investment income, fathers' occupation, and husbands' class origin, were unrelated to marital quality or marital problems at the bivariate and multivariate levels of analysis.

Terman and Oden's (1947) early longitudinal study of gifted children found no relationship between aspects of the family environment such as birth order, number of siblings, attachment to siblings, and religious training or sex education in the home and their later marital quality. However, they did find that if the discipline in the home was not irregular and if the person rated his or her childhood above average, he or she had higher marital success (Terman & Oden, 1947, as reported by Burgess & Wallin, 1953).

Vaillant (1978) reported that his composite measure of "childhood environment" was not related to middle-aged men's marital quality. However, his measure included a conglomeration of psychiatrists' and family workers' notes on the boys' report of their home life and included peripheral measures such as whether the men had done well in high school academically, socially, and athletically. It also included measures of the quality of the parent–child relationships that we conceptualize as distinct from, or at least a distinct aspect of, the family environments.

Holman and colleagues' (1994) global measure of home environment, which included occurrence of stressor events, childhood happiness, satisfaction with communication, leisure, work, discipline in the family, and parental alcohol use, was significantly related to the marital satisfaction of husbands and wives married 1 year. But their measure also included the parent–child relationship, and therefore measured more than what we conceptualized as home environment.

Bennett and her colleagues (Bennett, Wolin, & McAvity, 1988; Bennett, Wolin, Reiss, & Teitelbaum, 1987) demonstrated that alcohol abuse in the parental generation affects the child's ability to function in marriage. Brennan, Shaver, and Tobey (1991) reported that adults who avoid closeness and intimacy in adult relationships are more likely to report a parent with an alcohol problem than are other young adults.

Whyte (1990) reported that the level of family conflict wives remembered in their families of origin was related to their current marital quality, and this variable retained a significant relationship with marital quality even when controlling for other premarital and marital variables. Wamboldt and Reiss (1989) found that aspects of respondents' remembered family environment, including expressiveness, conflict, and cohesion in the family, were related to relationship adjustment.

Parents' Marital Quality

Despite the fact that some of the very earliest research noted a relationship between these factors (Burgess & Wallin, 1953; Terman & Oden, 1947), only a few studies have been done that examine the relationship between the quality of the parents' marriage and the quality of their adult children's marriages. For example, Overall, Henry, and Woodward's (1974) study of psychiatric outpatients found in their sample that a history of parental marital discord was related to marital complaints. This relationship held even when controlling for "relevant background variables and psychiatric symptom manifestations" (p. 450).

Most of the support for this relationship comes from case studies or in-depth qualitative interview research. This research strongly suggests that the quality of the parental marriage, along with other components of the family-of-origin experience, is related to who is selected for marriage and to the development of the resulting marital relationship (Bennett et al., 1988; Doxey, 1994; Fischer & Ayoub, 1996; Napier, 1971; Napier & Whitaker, 1978; Noam, 1996). However, these studies also note that patterns of interaction are not always transmitted intergenerationally, and each of them suggests that other mechanisms at work increase or decrease the likelihood of a generational transmission.

Parent–Child Relationships

The aspect of family of origin as it relates to adult children's marital quality that has received the most attention is the relationship between the parents and the child. Burgess and Wallin (1953), summarizing their own research and others' earlier research, found support for the quality of the parent–child relationship being positively related to adult children's marital quality in most cases. Since that time, other researchers, using composite family of origin measures that contained a number of measures of the quality of the parent–child relationship, found a significant positive relationship between their composite measures and later marital quality (Holman et al., 1994; Kelly & Conley, 1987).

Much of the research, particularly quantitative research, that looks at the influence of parent–child relationships on children's marital relationships has been drawn from attachment theory. Hazan and Shaver (1987) hypothesized that the three attachment behaviors that have been identified in infants and young children—secure, avoidant, and anxious-ambivalent—should also be evident in young adults, and that the type of attachment relationship they had with parents should be reflected in the quality of their close, romantic relationships. Hazan and Shaver's results supported this hypothesis. A number of other studies have also used these attachment styles and found similar results (Noam, 1996; see also Shaver & Clark, 1996, for a review of this research; Fischer & Ayoub, 1996; cf. Feeney & Noller, 1990).

Other studies that do not use the attachment perspective or the adult attachment styles developed by Hazan and Shaver have found similar results. In a 36-year prospective study of the relationship between child rearing and adult outcomes, Franz, McClelland, and Weinberger (1991, p. 592) found that "adults whose mothers or fathers were warm and affectionate were able to sustain long and relatively happy marriages." Rutter's (1988) study of English women reared as children totally or partially in an institution, showed that as a rule poor quality parenting was related to poor decision making in later choices about intimate partners and to poor quality marriages.

Coming from a psychoanalytic and family systems perspective, Napier (Napier, 1971; Napier & Whitaker, 1978) used case studies to demonstrate the complex and long-lasting relationship between parent–child interactional processes and the quality of the children's marriages. Doxey (1994) takes a social constructivist perspective in her qualitative, in-depth interview study of early married couples and their relationships with parents. She found that the remembered parent–child relationship continued to affect the evolving marital relationship for good or ill.

We have presented research evidence for relationships between four aspects of family of origin and adult children's marital quality. However, the simple direct relationships do not tell the complete story. We suggest that the rather modest relationship between some of the family-of-origin variables and marital quality results from *indirect* rather than direct relationship to marital quality. We now build a theoretical and empirical case for a proposed model that shows direct and indirect connections between family-of-origin factors and children's subsequent marital quality.

Theoretical and Empirical Ordering of the Family-of-Origin Factors

As we noted in Chapter 1, theoretical work on a prediction model of marital development initially lagged far behind the research. Bowerman's (1964) review of prediction research claimed that greater understanding of marital prediction would depend more on the development of a body of theory than on methodological advances. Burr (1973), responding to Bowerman's call for theory development, began that process, but did not include family-of-origin factors explicitly in his theoretical model of premarital prediction. Lewis and Spanier (1979) presented a model of marital quality and stability that included family-of-origin factors. They used a social exchange perspective to order their propositions, and they subsumed family-of-origin factors under the category of the premarital "social and personal resources" that the individual brought to the marital relationship. Burr, Leigh, Day, and Constantine (1979), responding to the Lewis and Spanier (1979) review, suggested that symbolic interaction provided a more parsimonious understanding of marital satisfaction (they preferred the concept of marital satisfaction to marital quality). They subsumed the premarital family-of-origin variables under the interactionist concept of role enactment.

However, as far as we can determine, neither the theoretical models nor the prediction research that has hypothesized or studied the relationship between family factors and later marital quality has explicitly suggested an ordering to the concepts seen as important aspects of the family of origin. We believe, however, that such an ordering is scientifically and practically useful. Furthermore, theory has developed since the time of Bowerman in the mid-1960s, and Burr, Lewis and Spanier, and Burr, Leigh et al. in the 1970s, which allows for greater specificity in our explanation of the interrelationship of the family-of-origin predictors of marital quality. Moreover, other research connects some of the family-of-origin variables with one another, even if the end goal of that research was not then to connect these variables to adult children's marital quality.

A number of theoretical perspectives have been used to explain the relationship between family of origin and children's individual and social development. The idea that parents influence their children's development is, according to Acock and Demo (1994, p. 42), "central to anthropological, developmental, structural-functional, symbolic interactionist, feminist, social exchange, social learning, social role, family systems, and psychoanalytic theories." Our own review of the literature revealed that five perspectives are used most frequently to explain how family-of-origin factors related to *adult* children's social competence: social exchange, symbolic interactionism, social constructivism, family systems, and most especially, developmental theories. Each of these is now explained to set up the ordering of variables.

Lewis and Spanier (1979) were the first to apply a social exchange perspective to this relationship. After reviewing all of the research on family of origin and later marital quality or stability, they inductively tie the findings to a more general idea out of social exchange theory by suggesting that premarital family-of-origin factors can be seen as "resources" the person brings or fails to bring to a relationship, and that "the greater these social and personal resources available for adequate marital role functioning, the higher the subsequent marital quality" (Lewis & Spanier, 1979, p. 275). Sabatelli and Shehan (1993, p. 396) suggest that a core assumption from the social exchange perspective about the nature of relationships is that "social exchanges are characterized by interdependence; that is, the ability to obtain profits in a relationship is contingent on the ability to provide others with rewards."

Sabatelli and Shehan build a model of relationship satisfaction suggesting that satisfaction is derived from a person's evaluation of the rewards in a relationship. Thus, the more resources a person has derived from the family of origin, the greater the rewards the person has to offer a partner, and therefore the more likely that person and the other should view the relationship as satisfactory. Lewis and Spanier (1979) did not use the exchange concept of comparison level (CL), but Sabatelli and Shehan (1993) introduce it into their model of relationship satisfaction. The CL is the standard a person uses to evaluate the rewards or costs associated with, and therefore the satisfaction derived from, a relationship. This standard is based on the person's understanding of social norms about what can be expected from relationships, and on the person's observations of other similar relationships, such as between parents, other relatives, or close friends.

Thus, social exchange suggests that family-of-origin factors can be seen as partially responsible for endowing individuals with rewards they bring to a relationship. The way in which individuals view these as rewards is then related to how these family-of-origin experiences become a part of the comparison level by which a person evaluates his or her satisfaction with the relationship. That is, on the basis of observations of the parents' marital relationships in the family of origin, persons will expect or not expect certain rewarding or costly behaviors in their own marital relationships. Social exchange does not explain how these expectations are learned, but seems to assume a social learning perspective, that is, people learn from observations of and experiences in relationships. Therefore, we could speculate that people learn from observing the parents' relationship and from their experiences in relationships with their parents and siblings.

However, a number of important issues are left unaddressed by social exchange theory. For example, it does not tell us how humans calculate the rewards, costs, and alternatives that are part of their relationship evaluation (Burr, Leigh, et al., 1979). We are not given any insight into how or why some relationships would be more salient than others (e.g., a parent–child relationship as opposed to a sibling relationship), nor any suggestion on ordering of factors.

Symbolic interaction theory assumes that humans behave on the basis of the meanings they create in interaction (Burr, Leigh, et al., 1979; LaRossa & Reitzes, 1993). People then act on the basis of the meaning they attribute to a situation or another person's behavior. Among the meanings developed are a sense of self and others. Thus, symbolic interaction, applied to the relationship between family of origin and adult-child marital quality, suggests that the family is a primary player in the development of how possible intimate others are seen, how structures interact between them, and the meaning inferred from such interaction.

As noted above, Burr, Leigh, et al. (1979) suggest that family-of-origin factors are indicators of a more general concept of role enactment, which they define as "how well a person performs a role relative to the expectations for that role" (1979, p. 58). Evidently they see the parent–child relationship as an important arena for developing a conception of and perceptions about roles one plays in marital relationships. Therefore, to the extent that couples are able to enact healthy and compatible spousal roles, they will experience marital satisfaction.

As we described in Chapter 1, family systems theory suggests that to understand marital quality as it is perceived by a spouse, we need to recognize the principle of wholism, that all parts of the system are interconnected and influence one another. Various family systems theorists have noted the peculiar interconnectedness of members of premarital couples as it relates to families of origin. Napier (1971) and Napier and Whitaker (1978), combining a psychoanalytic perspective with their family systems approach, suggest that individuals are drawn to other individuals as marital partners to satisfy some unmet need from childhood, to escape from some aspect of the family of origin, or to work out issues from their childhood. But in the process, they often "choose" someone whose deficits match or complement their own.

Bowen's family systems theory offers another variation on this same idea. Bowen describes individuals as differing in their ability to navigate through life's challenges based on their fusion with or differentiation from the family of origin's emotional climate. Thus, one's ability to form high-quality, intimate adult relationships depends on how well the relationships in the family of origin have been resolved and how well the person has "differentiated" from the family (Papero, 1995).

Closely related to family systems theory explanations is the social constructivist perspective put forward by Wamboldt and Reiss (1989). They begin by noting that findings concerning family background have yet to be well-integrated into a therapeutically meaningful understanding of the mechanism(s) whereby some marriages succeed while others fail. They cite two prominent models that suggest how this process may proceed: the socialization model and the social constructivist model. The socialization model suggests that children learn a repertoire of behaviors and schema from observation and modeling. These experiences then shape the structure of subsequent relationships. The socialization model, pushed to the extreme, views children and adolescents as passive recipients of an intergenerational legacy and emphasizes continuity rather than change. Social constructivism takes a more developmental and systemic approach by allowing for more of a possibility of change. Children are seen as capable, over time, of actively "constructing" their own models and altering previous models based on the multiple relational systems of which they are a part. Indeed, the transition into a marital relationship is seen as one of the best, if not the best, opportunity for a person to "reconstruct" a relationship model as the person and his or her partner combine two family-of-origin experiences (Wamboldt & Reiss, 1989, p. 321).

In our specific case this perspective helps us justify the inclusion of multiple relationship systems (parents' marital relationship and parent–child relationships) and to speculate that these relationship systems should be interdependent. Furthermore, it is clear from this perspective that to understand the quality of the marital relationship as it is influenced by family-of-origin factors, we also need to know about the partner's family of origin.

However, the most frequently used and most compelling arguments come from developmental perspectives. As an overarching perspective, developmental reasoning can be seen in traditional family developmental (life cycle) theory and life course analysis often used by family sociologists (Klein & White, 1996). But the particular developmental perspectives used to explain family-of-origin factors' influence on marital quality come largely out of developmental psychology. Bretherton (1993, p. 280) asserts that two of the most fundamental assumptions underlying developmental theories are (1) that the parent–child relationship plays a crucial role in the development of a sense of self and the capacity for relatedness to others and (2) that patterns of social interaction with parents are internalized and affect the individual's capacity for close relationships outside the family. Bretherton lists three other related assumptions and then concludes:

> In short, parent and child operate as a codeveloping two-person system embedded within also developing family and societal systems. Individual differences in the codevelopment of parent and child depend on the unique characteristics each brings to the initial relationship, as well as on the relationship patterns they create as each influences the other. The optimal outcome of this process for the child is not only a capacity for close relationships, but the internalization of parental-societal values. (p. 280)

Of particular importance to the development of theories about marital and family relationship are two of these developmental perspectives: attachment theory, and ecology theory of human development. There are, of course, more than these developmental perspectives, but their usefulness is in how they help us understand the issue of continuity and change across time and generations, how strong the relationships across time and generations should be, and how the family-of-origin variables should be ordered.

Attachment Theory

Attachment theory developed out of observations by John Bowlby (see Bowlby, 1988) of the behaviors of infants with their mothers or primary caregivers. He postulated that humans are social from birth, and that seeking a secure attachment is a fundamental part of our nature. "By conceptualizing attachment ... as a fundamental form of behavior with its own internal motivation distinct from feeding and sex, and of no less importance for survival, the behavior and motivation are accorded a theoretical status never before given them" (Bowlby, 1988, p. 27).

Attachment theory is often described as a developmental theory (Belsky & Pensky, 1988; Bretherton, 1993), a psychoanalytic theory (Bretherton, 1993; Miller, 1993), an object relations theory (Bretherton, 1993; Miller, 1993), and an ethological-evolutionary theory (Bretherton, 1993; Putallaz, Costanzo, & Klein, 1993). Bowlby himself says that attachment theory "was developed out of the object relations tradition in psychoanalysis; but it has drawn also on concepts from evolution theory, ethology, control theory, and cognitive psychology" (Bowlby, 1988, p. 120). Part of attachment theory's appeal and power is its ability to offer a fundamental explanation for behavior and its ability to incorporate ideas successfully from other theoretical perspectives that enlarge its explanatory power.

Literally hundreds of studies have been guided by attachment theory and all observers agree that the evidence supporting the importance of attachment in infants and young children is strong, and that there is a great deal of continuity between attachment styles developed in infancy and attachment styles in children up to age 6 (Bartholomew, 1993; Shaver & Hazan, 1993). However, attachment theory was not seen by Bowlby as simply a theory to explain the first few years of life . He felt that "attachment behavior is held to characterize human beings from cradle to the grave" (Bowlby, 1977, p. 203). Bartholomew (1993, p. 30) asserts that attachment theory makes "two bold hypotheses:" first, that attachment behavior characterizes human beings throughout life, and second, that "patterns established in childhood parent–child relationships tend to structure the quality of later adult–child relationships."

The first assertion, that attachment is a fundamental need cradle to grave, is an important nondevelopmental assertion in understanding why people marry, but the second assertion is the "more exciting (and controversial) implication of the theory" (Bartholomew, 1993, p. 31). Its implication is that a person's ability to form and maintain appropriate intimate relationships throughout life depends on at least the quality of the attachment relationship the person had with his/her parent(s). Indeed, Bowlby says that a basic premise of attachment theory is that internal representations of attachment formed during childhood and adolescence "tend to persist relatively unchanged into and throughout adult life" (Bowlby, 1977, p. 209). As noted above, there is a great deal of support for the continuity of attachment behavior or styles from infancy through early childhood (Bartholomew, 1993; Shaver & Hazan, 1993). Several pieces of research by Hazan and Shaver (1987), and those who followed their theoretical and methodological lead (see Shaver & Clark, 1996, for a review), have demonstrated convincingly that attachment behaviors continue in adulthood (Weiss, 1996). But whether these adult attachment behaviors are consistent with and derive from attachment behaviors learned in infancy and childhood from interaction with parents is not as clear. Bartholomew (1993, p. 31) contends that "there is as yet no direct evidence for continuity from parent–child to adult–adult relationships, and it will be some time before such evidence is available. However, extrapolating from the childhood attachment literature, it is possible to predict developmental pathways that may lead to specific patterns of problems in adult personal relationships."

Others find the evidence more compelling for the continuity of attachment behaviors learned in childhood. Miller (1993), in her review of the research, finds evidence for what she calls "relationship learning," which begins in childhood and continues into adulthood; and she provides an excellent explanation for both continuity and change, which we will describe below. Hazan and Shaver's (1987) groundbreaking study of attachment behaviors in young adults found that remembered attachments to parents were consistent with current attachment behaviors with romantic partners. They report that patterns of behavior labeled secure, avoidant, and anxious-ambivalent in children could be identified in adult romantic behavior. Numerous studies followed their line of research. Shaver and Clark (1996) summarize the research in a recent book chapter. This line of research demonstrates that avoidant adults had parents whom they described as rejecting and cold—and with whom they had a poor relationship. The avoidant adults were also more likely to have an alcoholic parent than were adults in the other styles of attachment. The avoidant adults were uninterested in seeking and developing intimacy and were cynical about relationships. Anxious-ambivalent adults described their parents as intrusive and unfair, which Shaver and Clark suggest may be due to inconsistent and unreliable parenting. These adults yearned for romantic relationships, seeming even desperate, but were argumentative, intrusive, and overcontrolling in romantic relationships. Secure adults spoke of their parents in generally favorable terms. Their adult romantic relationships tended to be more stable and demonstrated greater ability to resolve problems and work together than did the other two.

The mechanism by which early experiences influence later relationships is by means of what Bowlby (1988) called *representational models* or *working models*. A working model, according to Bowlby (1988, p. 129), is a "cognitive structure" a child builds based on his or her parents' ways of communicating and behaving toward him or her. This model governs how the child feels about him/herself, how he/she expects parents and others to treat him/her, and how he/she plans his/her behavior toward others.

Bowlby (1988, p. 130) emphasizes the unchanging nature of working models, seeing them as becoming "habitual, generalized, and largely unconscious," but he allows for "gradual updating of models." This is most likely with secure individuals, whereas insecure individuals are more likely to maintain their original working models. Most other attachment researchers suggest that working models resist change, but they can be changed (Bartholomew, 1993; Bretherton, 1993, 1996; Miller, 1993; Noam & Fischer, 1996; Putallaz et al., 1993; Shaver & Clark, 1996).

Miller offers the best explanation of the reasons for strong continuity and yet the possibility of change (1993, p. 29):

> Continuity in experience, which is a manifestation of assimilation processes, has received particular research attention because of interest in long-term impact of early relationship experience. Developmental evidence for continuity in social experiences is strongest for childhood, especially for aggressive-rejected children, but is beginning to accumulate for adulthood as well. Research results do not imply invariance in social outlook and behavior throughout life, but rather that outlooks and behavior change gradually due to the force of prior expectations. According to object relations theories (of which attachment theory is one), prior expectations can be difficult to alter due to their history of reinforcement, internal organization, and potential association with anxiety. Continuity, rather than discontinuity, in experience is to be expected because assimilation is a simpler, less threatening process than accommodation of novelty. Accommodation of experience, however, makes acquisition of skills and understandings possible, and we are only beginning to demonstrate some of the factors that facilitate or inhibit accommodation processes.

Miller mentions novelty and conflict in relationships as the types of experiences that can lead to accommodation. Other authors have mentioned important relationship experiences, breakup of important relationships, successful long-term psychotherapy (Shaver & Clark, 1996), emotionally significant relationships that contradict earlier relationship patterns, and major life transitions (Bartholomew, 1993). Thus these working models are not unmodifiable, but most authors suggest, as do Putallaz et al. (1993, p. 91), that we continue to need "to examine the processes by which models are both transmitted and modified."

Attachment theory and research provide strong support for a relationship between parent–child interaction and adult children's marital quality variables. We now turn to human ecology theory for help in ordering the variables.

Ecological Theory of Human Development

Two ideas from Bronfenbrenner's (1979) ecology theory of human development are useful to our task here. First, his theory, like other perspectives in the ecological tradition, posits that humans and their relationships have to be studied in their broader contexts (Bretherton, 1993). Thus, to understand family-of-origin effects on adult marital satisfaction, we need to recognize that the family is embedded within larger contexts such as the society in which the family resides. Also, parent–child relationships are embedded within the broader family context. The second helpful idea from Bronfenbrenner is the idea of interrelated levels of systems that describe the environment within which individuals and their relationship are embedded. They are differentiated with respect to their immediacy to the developing person or relationship (Bubolz & Sontag, 1993) and to the level of involvement the person or relationship has with them. Thus, the most proximate system to the developing young adult is the parent–child relationship. Next would be the broader family environment, since both parents and child are a part of that system, but so are other family members, and there will be behaviors and interactions that did not directly involve the young adult but inevitably influence the parent–child relationship. The parents' marital subsystem and the actual family structure are part of the broader family context, one in which the child has limited access and responsibility, but which should have an effect on the parent–child relationship.

From an ecological perspective, it is logical that the parents' marital relationship and family structure are more distal than the home environment. This is because the adult child played a role in and was a part of the home environment, but was not directly involved with the parents' marital relationship and the forming of the family structure. Research (Rhoades, 1994; Rutter, 1988) and theory (Easterbrook & Embe, 1988) support a relationship between parents' marital quality and parent–child relationship. There is also research support for a relationship between family structure and the parent–child relationship (Acock & Demo, 1994; Simons & Associates, 1996).

This reasoning and research suggest a rather complex path model. Indeed, it exceeds the complexity and comprehensiveness of any model heretofore presented. But it still does not adequately represent all we now know about the influence of family-of-origin factors on adult children's marital quality. As noted earlier, family systems theory and psychoanalytic theory and its offshoots, such as object relations theories and attachment theory, make it clear that the relationship between the parent–child and adult marital quality is more complex than we have thus far been able to model. Attachment theory posits that the quality of the parent–child relationship results in a "working model" of self and others that affects the (adult) child's ability to form long-lasting, quality attachments, such as in a marriage. But of course we "attach" to another person who also has an attachment style based on the quality of his/her parent–child relationship; and the "marital quality" that results from a marital union of two people is a function of the two people's relationship history. Therefore, the marital partner's family-of-origin variable should influence one's perception of one's own marital quality. According to clinical research and theory (Bowen, 1978; Napier, 1971; Napier & Whitaker, 1978), individuals tend to marry people at their same level, that is, with similar attachment needs. Thus, there should be some sort of connection between the quality of the partner's parent–child relationship and the adult child's marital quality. We suspect the relationship between partners' families of origin and marital quality is much more complex than we are able to model, but we believe we will extend our understanding by proposing a direct effect from partners' parent–child relationships to adult children's marital quality and a correlation between the two partners' parent–child relationships.

There is some limited empirical support for this hypothesis in existing literature. Couillard (1990) found that the couples with the best marital adjustment had highly healthy families of origin, and the least adjusted couples tended to have families of origin with low emotional health scores. Furthermore, a wife's perception of her marital adjustment was most dependent on her own family of origin's emotional health, but a husband's marital adjustment was usually influenced by the wife's family of origin emotional health as well as her own family of origin's emotional health. Wamboldt and Reiss (1989) found that premarital reports of conflict or expressiveness in the family of origin were frequently as highly related to later relationship adjustment of the spouse as to the relationship adjustment of the person. Holman et al. (1994) found that males' family-of-origin quality reported premaritally was more highly related to wives' marital satisfaction 1 year into marriage, than was the wives' own reported family-of-origin quality.

In another analysis of the same data set used in this study, we found an interesting interaction with males' marital quality. Men with poor parent–child relationship quality experienced significantly higher marital quality when their wives reported lower parent–child relationship quality than when the wives reported good parent–child relationship quality. Alternatively, when the men had good parent–child relationship quality, they experienced lower marital quality when their wives reported poor parent–child relationship quality. One plausible hypothesis we proffer is that men from good family-of-origin backgrounds feel responsible to help their wives deal with problems. With women reporting a poor parent–child relationship quality, this is likely to be a burden to the marriage. Given the cultural expectation that men be independent and strong, men with poor parent–child relationship quality may perceive their healthier wives as a threat to their masculinity, whereas when these same men have wives who also report poor parent–child relationship quality, they will more likely cooperate to help one another overcome the difficulties. Further research is needed to replicate this interaction and examine the several plausible hypotheses that could be generated to explain it.

We can represent the hypothesized relationships between family-of-origin factors graphically in a path model, represented in Figure 4.1. This model represents both what we are able to glean from research and theory, and what we are able to measure, given an extant data set.

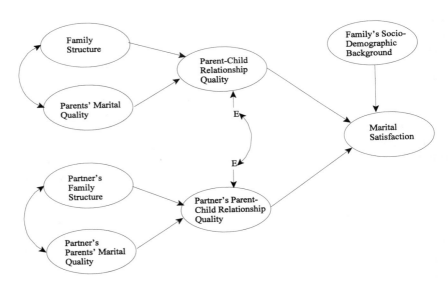

Figure 4.1. Conceptual model for family-of-origin factors relationship to marital satisfaction.

Table 4.1. Means (with Standard Deviations) for Marital Quality, Parent–Child Relationship Quality, Family Structure, and Parents' Marital Quality

	Female	Male
Marital Satisfaction		
Physical Intimacy*	3.95 (0.93)	3.64 (0.98)
Love	4.41 (0.83)	4.35 (0.71)
Conflict Resolution*	3.84 (0.89)	3.73 (0.85)
Equality*	4.16 (0.86)	4.06 (0.74)
Communication*	3.83 (0.94)	3.70 (0.87)
Overall	4.47 (0.67)	4.41 (0.67)
Parent–Child Relationship Quality		
Father–Child Relationship*	2.52 (0.93)	2.40 (0.87)
Mother–Child Relationship*	3.13 (0.74)	2.93 (0.68)
Parents' Discipline Quality	3.00 (0.71)	3.09 (0.60)
Satisfaction with Family Relations	2.65 (0.86)	2.67 (0.83)
Family Structure		
Father's Traditional (reference category) and Nontraditional Family Structure*	0.91 (0.29)	0.86 (0.35)
Mother's Traditional (reference category) and Nontraditional Family Structure	0.89 (0.32)	0.85 (0.35)
Parents' Marital Quality		
Father's Marital Satisfaction	3.07 (1.15)	3.10 (1.15)
Mother's Marital Satisfaction	2.95 (1.24)	3.01 (1.18)
Family Sociodemographic Background		
Father's Education*	4.97 (1.77)	4.61 (1.96)
Mother's Education	3.72 (2.36)	3.60 (1.39)
Father's Occupation Professional (reference category) or other	0.20 (0.40)	0.19 (0.39)
Father's Income	5.99 (1.85)	6.02 (1.72)

* Differences significant at $p < .05$ level.

Results

The measures for the latent variables used in the analyses in this chapter are described in Chapter 2. Structural equation modeling (SEM) was used to perform the analyses for our models. Models were run separately for wives and husbands. We followed a two-step process (Jöreskog & Sörbom, 1996; Schumacker & Lomax, 1996), estimating first the measurement model, and then the structural model. The measurement model's confirmatory factor analysis results demonstrated that some of the family environment issues were viewed by respondents as part of the parent–child relationship. Evidently, when answering our items about, for example, the quality of communication in the family, respondents were thinking in terms of their communication with their parents, rather than communication in the whole family. What we had conceptualized as part of the broader family environment was included as an indicator of the parent–child relationship.

Thus, the exogenous variables for the models consisted of family structure (a dummy variable), family sociodemographic background, and parents' marital quality for both the wives and husbands. The endogenous parent–child relationship quality and the criterion variable wives' or husbands' marital satisfaction. Estimation of the SEM is based on covariance matrices. Table 4.1 presents the means and standard deviations for the various indicators of the marital quality and family-of-origin latent variables. The results show that the wives generally had higher marital satisfaction than did their husbands, and also higher means on relationships with their mothers and fathers than did their husbands. The wives were slightly more likely to have been reared in an intact family than were their husbands, but the husbands saw their parents as having as high a quality of marriages as their wives. Wives' fathers had a little more education than their husbands' fathers, but they were similar in the three variables of mother's education, father's occupations being professional, and father's income.

Table 4.2 shows the bivariate correlations of the latent variables used to test the reestimated structural model. The highest correlations are generally between variables that are connected with arrows in the structural model, giving a preliminary indication that the hypothesized conceptual model should fit the data.

The path diagrams in Figure 4.2 for the wives and Figure 4.3 for the husbands show the results for the statistical models tested. Unstandardized and standardized path coefficients are reported. The unstandardized coefficients allow the husbands' and wives' models to be compared on a similar metric, while the standardized allow a more intuitive interpretation of the paths and a comparison of paths within the same model. Good model fit is indicated in both instances; nonsignificant chi-squares and fit indices are well above .90.

Most important for our purposes here is that, as hypothesized, the quality of the parent–child relationship in the family of origin, as reported premaritally, is positively and   significantly related to marital satisfaction several years into

Table 4.2. Bivariate Correlation Between Latent Constructs

	1	2	3	4	5	6	7	8
1. Marital Satisfaction	—	.12	.37	.01	.06	.06	.23	.02
2. Males' Parent–Child Relationship Quality	.22	—	.17	.21	.01	.70	.06	.02
3. Females' Parent–Child Relationship Quality	.16	.14	—	.00	.17	.06	.65	.20
4. Males' Family Structure	.05	.24	-.01	—	.10	.38	.02	.06
5. Females' Family Structure	.02	.01	.16	.09	—	.02	.39	.12
6. Males' Parents' Marital Quality	.15	.70	.04	.39	.01	—	.08	.04
7. Females' Parents' Marital Quality	.10	.05	.66	-.00	.39	.06	—	.31
8. Family Sociodemographic Background	.07	.18	.04	.17	.04	.26	.07	—

Note. Coefficients above the diagonal are for wives ($N = 355$), those below the diagonal are for husbands ($N = 367$).

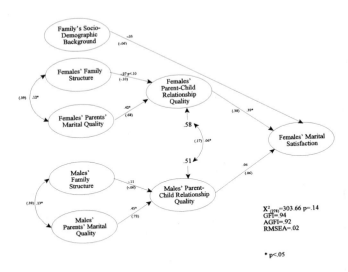

Figure 4.2. Female model of family-of-origin factors and marital satisfaction; unstandardized (and standardized) coefficients (*N* = 355).

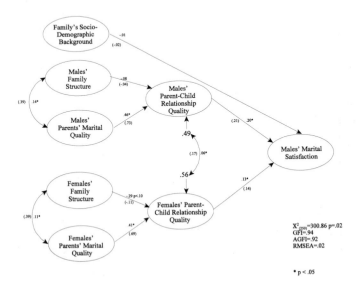

Figure 4.3. Male model of family-of-origin factors and marital satisfaction; unstandardized (and standardized) coefficients (*N* = 367).

marriage. The relationship between the wives' parent–child relationship quality and their later marital satisfaction is almost twice that of the husbands' parent–child relationship quality and their later marital satisfaction. However, while the quality of the husbands' parent–child relationships is not significantly related to wives' marital satisfaction, wives' parent–child relationship is almost as highly related to the husbands' marital satisfaction as the husbands' own parent–child relationship quality. Furthermore, as our theory suggests, the quality of wives' and husbands' parent–child relationship are correlated; partners do generally choose a mate with family-of-origin experiences similar to their own.

For husbands, being raised in an intact family by both biological parents did not influence the quality of the parent–child relationship, but being in a home where both biological parents were continuously present did slightly improve the quality of females' parent–child relationships. But husbands and wives from intact homes perceived their parents as having significantly higher marital satisfaction, and parents' marital quality was positively and significantly related to the quality of the parent–child relationship.

In neither model did family sociodemographic background have a direct effect on marital satisfaction. But this background variable was positively and significantly correlated with males' family structure, males' parents' marital quality, and males' parent–child relations. For the wives, their family socio-demographic background was positively and significantly related to their parents' marital quality and the parent–child relationship. These correlations, taken together with the small, insignificant direct paths from sociodemographic background and marital quality would indicate that future models should consider these background characteristics as predictors of the parents' marital structure and quality.

We also looked at the indirect and total effects for both models. Only wives' parents' marital quality had a statistically significant indirect "effect" on wives' marital satisfaction; and wives' parents' marital quality and wives' parent–child relationship quality had statistically significant total "effects" on wives' marital satisfaction. On the other hand, husbands' parents' marital quality, and wives' parents' marital quality both have statistically significant indirect "effects" on husbands' marital satisfaction. Both of those variables, along with husbands' parent–child relationship quality and wives' parent–child relationship quality, have statistically significant total "effects" on husbands' marital satisfaction.

Discussion

The most fundamental conclusion to be reached from our data is that the quality of the family-of-origin experience assessed premaritally does indeed influence the marital quality of the children who grew up in those families. We have not yet seen how family-of-origin factors fare when other factors are taken into account (as we will in the next several chapters), but that should not diminish the fact that knowing about and understanding the family of origin premaritally can help us understand marital quality several years into marriage.

Implications for Research and Theory

Family of origin has often been conceptualized and measured as an undifferentiated conglomerate of structural and process variables, often at different levels of analysis. It was our contention that some aspects of the family-of-origin experience would have a greater influence than would others. We based this contention largely on the developmental perspectives of attachment theory and ecology of human development theory. A fundamental assumption of develop- mental psychology is that the parent–child relationship is the most important relationship in a child's development (Bretherton, 1993). The attachment perspective, as well as a symbolic interactionist perspective, suggests that the primary family-of-origin factor influencing later marital quality will be the quality of the parent–child relationship. Furthermore, attachment theory suggests that the quality of this early relationship has long-lasting consequences, including the ability of a person to form high quality, intimate relationships as an adult. The ecology of human development perspective suggests an ordering of the family-of- origin factors from most proximate to most distal. While acknowledging the importance of the relationships that are the most proximate to the developing individual, such as the parent–child relationship, the ecology of human development perspective suggests that the more distal factors should also be important, including structural factors. Given these theoretical insights and adding to that the knowledge from available quantitative and qualitative research, we suggest the ordering of, and the relationships between, the variables noted in Figure 4.1.

Our analysis supported both the assertions of attachment theory and ecology of human development theory. We find that the quality of the parent–child relationship has the strongest relationship with later marital quality; such that the higher the quality of the parent–child relationship in childhood, the higher the quality of the adult child's marital relationship several years into marriage. Also, the family-of-origin factors in which the child did not participate as directly, did, as predicted from the human ecology perspective, make an important contribution. The most important of these factors is the quality of the parents' marriage. The higher the quality of the parents' marriage, the higher is the parent–child relationship quality. While being reared in an intact family versus any other family structure is not related directly to the parent–child relationship, it is related to the quality of the parents' marriage, such that parents in intact marriages have a better relationship with one another than do parents in other family structural arrangements.

Furthermore, we hypothesized, based on our review of existing research, that there is a direct relationship between family sociodemographic background and marital quality. Our results demonstrate that while no direct connection has been found, the correlations between this particular background factor and the structure and quality of the parents' marriage suggest that these sociodemographic factors may make an important contribution. They may establish a foundation for stable marriages and higher-quality marital relationships between parents which then affects the children's later marital relationships.

A family systems perspective and social constructionist perspective suggest that we cannot understand marital quality based only on the perceptions of one individual in the marriage. Indeed, not only should the person's relationship quality be influenced by the quality of the partner's parent–child relationship, but the two parent–child relationship qualities should be related to one another. Our results support these theoretical speculations, at least with the husbands. In fact, the quality of wives' parent–child relationships has almost as much influence on the husbands' marital quality as the husbands' own parent–child relationships, while the quality of the husbands' parent–child relationships has a minimal influence on the wives' marital quality. Additionally, the wives' parent–child relationships have almost twice as much influence on the wives' own marital quality as the husbands' parent–child relationships have on the husbands' own marital quality.

We interpret these results as supporting Wamboldt and Reiss's (1989) contention that wives are the "chief architects" of marital relationships. But our results allow us further theoretical speculations. We suggest that women's ability to be "architects" is much more influenced by the quality of their parent–child relationships, their attachment to parents, than that of the husbands. This assertion is based on the finding that the influence of wives' parent–child relationship quality on wives' marital quality is stronger than that of the husbands' parent–child relationship quality on husbands' marital quality. Husbands evidently depend on other factors to "construct" their sense of marital quality. This is not surprising in a culture that expects greater independence and individuation for males than for females.

The relationship between the childhood parent–child relationships of the wives and husbands lends support, albeit limited, to the object relations idea of partners "choosing" partners with similar deficiencies (or advantages) as themselves. The relationship, while statistically significant, is small, but the existing data set we used was not specifically designed to provide measures of Napier and Whitaker's idea of psychological needs or Bowen's idea of differentiation from or fusion to the family-of-origin's emotional climate. Given the somewhat general measures we used, we think that the fact that we have any statistically significant relationship in the hypothesized direction lends some support to this family systems idea, or at least calls for a more careful examination of these family systems ideas.

Implications for Practice and Policy

Given that 28% of clinicians take a primarily intergenerational approach (Nelson, Heilbrun, & Figley, 1993) and that 82% report the family-of-origin theory moderately to considerably influences their practices (Wilcoxon, 1989), we think it is no small matter, especially to practitioners who work with couples and families, that longitudinal research in the 1990s is showing the continued importance of family background, especially of the parent–child relationship on marital quality. Clergy, educators, premarital counselors, social workers, and others who teach and counsel couples considering marriage should find our results useful for designing educational or therapeutic interventions. A postmodern, constructivist approach suggests that individuals can "restory," "remember," or "reframe" their family-of-origin experience. While a parental divorce cannot be undone, the meanings attached to that divorce can be changed, and consequently, the negative influence of the divorce lessened. Even more so, the quality of the parent–child relationship can be told differently, can be seen through different lenses, or different aspects of the relationship can be emphasized, so that the negative consequences of the parent–child relationship do not unduly negatively influence the impending marriage. Additionally, the work of such authors as Framo (1992) cogently argues that only through directly working with the families-of-origin of each spouse can progress be made in resolving current conflicts in a marriage.

Furthermore, this is especially important for females. Wamboldt and Reiss (1989, p. 332) interpreted their similar results to suggest "the awesome, unfair responsibility that the role of relationship specialist confers upon women." They suggest that greater attention needs to be paid to gender differences in the practice of marital therapy, and special note needs to be given to the gender differences in connectedness to families of origin and how that connectedness influences adult children's marital quality. We believe Wamboldt and Reiss's suggestions are good, but they are only one possible way to view data.

We two authors disagreed on alternate explanations. Holman's thinking is that instead of viewing the results as demonstrating an "awesome responsibility," they could also be seen as a "wonderful opportunity," an example of the real power of females in the most important of human relationships—their own marriages and their parent–child relationships (with their parents and with their children). Indeed, given that women clearly need and seek for greater power in their relationships with men, it seems strange that Wamboldt and Reiss see this power not as power, but as simply another unfair responsibility. Birch, on the other hand, thinks that a more compelling explanation concerns the operation of transference. Perhaps women with poor parent–child relationships engage in transference with their husbands, provoking males in ways that elicit the same troubling behavior as she experienced with her father (for example). As these conflicts are resolved, the female may feel a sense of satisfaction at working through an issue she never was able to with her father. However, the male may feel frustrated and confused by the whole interaction, inasmuch as it makes no sense to him in the context of his relationship with her and thus his marital satisfaction suffers. Of course further research will be necessary to examine these and other hypotheses more carefully.

Males' and females' parent–child relationships are equally influenced by their parents' marital quality. Therefore, it is important to help individuals understand, deal with, and see in a positive light, their own parents' relationships. Given our findings, doing this should assist them in redefining their own relationships with their parents. The work of Framo (1992) is again relevant. These are the types of conflicts that he believes should be addressed directly with members of the family of origin present in a family-of-origin session. Thus these findings can guide therapeutic work in helping individuals understand and deal with their perceptions of family-of-origin factors as well as to confront those perceptions directly.

Although our results are limited, and we will be able to say more about implications after information in succeeding chapters has been added, there is at least one broad implication for policymakers that can be extracted from our findings. If high-quality marital relationships are valued, whether for intrinsic reasons or economic reasons, government and industry should consider what can be done to strengthen parent–child relationships. Both the relationships of adults with their own children, and the emotional "baggage" these adults carry from their own childhood experiences in their families, should be addressed. We say more about this in Chapter 9.

5

Individual Characteristics Influencing Marital Quality

Thomas B. Holman, Jeffry H. Larson, and Joseph A. Olsen

> *He had a bad temper, he was power oriented and controlling. I really thought that he would abuse me or my children if I married him. He didn't respect my body because of his temper.*
>
> —Female respondent

> *She was mentally unstable.*
>
> —Male respondent

> *I love him and I hope he will change. He has a poor self-esteem. Any discussion of problems in our relationships, he puts up defenses and throws everything back or says he is worthless.*
>
> —Female respondent

> *We were very in love but we had a lot of differences in what we valued and how we wanted to live our lives. Also his upbringing and attitudes toward women were not the same as mine. It took me a long time to realize these things because I loved him so much.*
>
> —Female respondent

Findings presented in Chapter 4 demonstrate that family-of-origin factors such as the quality of the parent–child relationship predict later marital satisfaction. But, as the above comments by our respondents and the model in Figure 1.1 indicate, there is more to understanding premarital prediction of marital quality than just the family of origin. Indeed, Auhagen and Hinde (1997) recently commented on the importance of understanding individual characteristics' link to personal relationship dynamics:

> The course of a dyadic relationship depends in large measure on the psychological characteristics of both participants. That is a truism, yet our understanding of just how relationships are affected by personal characteristics, and vice versa, is still meagre. Clearly the issue is critical, but it is also a matter of very considerable complexity. (p. 63)

The purpose of this chapter is to learn how the premarital individual characteristics of each person relate to later marital satisfaction. First, we look at the direct effects of a number of individual characteristics, including personal attributes and attitudes about marital and family issues, on marital satisfaction. Besides hypothesizing a direct relationship from individual characteristics to marital satisfaction, the model in Chapter 1 suggests that these individual characteristics are influenced by family-of-origin factors and that those two factors together simultaneously impact later marital quality. Therefore, we also test a model that includes family-of-origin factors' effects on individual characteristics, and both factors' simultaneous effects on later marital satisfaction. Separate models for males and females are estimated. Tests of individual characteristics' indirect effects on marital satisfaction are investigated in Chapter 8.

Premarital Individual Characteristics and Marital Quality: Research and Theory

We use the conceptual label *individual characteristics* to encompass factors such as personality traits, temperament, feelings about oneself, and individually held values, attitudes, and beliefs (Auhagen & Hinde, 1997). These things are conceptualized as part and parcel of who the individual is and how he or she sees him- or herself as an individual. These conceptual areas are seen as primarily "belonging" to the individual, rather than to the relationship.[1]

Much of the very earliest research about premarital and marital relationships was guided by a psychological perspective. This is not surprising. Psychology and psychiatry were coming into their own in the decades just before World War II. As Stahmann and Hiebert (1997, p. 7) note, "At that time, any problem in the marital relationship was seen as a by-product of a problem with an individual.

Neurotic or psychotic individuals caused problematic marriages." This emphasis was naturally translated into a focus on individual personality traits and disorders by researchers, and they hypothesized that premarital personality traits would have a direct effect on later marital quality.

Longitudinal research that was begun in the 1930s confirmed many of these ideas. One of the earliest longitudinal studies published was done by Adams (1946). He collected premarital data from a sample of college students beginning in 1939 and continuing into the 1940s. One hundred married couples completed a marital survey approximately 2 years into the marriage. He found that men who were more "tranquil, frank, and steady" before marriage were happier in their marriages than were men who were irritable, evasive, and emotional. Women who were "frank, stable, and contented" before marriage were more likely to be happy in marriage compared with women who were "evasive, unstable, and worried or discontent" (all quoted material from p. 189).

Terman was one of the major proponents of the importance of personality. In his study of gifted children, he investigated the relationships between several childhood or adolescent personality and attitudinal factors and marital happiness (Terman & Oden, 1947). Men's childhood "masculinity" scores were unrelated to their marital happiness at about 4 years into marriage. However, females with higher-than-average masculinity scores tended to have lower marital happiness scores. Men with lower "sociability" (low on extroversion) scores had lower marital happiness scores, but sociability in childhood was not related to women's marital happiness. Emotional stability as children was related to both men's and women's marital happiness. Women with high intellectual interests were less happy in their marriages.

Terman and Oden found that trait ratings from subjects' parents and teachers at two times during childhood were not correlated with marital happiness. Furthermore, childhood nervous symptoms and social adjustment were also not related to marital happiness.

The last of the large-scale premarital prediction studies was done by Burgess and Wallin (1953). Premarital data, including data on personality features, evaluations of the self, and attitudes about marital and family issues, were collected in the late 1930s and marital data were gathered in the early 1940s when the couples had been married 3–5 years. The researchers found that happily married individuals tended to be emotionally stable, considerate of others, yielding, companionable, self-confident, and emotionally dependent. They also found that some premaritally held values or attitudes were related to later marital happiness. If the men were confident of success in marriage, they consequently had happier marriages. Also, a desire for children was related to marital happiness for both men and women.

Three other smaller studies that began in the 1930s or 1940s were published in the decades after the Burgess and Wallin tome. Vaillant (1978) studied the adult lives of 95 men who were young adults in the late 1930s and in their mid-50s in 1975. He found that the unhappily married men in his sample were the most delayed in establishing independence from their mothers. It is unclear whether this is an indicator of a feature of the men's premarital personality or mental state, or more reflective of the early and ongoing relationship with their mothers.

Skolnick (1981) investigated the premarital predictors of marital satisfaction of middle-aged men and women. She found that men and women who had aggressive personalities premaritally were less satisfied in marriage, but that premaritally high nurturant men and women were more satisfied in their midlife marriages. Men who had low self-confidence premaritally had lower marital satisfaction, whereas women with lower marital satisfaction had the highest early adolescent self-esteem.

The last of the "early studies" was published by Kelly and Conley in 1987. Premarital data were gathered between 1935 and 1938, when the couples were engaged, from an all-white sample in the northeastern United States. The final sample consisted of 249 couples for which they had both premarital and marital data. They found that men's and women's premarital neuroticism was negatively related to marital adjustment, as was men's lack of impulse control.

The growth of theorizing about marriage in the 1970s resulted in attempts to theoretically explain many of the early findings. Burr's (1973) important theoretical summary suggested that these personality features or personal attitudes could be subsumed under the conceptual label of "conventionality." He argued that the behaviors or acts themselves are not the cause of variation in marital adjustment, but whether the behaviors were "conventional" for that culture or subculture. Thus, Burr argues that traits associated with marital adjustment in one culture can be radically different from traits that promote marital adjustment in another culture, and he uses Margaret Mead's study of three cultures in New Guinea as an example.

Lewis and Spanier's (1979) review of factors related to marital quality and stability a few years later summarized this early research on individual characteristics as finding that premarital neurotic behavior, emotional health, self-concept, and conventionality were all related to later marital quality. Using a social exchange perspective, they conceptualized these factors as indicators of "premarital resources" (or the lack thereof) brought to the marriage. Burr, Leigh, et al. (1979), in a critique of Lewis and Spanier's theoretical position, suggest that these personality features and personal attitudes are more parsimoniously seen from a symbolic interactionist perspective as skills that indicate perceived "role enactment," and this role enactment is related to marital satisfaction. In any case, we see that marriage theorists had moved from the individual psychological and psychiatric explanations that emphasized the individual's mental or emotional health to explanations that viewed these individual factors as "conventionality," "skills," or "resources." But these latter explanations still hypothesized a direct relationship between premarital individual factors and later marital quality.

Research coming after the Burr and the Lewis and Spanier theoretical summaries, and using samples drawn during the 1970s and 1980s, mostly found support for the earlier research. Bentler and Newcomb (1978) found that sociability (extroversion) was positively related to marital quality. Others have found that premarital depression is related negatively to marital quality (Beach & O'Leary, 1993; Markman et al., 1987). Holman et al. (1994) found that their composite measure of "personal readiness" (which contained indicators of emotional health, impulse control, and self-esteem) was positively related to marital satisfaction. There is also some indication that dysfunctional beliefs and (un)conventional attitudes were related to marital outcomes like marital satisfaction (Bentler & Newcomb, 1978; Kurdek, 1993). Also, a strong desire to marry and certain premaritally held attitudes about marriage, such as how liberal or conservative one's views toward marriage and family are, were related to marital satisfaction in a sample of Israeli couples (Shachar, 1991).

In sum, past research and theory suggest that certain premarital personality features such as impulse control, agreeableness, and extroversion/sociability are related to later marital quality. Also, mental or emotional states such as depression, self-esteem, and emotional health are related to marital quality. There is also support for premarital values, attitudes, and beliefs having a long-term effect on marital quality.

Family-of-Origin Factors and Individual Characteristics

The model in Chapter 1 predicts that family-of-origin factors have an effect on individual characteristics and that the two factors—family of origin and premarital individual characteristics—simultaneously affect later marital satisfaction. In this section we will first review the research and theory that connect happenings in the family of origin with the development of individual characteristics. Second, we will consider the evidence for both family of origin and individual characteristics simultaneously having effects on marital satisfaction even when the other is statistically controlled.

Family-of-Origin Effects on Individual Characteristics

Belsky and Pensky (1988) summarize both longitudinal and cross-sectional evidence that suggests that "emotionally-laden and socially-based learning (primarily from the family of origin) shapes personality development and that personality plays a central, causal role in the intergenerational transmission process" (p. 193), such as marital relationship quality. They say that social learning processes of imitation and reinforcement help explain how marital processes, for example, could be intergenerationally transmitted. But modeling theory in and of itself is not enough. They believe that a framework like attachment theory with its ideas about working models of self and other is needed to fully explain transmission. Using these ideas, they expect personality characteristics of individuals to be affected by rearing experiences in their families of origin and for these personality characteristics to affect marital functioning. Their review yielded both cross-sectional and longitudinal support for these ideas, although they found that with "corrective emotional experiences" the transmission of negative aspects of the family of origin could be overcome. They conclude with this statement:

> Without such "corrective emotional experiences" it is difficult to imagine how a history of rejection and disregard would enable one to develop positive feelings about self and others, learn to manage emotional impulses, and take the perspective of and as a result, develop the ability to care for and nurture another, be it a spouse or child. (Belsky & Pensky, 1988, p. 209)

More recent support for a connection between family-of-origin factors and individual characteristics is also available. Amato and Keith (1991) conducted a meta-analysis of studies dealing with the long-term consequences of parental divorce. Their finding is that adults who experience parental divorce exhibit lower levels of adult psychological adjustment (emotional adjustment, anxiety, life satisfaction). Amato (1994) also looked at the father–child relationship and found that the closer that relationship the better the adult child's psychological state. This was a "modest, but not trivial" relationship according to Amato, and was essentially the same for daughters and sons. Acock and Demo (1994) reported similar results using a national data set. They found that children and adolescents in first-marriage families scored higher on five of six measures of adjustment and well-being compared with youth in divorced families. However, they found that family process variables like mother–child relationship are much more important in youth's adjustment than is family structure. Also, Parker and Gladstone (1996) cite a number of studies using a measure of parental care and protection/control. These studies generally show a relationship between low parental caring and high overprotection with adult depression, anxiety, phobic disorders, and eating disorders, although other factors can mediate the relationships.

Simultaneous Effects of Family-of-Origin Factors and Individual Characteristics

Very few studies have tested the simultaneous effects of individual traits and other premarital predictors. We only found three. Bentler and Newcomb (1978), testing a model containing both family-of-origin structural variables and individual personality characteristics, found individual characteristics to be more predictive of marital success. The other two studies are unpublished and contain multiple predictors, not just family-of-origin factors and individual characteristics. Both of these studies are presented in more detail in Chapter 8. The first is a study by Holman (1981). He found that a family-of-origin scale that contained indicators of both the parents' marital quality and the parent–child relationships, and a premarital emotional health variable were both unrelated to marital satisfaction at 1 year of marriage, when other premarital and marital variables were included in the path analysis. However, Rhoades (1994) found that both the parent–child relationship quality and premarital emotional health were related to marital satisfaction at 1 year of marriage, even when premarital social approval and premarital couple communication were also simultaneously in the model.

Given the literature and theory reviewed above, we tested the following hypotheses in this chapter.

1. There is a positive relationship between premarital individual characteristics, like personality traits and personal attitudes, values, or beliefs, and later marital satisfaction.
2. Premarital individual characteristics and family-of-origin factors have significant simultaneous effects on later marital satisfaction.
3. Family-of-origin factors have an indirect effect on marital quality through individual characteristics.

Results

We report our test of these hypotheses sequentially. First, we investigated in detail the effects of various indicators of individual characteristics on later marital quality, both alone and in concert with one another. After we identified the most predictive individual characteristic(s), we tested a multivariate path model with the best individual characteristic variables. Then we added the parent–child relationship variables and tested a model of its simultaneous effect with an individual characteristic variable on marital satisfaction, and its indirect effect on marital satisfaction through the individual characteristic.

The data collection, measures for latent variables, and methods of analysis have been described in Chapter 2. We began our analyses by examining bivariate correlations between scales representing individuals' characteristics of impulse control, self-esteem, depression, and several single-item indicators of attitudes about happiness in marriage, religion, premarital sex, wife/mother employment, ethical behavior, and desire to have children. These bivariate analyses showed that premarital impulse control, depression, and most of the premarital attitudes variables were not related to later marital satisfaction. Premarital self-esteem and the expectation that marriage would bring greater happiness than almost anything else were both significantly related to later marital satisfaction. Therefore, we constructed a path model with two latent predictor variables—premarital self-esteem and premarital expectations that marriage would bring more happiness than almost anything else.

The results for females and males are shown in Figures 5.1 and 5.2. For both genders, the greater the premarital self-esteem, the greater is the marital quality. The premarital attitudinal variable, expectations of marital satisfaction, is not related to the females' marital satisfaction, but it is positively related to the males' marital satisfaction. Thus, the greater the expectation that marriage would bring more personal satisfaction than would almost anything else, the greater is the later marital satisfaction of the males.

Since only parent–child relationship quality had a direct relationship to marital quality in the family-of-origin models tested in Chapter 4, we used that latent variable to test hypotheses 2 and 3. The results for males and females are shown in Figures 5.3 and 5.4 for the models containing the family-of-origin predictor, parent–child relationship quality. In these models, self-esteem and marriage expectations were considered as predictors of marital satisfaction, as well as potential intervening variables that might also mediate the effect of parent–child relationship quality on marital quality.

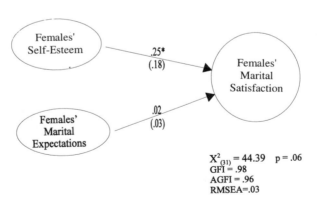

Figure 5.1. Female model of individual characteristics and marital quality; unstandardized (and standardized) coefficients ($N = 368$).

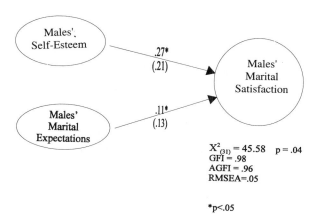

Figure 5.2. Male model of individual characteristics and marital quality; unstandardized (and standardized) coefficients ($N = 371$).

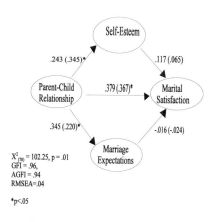

Figure 5.3. Female model of self-esteem and parent–child relationship quality with marital quality; unstandardized (and standardized) coefficients ($N = 368$).

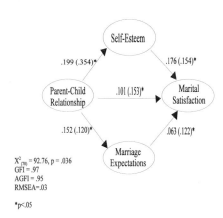

Figure 5.4. Male model of self-esteem and parent–child relationship quality with marital quality; unstandardized (and standardized) coefficients ($N = 371$).

Both models fit quite well, with goodness-of-fit indices above .96. Parent–child relationship has a strong effect on self-esteem for both males and females. A significant effect of parent–child relationship on marriage expectations is also seen for both males and females, although it is somewhat stronger for females. The direct effect of parent–child relationship on marital quality is also significant for both males and females, but is much stronger for females. Among males, both self-esteem and marriage expectations have significant and positive direct effects on marital quality, while neither of these effects is significant for females. The effect of the parent–child relationship on marital quality was stronger and more direct for females, and more likely to be mediated by self-esteem and marriage expectations for males.

Discussion

The hypothesis of the relationship between premarital individual characteristics and marital satisfaction was largely supported. While several personality characteristics and attitudinal factors were not related— such as depression, impulse control, and attitudes about religion, premarital sex, women's employment, ethical behavior, and children—two were: self-esteem and marital expectation of happiness. This was especially true for males. Both males' premarital self-esteem and their expectation that marriage would bring them more personal satisfaction than would almost anything else were related to the males' later marital satisfaction. However, for the females, while their premarital self-esteem was related to their marital satisfaction at about the same level as with the males (compare the unstandardized coefficients), the females' marital expectations were unrelated to marital satisfaction.

When parent–child relationship quality was added to the models, several interesting things happened. First, unlike some earlier research has reported (e.g., Bentler & Newcomb, 1978), we found that family of origin *and* individual characteristics are important predictors, at least for males. Second, we are the first to hypothesize an indirect relationship between family of origin and individual characteristics, and our models demonstrate such a relationship.

Implications for Theory, Research, and Practice

The results reported here support our ecological theory of premarital prediction in that two dimensions of premarital relationships—individual *and* family-of-origin characteristics—were shown to simultaneously affect later marital quality.

A limitation of our research reported here on individual characteristics is that we tested for only a limited number of personality traits. In addition, our scales were brief (usually three items). This may result in some measurement error, as several dimensions of personality (e.g., depression) are multifaceted and we could not measure all of those facets in this research. For example, depression can be displayed not only as a depressed mood but also as irritability, especially in late adolescents. It is also reflected in apathy, loss of pleasure or interest in most things, sleep disturbances, appetite changes, suicidal thoughts, hopelessness, and so on. Impulsivity is another example of a multifaceted trait. Perhaps impulsive spending is more related to later marital problems than is impulsive thrill-seeking. Thus, future research should include more in-depth assessments of individuals' personality traits.

Our results have several important implications for clinical practice and education. Self-esteem appears to be especially important for clinicians and educators to assess premaritally. Of all personality traits, it may be the key trait to assess and enhance before marriage. Poor self-esteem may predispose an individual to distort relationship events or to overreact to negative relationship events (Kurdek, 1993). This may contribute to him/her being someone with whom it is very difficult to live.

Improving self-esteem before marriage can best be accomplished using two approaches: (1) individual cognitive therapy (Beck, Rush, Shaw, & Emery, 1979) and/or (2) family-of-origin cognitive therapy (Bedrosian & Bozicas, 1994). Family-of-origin cognitive therapy focuses on the negative cognitions individuals developed as a result of dysfunctional family of origin experiences. For example, an individual who was emotionally abused by his/her parents may develop negative cognitions about the self (e.g., "I'm unworthy of anyone's love"). Or, a child may learn dysfunctional rules in the family (e.g., "Don't trust yourself or others," "Don't get close to others," or "Don't talk about what you're thinking or feeling"). As an adult, he/she must identify where these dysfunctional rules came from, determine if they work to increase intimacy in current adult relationships, and learn how to discard them and replace them with more functional rules about close relationships. This emphasis in family-of-origin cognitive therapy on assessing and overcoming the negative effects of family dysfunction as part of self-esteem enhancement coincides with our research results that have demonstrated an indirect effect of family-of-origin on marital quality through individual characteristics such as self-esteem.

The finding for men that unrealistically high expectations of marriage are positively related to later marital satisfaction research supports other literature that men are more easily and quickly romantically involved in relationships than are women (Canary & Emmers-Sommer, 1997). It may be that such premarital perceptions of marriage help men commit to the relationship more easily, at least in early marriage. Many premarital counselors emphasize that such unrealistic beliefs are dangerous to the health of the future marriage because they set up unrealistic expectations of self, partner, and the relationship. Thus, they may try to help individuals "exorcize" such beliefs before marriage. Our research suggests that this may not be warranted, at least for men. Mens' early marital satisfaction may actually benefit from such idealistic premarital beliefs.

Clinical research has shown that other types of dysfunctional beliefs may negatively affect marriage (e.g., Eidelson & Epstein, 1982). These beliefs include themes such as "People cannot change," "Perfect sex is important," and "Disagreements indicate failure in the relationship." Such beliefs bias a person toward filtering, processing, and appraising marital events in a dysfunctional manner (Kurdek, 1993). We did not test for the effects of these kinds of premarital beliefs on later marital quality but believe that such dysfunctional beliefs will have a strong negative effect on both marital quality and marital stability. Thus, these kinds of beliefs should be assessed in premarital counseling and cognitive therapy approaches utilized to change them.

In summary, a major portion of premarital counseling should focus on the assessment and treatment of individual characteristics identified in this chapter. Some individuals may need to be referred for more intensive individual therapy to overcome dysfunctional beliefs, low self-esteem, depression, and related neurotic traits such as exaggerated anger/hostility, severe anxiety or impulsivity, and unusual difficulty coping with stress.

Endnote

1. There is research to suggest that personality features are not just "traits," but that expressions of the personality feature may depend on the situation (Auhagen & Hinde, 1997). However, as Auhagen and Hinde (1997, p. 65) say, "The longitudinal consistency of characteristics over time is considerable."

6

Social Contexts Influencing Marital Quality

Cynthia Doxey and Thomas B. Holman

We felt neither set of parents really liked the significant other very much. They didn't disapprove of us dating. They just probably saw what we couldn't: that we weren't the "ones" for one another.

— Female respondent

We came from very different economic conditions. My parents were very bothered by this and didn't hesitate to tell me this.

—Female respondent

Peer pressure. The friends he kept influenced him how the marriage should be.

—Female respondent

His parents never fully accepted our getting married. He felt obligated to do as his parents told him. He always put them first in our relationship.

—Female respondent

In the study of personal relationships over the past several years, the approach has evolved from an emphasis on individual constructs to a focus on interactional and relational processes. However, this new approach has examined relationships as discrete units, separated from their contexts (Allan, 1993). Allan (1993) states that the research and theory of personal relationships in Western culture have been guided by the concept that relationships are "voluntaristic ties that those involved construct according to their own private agendas.... There is an emphasis on agency over and above structure" (p. 1).

This absence of connection to context is similar to Giddens's (1991) concept of a "pure relationship" which appears to be part of modern industrial societies. Giddens articulates a "pure relationship" as one that is not anchored in external conditions of social or economic life. It becomes a relationship which is "initiated for, and kept going for as long as it delivers emotional satisfaction" to the two individuals involved (Giddens, 1991, p. 89). In other words, from modernity's point of view, personal relationships including marriage, should be free from constraints from the society, culture, and even from family connections. When relationships are not "free-floating" they lose some of their "purity," according to Giddens (1991). In the contemporary United States, as Elshtain (1990) states, in some respects family ties have "become a drag on the freedom of the sovereign self: something to get out of, reduce in importance, or redefine as simply one choice among many" (pp. 260–261). Thus, one of modernity's influences on relationships is to permit and encourage the separation of dyadic relationships from their context, from their connection to other social systems, and even from the binding ties within the relationship.

Despite the influence of modernity in our culture and, hence, in much of our research, as discussed in Chapter 2, there has recently been a renewal of interest in how relationships are embedded within their larger contexts (Allan, 1993; Duck, 1993; Larson & Holman, 1994; Milardo & Wellman, 1992; Surra, 1990). Although most people would agree that agency, or the ability to choose, plays a part in developing and maintaining relationships, one should also realize that the choices available to us depend on our situations, including our culture, society, and economy (Allan, 1993). In fact, philosopher and social critic Wendell Berry (1983) proposes that marriage is actually as much a commitment to the community at large as it is a commitment to each other, and when we are faithful to those commitments, we make the community better. The community within which we live has a stake in the way relationships such as marriage work out because the government or communities often have to pick up the pieces of unsuccessful relationships. Therefore, societies' conceptions of what makes a good relationship will influence the way individuals and couples within those societies make choices and interact with each other (Allan, 1993). According to Milardo and Wellman (1992), relationships function within social networks, and those social contexts affect the nature of the premarital and marital relationships. In addition, individuals are influenced by their social networks, meaning their relationships with family and friends, in their choices for developing and maintaining dyadic romantic relationships (Milardo & Wellman, 1992; Parks, Stan, & Eggert, 1983;

Sprecher & Felmlee, 1992; Surra, 1990). Thus, unlike the modern concept focusing on pure relationships that are free from the contexts surrounding them, many researchers now acknowledge that the contexts in which relationships are embedded are inextricably tied to the relationship.

This literature review focuses on the social context of personal relationships, rather than other possible contexts such as the physical, biological, economic, or other contexts. Although we acknowledge that those other contexts are also important in the development and maintenance of relationships (Werner, Altman, Brown, & Ginat, 1993), we examine how individuals in relationships are influenced by the social support they receive from their family and friends (Sprecher & Felmlee, 1992), as well as by the sociocultural climate around them (Larson & Holman, 1994). The review examines the findings of previous studies focusing on the social context of relationships, with special emphasis on premarital and marital relationships. We discuss the constructs of the social context of relationships that have been measured previously. Then, we consider how those constructs of the social environment are related to relationship quality, as has been found in earlier research. Finally, we propose three hypotheses that we tested with the premarital and marital data used throughout this study, focusing on how the premarital social context is related to the ratings for marital satisfaction and stability.

Definitions

Social Networks

As we discuss social networks, we will include the definition of networks as described by van Tilburg (1997), which takes into account not only those individuals who have direct contact or influence with an individual, but also the linkages between others in that individual's network. These connections are somewhat similar to the concept of mesosystems, the links between microsystems in a child's life, as developed by Bronfenbrenner (1979) and Garbarino (1982) in their ecosystemic theory. Most research has not conceptualized the social environment in such a way as to include all of those linkages with others. While we agree with van Tilburg, we are not able to measure the entire network. Generally, social networks have been examined as a group of discrete and separate dyadic relationships between the focal individual and the others with whom they have relationships (e.g., parent, sibling, friend, co-worker). In this review and study, we will focus on the family-of-origin and friendship contexts.

Stein, Bush, Ross, and Ward (1992) state that researchers have investigated social contexts of couples in three ways, using either an individual perspective, a dyadic perspective, or a configural approach. The individual perspective is to examine a couple's social ties in terms of their separate personal networks. When using a dyadic perspective, on the other hand, researchers investigate the relationships with individuals that are jointly shared by the couple. Lastly, a configural approach conceptualizes the couple's network as being a composite of both the shared and separate links they have with others. However, even though the configural perspective appears to be the most useful in understanding how the interrelatedness of each partner's social ties exerts a collective influence on the couple's relationship, it is empirically unwieldy and complex, and is therefore infrequently used (Stein et al., 1992).

Social Support

Social support is often characterized as behavior carried out to either emotionally or instrumentally help someone else (Pierce, Sarason, Sarason, Joseph, & Henderson, 1996). Emotionally supportive behaviors usually communicate love or concern for the individual. Instrumentally supportive behavior, on the other hand, provides assistance for specific tasks or problems. In this research, we focus on approval of another's premarital partner as one way to measure emotional support. Discouragement or interference in someone's life goals or relationships would be seen as non supportive behavior.

Sociocultural Context

In the review of premarital research by Larson and Holman (1994), the authors conceptualized some demographic factors as indicators of the sociocultural context of relationships, rather than as individual traits, which is how they are often treated. Those constructs that they saw as sociocultural in nature were: age at marriage, education, income, occupation, socioeconomic status, race, and gender. These factors, determined by birth, family, or culture, are brought forward into a relationship. In addition, these factors, such as race or gender, are sociocultural designations that have been given meaning by the culture. As mentioned in Chapter 1, we attempt to see these factors as an indication of how individuals see themselves or believe others see them because of their membership in a particular group, rather than using those designations solely as "grouping" factors.

Direct Effects of Social Contexts on Marital Quality

Several constructs associated with premarital social contexts have been found to have direct effects on marital quality. The following review focuses on those constructs seen premaritally in the social network and sociocultural context that have been found to have an effect on individuals' later relationship or marital quality.

Social Network Support

Empirical attention given to the importance of social support from family and friends dates back to early research done by Burgess and Wallin (1953), who found that if the individuals in a relationship liked their in-laws, they were more likely to have a better relationship with each other. Theorizing about the issues of marital quality and stability, Lewis and Spanier (1979) proposed that the more support that significant others give to the couple, the higher is the subsequent marital quality. In addition, they proposed that parents' approval of their child's mate, and the level of liking of in-laws would also be associated with higher marital quality. These propositions have been supported in much of the research cited below.

Social networks include family, friends, acquaintances, co-workers, and others with whom we interact. Obviously, certain members of social networks have more influence over or offer more support to an individual or couple than other members. Surra (1990) states that an individual's social network consists of the linkages between the individual and his or her associates. There is an interactive network: those people with regular contact and personal interaction with an individual. There is also a psychological network, or the significant others who are close or important to an individual, even if they do not interact frequently with each other (Milardo, 1986; Surra, 1990). The psychological network's interference or support appears to be more closely associated with decreasing or increasing the stability of the relationship than the interactive network, which may not include many important and close relationships (Johnson & Milardo, 1984; Sprecher & Felmlee, 1992). In other words, family members' interference with a premarital relationship is more likely to influence an individual to stop dating a person than is interference from the network of friends and work associates.

Both Surra's review of literature in 1990 and Larson and Holman's review in 1994 cited studies showing support for the hypothesis that receiving positive support from one's own and the partner's social network was positively related to measures of love, commitment, relationship satisfaction and stability (Booth & Johnson, 1988; Parks et al., 1983). In addition, discouragement or opposition from the social network toward a relationship has been found to be linked to problems within the relationship, including separation or divorce (Surra, 1990; Whyte, 1990).

In research on premarital relationships, the same association between social networks and the quality of the couple's relationship held. In a longitudinal study of the influence of social networks on love, satisfaction, and commitment in premarital relationships, Sprecher and Felmlee (1992) found that perceived support from one's own family and friends had a larger influence on one's love, commitment, and satisfaction in the relationship than did perceived support from one's partner's friends and family. In addition, the study demonstrated that social support from friends and family was a positive predictor of later relationship quality, even up to 18 months after the researchers' initial contact with the couples. Parents' approval of their child's partner, especially for a female child, was subsequently associated with higher premarital relationship quality. These findings show that parents and extended social networks have an influence on relationships, and that support can be effective in developing greater relationship quality for a couple over time.

Other researchers examining social network support for dyadic relationships have found similar results. In general, network interference impedes relationship progress while support promotes relationship development (Surra, 1990). In a study of over 400 undergraduate students at a university, the researchers examined the reasons for the breaking up of the students' premarital relationships (Felmlee et al., 1990). They found that the causes of breakup were from a variety of sources, one of which was the social network's lack of support for their relationship. Whyte (1990), in his retrospective survey of women's marriages in Detroit, found that parental opposition to the mate they chose and to their marriage was positively related to later marital problems, and negatively related to marital quality, even when taking other factors into account.

In a study of premarital predictors of later marital quality and stability, Rhoades (1994) found that approval of the relationship premaritally from parents and friends was related to marital quality after 1 year of marriage. This association held even when a more comprehensive model was included, using factors from the family of origin, individual traits and characteristics, and couple processes included as other variables in the analysis.

Sociocultural Context

As mentioned earlier, the review by Larson and Holman (1994) conceptualizes demographic factors such as age at marriage, education, income, occupation, race, religion, and gender as part of the sociocultural context. This perspective of the social context is supported by Allan (1993):

> Despite the tendency in much social research to view many [personal relationships] as voluntary, as choice driven, and as essentially dyadic, in the end, all relationships are embedded within structural contexts that govern their patterning. (p. 24)

In other words, the experiences we have as members of certain groups, whether based on race, gender, educational level, or something else, give meaning to, and may permit or constrain, our actions as individuals and couples. Our choices in marital partner, along with our choices for behavior in marriage are influenced by the society in which we live, as well as by the groups to which we belong. As Surra (1990) discussed in her review of mate selection studies, the way certain social characteristics are distributed in a population influence social interaction as well as marriage outside the group. For example, the choice to marry someone within your own religious group is limited if your religious group is a small minority of the general population in which you live. Thus, when a minority group lives within a larger majority population, there is a greater chance that people in the minority group will marry outside their group. This in turn will affect the extent that parents and friends support or approve of their relationship.

Age at Marriage

Of all of the above sociocultural variables, age at marriage is one of the strongest and most consistent predictor variables for marital instability. The average age at first marriage has risen over the past 30 years, and the increase has been more pronounced for blacks than for whites (Surra, 1990). However, age at marriage is still a good predictor of marital stability because individuals who marry at a very young age, in comparison to the average, have a higher propensity to separate or divorce (Booth & Edwards, 1985; Sweet & Bumpass, 1988). The effect remains strong even when controlling for the effects of education and premarital pregnancy (Martin & Bumpass, 1988).

There is much less research on the relationship between age at marriage and marital *quality*. Whyte's (1990) study of Detroit women showed that age at marriage had a positive bivariate correlation with marital quality and a negative correlation with marital problems. But when age at marriage was included in a multivariate model containing indicators of premarital and marital variables, age at marriage dropped out as a significant predictor of marital quality and problems.

Socioeconomic Factors

Premarital education level, income, and occupational status have some predictive ability of marital stability. In a national sample of young men, Bahr and Galligan (1984) found that those with a higher premarital education level and who had not been unemployed were the most likely to still be married after 9 years. However, the relationship with education and marital stability is not always linear, and may be related to gender. Houseknecht and Spanier (1980) found that women with graduate degrees have higher separation rates than women with undergraduate degrees. In addition, Whyte (1990) showed that a wife's educational level was unrelated to marital stability or quality; however, wives with well-educated husbands were more likely to have stable marriages than wives with less-educated husbands.

Race

Race has not been a strong predictor of marital outcomes, but there have been some small effects associated with race and marital stability (Larson & Holman, 1994). Whyte (1990) found that African American marriages were less stable and lower in quality compared with whites, even when controlling for age at marriage, premarital pregnancy, and income. However, a possible reason for this difference between races is the fact that African Americans are living in a predominantly Caucasian society, which may give pressure or constraints on the choices they have for marriage and marital behavior. Not only are they a minority, but less than 150 years ago they were treated as slaves, having been uprooted from their native African culture. Racial biases and prejudices in the wider American culture may have given rise to adaptations that are not supportive of marriage quality and stability. Other research has suggested that African American marriages have more affective intensity than do Caucasian marriages, leading to more open and direct interaction (Oggins, Veroff, & Leber, 1993). The result of this kind of interaction may be that there are more apparent marital difficulties than in Caucasian families who may be less likely to be open about their conflict.

Race may also be a factor in the social context of marriage because of the issues of homogamy and whether social networks support or disapprove of marriage outside one's race. A study on dating preferences of students of multi-ethnic backgrounds demonstrated that some degree of ethnocentrism was related to who they desired to date, especially with respect to whether their social network would approve or disapprove (Liu, Campbell, & Condie, 1995). In addition, premarital relationship breakup was often associated with dissimilarity in race, along with support or interference from the individuals' social network (Felmlee et al., 1990).

Gender

Gender is basic to our identity, and has to do with the understanding of what it means to be female or male within a culture (Wood, 1993). Gender is a social variable because societies and cultures prescribe what men's and women's positions in the society are, along with what is accepted as appropriate ways of "thinking, acting, and feeling" in relation to each other (Wood, 1993, p. 28). Because of the differences that exist in the way males and females are socialized to think about their identity and their relationships with others, the understanding of gender and life as a gendered individual is likely to have an influence on later marital experiences, stability, and quality (Wood, 1993).

Wood (1993) emphasizes that the traditional feminine identity is defined within relationships and through connections with others. This definition of self fosters empathy, sensitivity to relationship dynamics, "loyalty, responsiveness to others' needs, and a tendency to experience other feelings as [one's] own" (p. 33). This definition of self within relationships promotes a tendency for women to be the "relationship specialists" because they are involved in relationships and attentive to interpersonal dynamics and communication (Wamboldt & Reiss, 1989). In contrast, masculine identity grows out of a differentiation of oneself from relationships (Wood, 1993). Autonomy becomes important in relationships, which may foster competition, control, and repression of feelings. Intense closeness may be uncomfortable for the masculine identity. The result of putting two such disparate identities together in marriage is that males often appear to withdraw from working on the dynamics of the relationship while females desire to examine and discuss all of the nuances that they see in the relationship (Wood, 1993).

One of the difficulties in studying how gender is related to marital quality and stability is that researchers generally have accepted the feminine way of relating as being the "better" way to have a relationship (Wood, 1993). Most research on marriage focuses on feminine communication patterns, and feminine ways of expressing care to others, and achieving closeness as being the best measures of how well the marriage is faring. However, as Wood points out, the masculine identity also expresses care, communicates, and achieves intimacy, but the focus is on action, or "doing" things for or with the other, rather than on talking, which is more typical of femininity. Although researchers have recognized the distinctions between feminine and masculine styles of intimacy, they often have not given equal value to the masculine style. Therefore, the possibility arises that some gender differences that are found in research with respect to marital stability and quality may actually be associated with the way intimacy and caring for the other were measured (Wood, 1993).

Having said this, we turn to the gender differences that have been found in premarital and marital relationships, according to the Larson and Holman (1994) review. Gender has often been used merely as a control variable, or has been ignored altogether. However, Wamboldt and Reiss (1989) discussed the role of women in maintaining and developing relationships because they tend to be the "relationship architects." They view women as having an unfair responsibility to have the success or failure of a relationship depending largely on them (Wamboldt & Reiss, 1989). Gender also appears to be indirectly related to relationship outcomes through personal characteristics, family-of-origin factors, or interpersonal processes (Larson & Holman, 1994).

Effects of Family of Origin on Social Context

The family of origin, specifically the relationship between parents and children, is part of the influence of the social context on premarital relationships. As shown in Chapter 4, of all of the family-of-origin variables studied, the best predictor of later marital outcomes was the quality of the parent–child relationship. Since one of the primary social contexts of individuals is their family of origin, there is reason to expect that the quality of the parent–child relationship is influential in determining the kind of social support and approval the child receives when choosing a spouse.

As was shown in Chapter 4, the data in this study have supported the idea that romantic love can be conceptualized as part of attachment theory (Hazan & Shaver, 1987; Shaver & Clark, 1996). Hazan and Shaver (1987) proposed that just as attachment to a parent figure in infancy and early childhood is important for the growth and social development of a child, similarly, attachment can be used as an underlying theory for the development and growth of adult romantic relationships. They, along with their colleagues (see Shaver & Clark, 1996, for a review of other studies), have found evidence that individuals who appeared to be securely attached to their parents in childhood were more likely to be secure in their romantic relationship attachments. They had more positive and accurate views of themselves and of others in their relationships, and were more likely to be stable in their relationships than were either of the other groups of attachment patterns (avoidant or anxious-ambivalent). In the results of the study discussed in Chapter 4, the evidence was in support of the theory that romantic relationships are an extension of attachment to parents. Holman and Birch (Chapter 4, this volume) found that the parent–child relationship prior to marriage had the strongest relationship with later marital quality than did any of the other family-of-origin factors that were tested in the model.

As was discussed earlier in this chapter, social context includes both the social support of the social network as well as sociocultural variables. One of the most important social environments for any individual is the family of origin because that is where we receive our first experiences of family life, and that is where we learn more about what families are (Marks, 1986; Wamboldt & Reiss, 1989). In addition, the relationships with members of the family of origin are some of the more important and long-lasting relationships in our lifetime, and therefore, greatly influence the development of individuals (Bowlby, 1988). When examining the social context of an individual's development, it seems only natural to focus on the importance of family-of-origin relationships, as has been done within the ecological framework (Bronfenbrenner, 1979; Garbarino, 1982). As previously mentioned, Wamboldt and Reiss (1989) argue that marriage is an individual's second chance to have a family experience and to make changes in his or her relationships with others. However, relationships and patterns of experience within families of origin still continue to influence the person even after marriage, and they have been found to influence later marital quality (Doxey, 1994; Holman et al., 1994).

Holman and Li (1997) found that earlier parent–child relationships were related to the perceived support for the current premarital relationship. Therefore, we would also concur that early parent–child relationships would influence the perceived support from the parents for the choice of marital partner (the social context of the premarital relationship) and would influence later marital quality.

Hypotheses

Based on the literature reviewed above, we expected to find direct effects of the premarital social context on later marital quality as follows. First, the social network support from family and friends for the premarital relationship (specifically, approval and support of their upcoming marriage and choice of marital partner) is associated with later marital quality. We expect that more approval and support from the social network is related to higher marital quality.

Second, premarital sociocultural variables (socioeconomic status, age at marriage, gender, and race) will be associated with later marital quality. That is, the higher one's socioeconomic status and age at marriage, the greater is the marital satisfaction. Gender was also hypothesized to affect later marital satisfaction. Indirect effects were also expected. The family of origin was expected to be associated with the social context of the premarital relationship, in that the reported quality of the parent–child relationship was related to the support and approval the couple received premaritally from their social network, which was, in turn, associated with later marital quality.

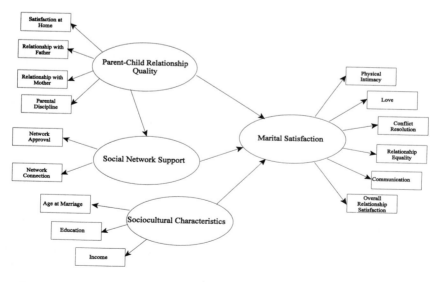

Figure 6.1. Proposed model of premarital parent–child relationship quality, social network support, sociocultural variables, and later marital satisfaction.

The model of the relationships between social network support, sociocultural variables, family-of-origin factors, and marital satisfaction is presented in Figure 6.1. We are proposing that Social Network Support and Sociocultural Characteristics at Time 1 will be directly related to Marital Satisfaction at Time 2. Furthermore, the Parent–Child Relationship Quality at Time 1 will be indirectly related through Social Network Support to Marital Satisfaction at Time 2.

The data collection, measures for latent variables, and methods of analysis have been described in Chapter 2. For this particular chapter, we used the following latent variables with the premarital data: Social Network Support, Sociocultural Characteristics, and Parent–Child Relationship Quality (as described in Chapter 4). From the marital data at Time 2, we used the measurements for the latent variable of Marital Satisfaction. Structural equation modeling (SEM) was used to perform the analyses for our proposed model, and the models were run separately for husbands and wives. However, since the literature has suggested that gender is a sociocultural characteristic, we also performed a test of a comparison model between males and females to find out how similar or different the husbands' and wives' perceptions are from each other. We followed the two step process of SEM (Jöreskog & Sörbom, 1996), estimating first the measurement model and then the structural model. In estimating the measurement models, we decided not to include race as a sociocultural variable because our data did not have enough variability in race, since the large majority of respondents were Caucasian.

Results

The means, standard deviations, and paired t-values for the various indicators of social network support and sociocultural characteristics are presented in Table 6.1. The results show that the only significant differences between the husbands and wives for these indicators are that males are generally older and have a higher income before marriage than do females. There are no significant differences between males and females on the other variables.

Direct Relationships

The path diagrams of the direct relationships between social network support, sociocultural characteristics, and marital satisfaction for the wives and husbands are presented in Figures 6.2 and 6.3, respectively. Both the unstandardized and standardized path coefficients are reported in the figures. Good fit of the models is indicated in both instances with nonsignificant chi-squares and the goodness-of-fit indices well above .90.

Table 6.1. Means (with Standard Deviations) for Marital Satisfaction, Social Network Support, and Sociocultural Characteristics Compared for Males and Females

	Males	Females
Marital Satisfaction*	3.98 (0.60)	4.11 (0.68)
Social Network Support		
Network Approval	3.36 (0.61)	3.41 (0.62)
Network Connection	3.30 (0.51)	3.34 (0.51)
Sociocultural Characteristics		
Age at Marriage*	23.98 (2.20)	22.15 (2.25)
Education	3.37 (0.85)	3.35 (0.80)
Income*	1.82 (1.17)	1.25 (.94)

*Differences significant at $p < .05$.

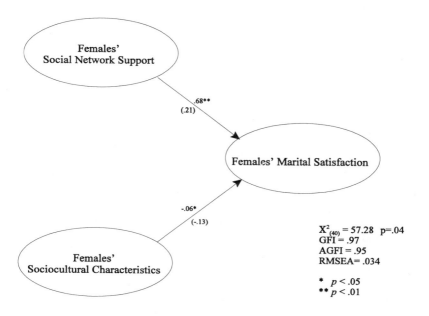

Figure 6.2. Females' premarital social network support and sociocultural characteristics, and later marital satisfaction; unstandardized (and standardized) path coefficients ($N = 355$).

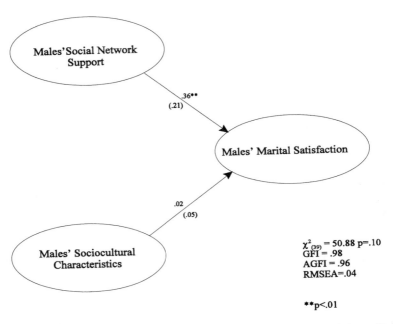

Figure 6.3. Males' premarital social network support and sociocultural characteristics, and later marital satisfaction; unstandardized (and standardized) path coefficients (N = 356).

As was hypothesized, there is a direct relationship between the social network support received premaritally and their later marital satisfaction for both husbands and wives. The unstandardized coefficients allow the husbands' and wives' models to be compared on a similar metric, and for the wives, this relationship was nearly twice as strong as for the husbands. The influence of social network support for females comes more from the premarital relationship with the parents and in-laws than just from approval from family and friends. However, for the males, the opposite occurs, with a stronger influence coming from the approval for the premarital relationship by significant others.

The relationship between the sociocultural characteristics and marital satisfaction is not as strong as that for social network support. Sociocultural characteristics included age at marriage, education, and premarital income as indicators. Each of the indicators' lambdas across models is quite similar, but one interesting feature is that, for females, having a higher age at marriage, higher education, and higher income premaritally is negatively related to marital satisfaction. This effect is positive, but not significant for the males.

Indirect Relationships

Figures 6.4 and 6.5 show the path models for wives and husbands, respectively, including the latent variable of parent–child relationship quality with the latent variables of marital satisfaction and social network support. We chose to include only the social network support in this model without the sociocultural characteristics because the literature and our hypotheses suggest that the social network support received will be associated with the kinds of relationships experienced in the family of origin. In addition, network support had a stronger relationship with marital satisfaction than did the sociocultural characteristics. As with the previous models, these models also have a good fit with the data, with nonsignificant chi-squares and the goodness-of-fit indices above .90.

As can be seen from the results in Figures 6.4 and 6.5, when the parent–child relationship is added into the model, the relationship between social network support and marital satisfaction becomes insignificant for both husbands and wives. The parent–child relationship is significantly related to both marital satisfaction and social network support. From the findings in Chapter 4, we knew that there would

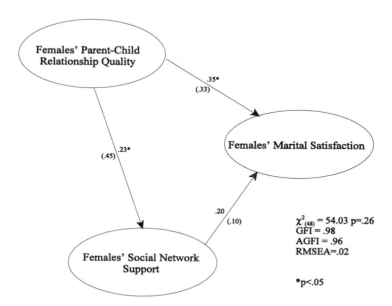

Figure 6.4. Females' premarital parent–child relationship quality, social network support, and later marital satisfaction; unstandardized (and standardized) path coefficients ($N = 357$).

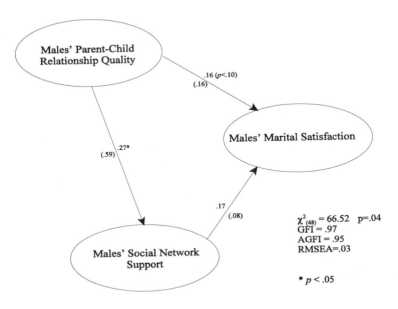

Figure 6.5. Males' premarital parent–child relationship quality, social network support, and later marital satisfaction; unstandardized (and standardized) path coefficients ($N = 356$).

be a significant relationship between the family-of-origin variables and marital satisfaction. This model shows that a higher-quality parent–child relationship is also associated with higher social network support for both husbands and wives. For the females, including the parent–child relationship with the social network support accounted for 14% of the variance in marital satisfaction. The model for the males accounted for 5% of the variance, similar to the previous model shown in Figure 6.3.

In Chapter 4, one of the results from the analyses showed that, for the husbands, marital satisfaction was not only related to their relationship with their parents, but also was related to the relationships between the wives and their parents. Because of this finding, we decided to include the wives' parent–child relationships in a model for the husbands. This model had both husbands' and wives' parent–child relationship as exogenous variables, and then used the husbands' social network support and the husbands' marital satisfaction as the endogenous variables. Again, the relationship between social network support and marital satisfaction was not significant. There was a significant relationship between the females' parent–child relationship and the males' social network support ($\gamma = .12$), as well as a relationship that was approaching significance ($p <$ .10) between the females' parent–child relationship and the males' marital satisfaction. This model may demonstrate that wives' family experiences have some influence on how the husband perceives the social network support, which includes both the family-of-origin relationships as well as how they got along with the in-laws and others.

Comparison between Male and Female Models

Since the literature suggests that there may be differences between the way females and males perceive their relationships with each other and with others around them, as well as the way they go about developing and maintaining relationships, we also carried out an analysis that would statistically compare the models for husbands and wives. Looking at the male and female models in Figures 6.2 and 6.3, and we see that there are some differences, where certain indicators are stronger than others, or that the path coefficients between the latent variables appear to be stronger for the females than for the males. However, without a statistical test we do not know if the differences are significant.

In the test of the gender models based on gender differences, we included both the husbands' and wives' variables for social network support, sociocultural characteristics, and marital satisfaction into one model. We allowed the wives' marital satisfaction to correlate with the husbands' marital satisfaction. Then we assumed that the error covariances would be correlated between indicators of the male latent variables and those for the female latent variables. While the Chi-square was significant, the other goodness-of-fit indices were above .90 for the model. After establishing a base model, we set each of the path coefficients equal for males and females, one at a time, for the relationship between social network support and marital satisfaction, and then for sociocultural characteristics and marital satisfaction. There was not a significant change in the Chi-square as each modification was made in the path coefficients. This means that there is not a significant difference between the male and female models. Thus, despite what appears to be different by running the models separately for each sex, there was no gender difference in how the premarital social context influences marital satisfaction.

Discussion

The hypotheses of the relationships between the social context of premarital relationships and later marital satisfaction were supported to some degree. For both husbands and wives, premarital social network support was more influential in predicting later marital satisfaction than were their sociocultural characteristics prior to marriage. Both of the models had good fit with the data, and both accounted for some variance in later marital satisfaction. These findings show that the premarital social context defined as social network support and sociocultural characteristics were predictors of marital satisfaction.

The relationship between premarital social support and marital satisfaction was found to be somewhat stronger for females than for males, supporting the idea that females tend to be the "relationship architects," as suggested by Wamboldt and Reiss (1989). In addition, for wives, the influence of social network support comes more from the premarital relationship with parents and in-laws, than from approval from significant others. The opposite is true for husbands, with more influence for the latent variable of social network support coming from the approval for the premarital relationship than from the connection they have with their parents and in-laws. While the relationship between the indicators of latent variables may not be important for the overall models, it is interesting that the husbands' perceptions of approval from their significant others is more important to them than to their wives. The wives appear to have recognized the importance of their ongoing relationships with their families of origin as well as with their in-laws. One reason for this may be that females tend to define themselves within their relationships and connections with others, while males tend to define themselves through differentiating themselves from others (Wood, 1993). But, according to our findings, the males still appear to need some approval from their friends and relatives when they make important choices such as continuing or fostering a premarital or marital relationship.

Interestingly, although much of the research cited earlier in this chapter showed that factors such as age at marriage, education, and income were generally related to marital satisfaction, the results of our analyses suggest that sociocultural characteristics may not be as important as we expected. In fact, contrary to our expectations that older age at marriage, higher education level, and higher income should be positively related to higher marital satisfaction, we found that for males there was a positive, nonsignificant relationship, while for females the relationship was significant but negative. Although our culture suggests that readiness for marriage includes older age at marriage, financial and educational readiness, our results indicate that at least for males, these sociocultural characteristics prior to marriage do not have as much influence on later marital satisfaction. One possible explanation for this finding may be that many of the husbands in our sample were actually attending college when they got married. Their expectations for higher income and education may not be reflected in their actual level of education and income prior to marriage. Perhaps, if we had compared their current sociocultural characteristics at Time 2, we would find a relationship of education and income with their marital satisfaction, as has been found in other studies.

On the other hand, the wives' premarital sociocultural characteristics were found to be negatively related to later marital satisfaction, suggesting that being "ready" for marriage in terms of age, education, and income, according to what our culture would suggest, is not important for females' lasting happiness in marriage. This negative relationship for females may have some explanation from social exchange theory. The results from our analyses suggest that the wives in our sample who were older, more educated, and had a higher income premaritally may be comparing their marital situation with the other possible alternatives that they could have due to their education and income. Perhaps they do not perceive their marriage as favorably in comparison with the fact that they could do something else. According to many exchange theorists, women in marriages who do not have other alternatives such as a career, or a possibility to make it through life on their own (i.e., women who are younger, less educated, and with a lower income), would be more likely to stay in a marriage. Women who have other alternatives due to their social status, education, or income could be more dissatisfied with a marriage, or be more prone to leave an unsatisfactory marriage. (See Klein & White, 1996, or Sabatelli & Shehan, 1993, for discussions of social exchange theory.)

With respect to the indirect relationships found between the parent–child relationship, social context, and marital satisfaction, we did not find support for a strong indirect relationship. The relationship between the premarital parent–child relationship and social network support was positive and significant for both wives and husbands. When the parent–child relationship was added into the model, the social network variable dropped from significance in the model. In other words, the parent–child relationship appears to be important enough to the marital satisfaction of the wives that it diminishes the relationship between the social context and marital satisfaction to nonsignificant levels. For males, the parent–child relationship is influential in the social network support, and it approaches significance in its direct relationship to marital satisfaction. One possible reason for these findings is that receiving social network support includes how connected you feel to your family and in-laws, as well as how much approval you receive from them and from your friends. Conceivably, the kind of relationship you have had with your own parents would be associated with how much approval and connection you have with them. Having a good relationship or a bad relationship with one's parents influences how one perceives their support of one's life choices. Thus, these results appear to support the attachment theory that relationships between parents and an adult child can have an influence on that child's relationships with others (Hazan & Shaver, 1987).

Implications for Theory, Research, and Practice

This chapter has examined the relationship between the premarital social context and later marital satisfaction. Our findings generally concur with previous theory and research, emphasizing that more support from social networks is associated with higher marital satisfaction. The approval from friends and family about the premarital relationship and the respondents' feelings of connection to their social networks were found to be more important than were the sociocultural characteristics of age at marriage, education, and income for later marital satisfaction. This finding is of itself interesting because much of the literature reviewed previously emphasizes that age at marriage and other socioeconomic factors play a part in marital satisfaction, and especially marital stability. These results show that those factors may not play as big a part as expected, and in the case of females, more education and older age at marriage might actually work against marital satisfaction. One of the reasons for the differences in these results is that we see these sociocultural characteristics as being phenomena of social contexts, whereas much previous research uses them as static groupings that are compared. If we had also used that information in the same statistical manner, they may have had more effect. These data are perhaps skewed due to the relatively high average socioeconomic status in our sample, and therefore, it is important to examine these issues more fully in further research.

The support from the social network becomes insignificant when the family-of-origin factor of the parent–child relationship is included in the analysis. The parent–child relationship confounds the social network support variable, most likely because support from family members is connected to the kinds of relationships one has with those family members. According to attachment theory discussed previously, the relationships we have in our families of origin are carried over into the present relationships in the way that we relate to others as adults. Similar to the findings in Chapter 4, we have found this pattern occurring in the way those family-of-origin relationships also influence the supportiveness of the premarital social networks.

The practical applications of these findings could be useful for therapists, clergy, and educators alike. According to this research, in order to promote higher marital satisfaction, professionals should also encourage better premarital relationships with family members, especially with parents. If couples have better relationships with their families and other social network members, they will probably receive more support from them as their premarital relationship develops. We should encourage premarital couples to get to know the families of their partners, to try to get along well with them, and to solve problems prior to marriage. It would probably be best for individuals who intend to marry to try to work through their problems with their families of origin prior to marrying, if possible. One implication of these findings is that in order to help couples have greater marital satisfaction, therapists and educators should teach dating couples about the importance of their relationships with their parents and with other social networks. Another method would be to suggest that when choosing a marital partner, it is best if both partners have strong and positive relationships to their families of origin. However, many individuals would be unable to get married if that were a requirement for marriage. There are many who have not had good experiences in their families of origin, but see marriage as a second chance for happiness in family life.

Individuals who have negative family-of-origin memories and experiences need to have some hope for change. As was suggested in Chapter 4, that negative family background can be reframed so that the influence is not as detrimental to the marriage. For example, Doxey (1994) found that although some respondents had negative experiences in their family life, they were able to "change their hearts" toward their parents and look on them with greater love. If this change of heart had occurred for the individuals, it also influenced the way they lived with their marital partner, so that they may experience more satisfaction in their marriage. Those individuals who were still harboring anger and resentment toward their parents also had lower satisfaction in their marriages. Some may be unable to make such "reframes" and need more in-depth family-of-origin therapy to overcome a negative legacy.

These findings imply that the social context of families, and even of friends, is an ongoing and important aspect of marital relationships, and should be given more attention in our research, theory, education, and therapy. These results also imply that more premarital counseling specifically addressing family-of-origin and social context issues should be made available, and should be encouraged in the community and churches.

7

Premarital Couple Interactional Processes and Later Marital Quality

Jason S. Carroll and Thomas B. Holman

> *Brian and I have always loved to talk to each other, and we still do.*
>
> —Female respondent

> *Our marriage and relationship is the happiest one I know. We are constantly amazed at the signs of unhappiness we see in our friends' relationships. We didn't realize how special and unique ours was. I think our greatest reason for our happiness is the fact that we are so alike in so many things, from our music tastes to styles of homes to raising children techniques. We agree on almost everything.*
>
> —Female respondent

If asked what the most critical element in the success or failure of marriage is, most people would simply say, "Communication." Communication is the metaphor we use in the contemporary United States to describe marriage (Bellah et al.,1985). For many people, marriage *is* communication. If a couple is having marital problems, the typical solution the man or woman on the street offers is that "you need to learn to communicate better," or "share your feelings with him (or her), " or "you just have to let him (her) know what your needs are," and the like. Improved communication is seen as the simple answer to most relationship problems.

This commonly held belief that quality communication is the main ingredient of marital success and the primary solution to marital problems is not without foundation in social science, and clinical research and theory (e.g., Raush, Greif, & Nugent, 1979). But our interest here is both broader and narrower than the proposition that communication quality is positively related to marital quality. Our interest is broader in the sense that we are interested in more than the process of communication between partners. We are also interested in resulting couple interactional characteristics such as the degree of an established sense of couple-ness, the degree of consensus on marital and family issues, social homogamy, and the level of similarity on fundamental values, and personality characteristics, as they relate to marital quality.

Our interest is narrower in the sense that we are concerned only with the relationship between these couple processes and characteristics *premaritally* and later marital quality. Specifically, in this chapter we address the question of whether couple interactional processes, including communication, consensus, similarity, and relationship identity formed before marriage, influence marital quality several years into marriage.

Literature Review

Communication Processes

Communication processes have long been recognized as a significant cross-sectional predictor of a couple's *current* level of marital satisfaction. In their review of literature from the 1950s, 1960s, and 1970s, Lewis and Spanier (1979) found that communication skills such as self disclosure, accuracy of nonverbal communication, frequency of successful communication, understanding between spouses, and empathy were all positively related to a couples' marital quality.

In more recent years, several studies have shown that current couple communication patterns are consistently reliable in distinguishing between distressed and nondistressed couples (Birchler, Weiss, & Vincent, 1975; Gottman, 1994a; Markman, 1991; Markman & Notarius, 1987; Smith, Vivian, & O'Leary, 1991). These studies have demonstrated that compared with non-distressed couples, distressed couples rate their communication more negatively (Gottman et al., 1976) and engage in more negative verbal and nonverbal interaction (Birchler et al., 1975; Gottman, Markman, & Notarius, 1977). More specifically, Weiss and Heyman (1990) found that unhappily married couples, compared with happily married couples, enter into more negative sequences of interaction, reciprocate their partner's negative affect, and respond more negatively to their partner.

While there is a substantial amount of research that supports an influential relationship between couple communication patterns and *current* relationship satisfaction, there is relatively little research that sheds light on how these processes influence marital quality *over time*. This is of particular significance given that recent studies on couple communication processes have indicated that the longitudinal predictors of marital satisfaction differ from its cross-sectional correlates (Gottman & Krokoff, 1989; Markman, 1984; Smith et al., 1990,1991). In other words, there is evidence to suggest that some predictors of current levels of marital satisfaction do not generalize to the prediction of changes in marital satisfaction *over time*. Therefore, in keeping with our focus on prediction of marital quality over time, we limit our research review in this section to longitudinal studies that have investigated premarital couple communication processes and their relation with marital dynamics and satisfaction. The studies reviewed are primarily ordered according to their conceptual orientations and linked together by how they have shaped marital prediction research.

Negativity/Positivity Models of Communication

During the last 20 years, much of the research that has investigated the influence of premarital couple communication processes on later marital quality has focused on levels of negativity and positivity in couple interactions. Traditionally, this method of conceptualizing communication places couple interactions on a continuum between positive and negative effects for the relationship. In this perspective, positivity and negativity are seen as dichotomous components of communication that are inversely related with one another. However, in more recent years, conceptual thinking has shifted and communication researchers have begun to conceptualize positive and negative communication as two separate measures that are influenced by, but not inversely correlated with, one another (Birchler et al., 1975; Gottman, 1994a; Orden & Bradburn, 1968).

For the most part, studies utilizing the "negativity/positivity perspective" have been grounded in behavioral and/or social learning models of couple dynamics and have set out to test the assertion of these theoretical frameworks that negative communication (i.e., the expression of negative affect, dissatisfaction, and so on) *precedes* marital distress. The majority of studies in this line of research have been experimental in design and have utilized observationally coded measures with relatively small samples of couples.

Markman (1979, 1981, 1984) is widely credited with initiating the first longitudinal research designed specifically to investigate the power of premarital communication patterns in predicting marital satisfaction. Conceptualized within a behavioral model of marriage, there were four stages in the design of this study: initial interview and laboratory sessions (Time 1), 1-year follow-up (Time 2), 2-½-year follow-up (Time 3), and 5-½ - year follow-up (Time 4). The study originally began with 26 premarital couples; however, due to couple breakup and missing data, results were drawn from 14 couples at Times 2 and 3, and only 9 couples at Time 4. In this study, couples were asked to briefly discuss five tasks, plus the major problem area in their relationship that they had previously determined. While they talked, each couple used a "talk table" (Gottman et al., 1976) to rate the intended impact (intent) and actual impact (impact) of their statements on a five-point scale ranging from supernegative (1) to superpositive (5). The "impact ratings" were designed to create a measure of perceived positivity of the interaction from the listener's perspective, while the "intent ratings" were designed to measure the intended positivity from the speaker's perspective. The two earliest reports on this study (Markman, 1979, 1981) only reported the "actual impact" or the listeners' ratings. The results indicated that while perceived positivity/negativity of communication when discussing a current problem area was not associated with relationship satisfaction at follow-up 1 year later, it was highly correlated with the level of marital satisfaction reported at follow-up after 2½ and 5½ years. In other words, the more positively couples rated their communication premaritally, the more satisfied they were with their marital relationship 2½ and 5½ years later. From these findings, Markman (1981) concluded that "communication and problem-solving deficits are etiologically related to the development and maintenance of marital distress" (p. 761).

In a later report, Markman (1984) presented the data from the "intended impact" or speaker's ratings. For the males' intent ratings, there was no significant relationship with Time 1 (Premarital), or Time 2 (1-year follow-up) couple relationship satisfaction. However, there was a significant relationship with Time 3 (2½-year follow-up) relationship satisfaction. This relationship was still positive at Time 4 (5-½-year follow-up), but was no longer significant. The females' intended positivity ratings followed a similar pattern, but the Time 3 correlation failed to reach the .05 level of significance. Markman (1984, p. 261) concludes that "the more positive the males intended their communication to be at Time 1, the more satisfied the couple was at Time 3 (2.5 years later)."

In this later report on his earlier longitudinal data, Markman (1984) also reported the predictive power of the intended impact in terms of the relative frequency of each button (superpositive, positive, negative, supernegative) pressed. These findings showed that the best predictor of Time 3 (2½ year follow-up) relationship satisfaction was the relative frequency of use of the negative buttons. This finding held true for both male negative intent and female negative intent.

In an effort to build on Markman's early longitudinal studies, Filsinger and Thoma (1988) followed 21 premarital couples over a 5-year period to investigate if couple interaction processes would predict later relationship adjustment *and* stability. Using an observational design to rate communication patterns, couples were asked to engage in a 15-minute discussion about a specific problem in their relationship that they had previously determined to be a "medium problem." In addition to investigating negativity and positivity, this study also investigated negative reciprocity, positive reciprocity, and rate of interruptions. The concept of reciprocity refers to how partners immediately respond when their partner makes a positive or negative statement. According to Filsinger and Thoma (1988), "if the other partner immediately follows a negative [comment by his/her partner] with his or her own negative, it is called negative reciprocity. If the response is positive to the initial positive, it is called positive reciprocity" (p. 786). In summary, it was found that marital *instability* measured at 1½-, 2½-, and 5-year follow-ups was predicted by premarital indicators of negative reciprocity, positive reciprocity, and level of female interruptions. Marital adjustment or quality, however, was only significantly predicted by female interruptions measured premaritally. The authors concluded that these findings suggest that relationships that have a "tit-for-tat" style of communication, whether it be positive or negative reciprocation, are the most endangered for future marital distress.

Similar to these findings, Kelly et al. (1985) reported that negative communication in premarital interactions is related with later marital satisfaction. Drawing conclusions from a self-report study that measured the premarital relational characteristics of 21 couples retrospectively (during early marriage), as well as 2½ years later, these researchers found that premarital conflict and negativity is a significant predictor of lower relationship satisfaction in early marriage. This finding was stronger for women than it was for men.

While these pioneering studies support the idea that negativity and positivity of communication affects later marital satisfaction, their findings have not been fully supported in later research. In a partial replication of these studies, Markman et al. (1987) found only weak support for the idea that positivity and negativity in premarital communication is related to later relationship satisfaction. In reporting their findings on the link between premarital couple communication patterns and marital quality at 1½- and 3-year follow-ups, the authors concluded "the results indicated a weak to moderate relationship that declines over time" (p. 275).

Smith et al. (1990) were also unable to substantiate that levels of negativity and positivity in premarital communication are associated with later marital satisfaction. Their longitudinal study was designed specifically to evaluate the association between affective or emotional expressive features of premarital communication and marital relationship satisfaction. Using a sample of 91 Caucasian couples about to be married for the first time, this study utilized a four-stage design: Time 1 (Premarriage), Time 2 (6 months into marriage), Time 3 (18 months into marriage), and Time 4 (30 months into marriage). At Time 1, each couple participated in a 10-minute focused discussion on a relationship issue about which they disagreed. Interviewers assisted each couple in selecting an issue and prompted interaction that would provide representative conflict and problem-solving efforts. These discussion sessions were then observationally coded using a system designed to measure the affective processes (e.g., pleased, sad, calm) rather than the actual content of the interaction. Confirmatory factor analysis was used to analyze these affective processes and create groupings or factors. This process resulted in three factors: Negativity, Positivity, and Disengagement. Negativity and Positivity were not significantly associated with marital satisfaction at any of the follow-up phases of the study. However, disengaging behaviors (e.g. quiet, sluggish, silent, tired) were negatively related to marital satisfaction at Time 3 and Time 4 (18 and 30 month) follow-ups. From these findings, the authors concluded that while negative communication proves to be "truly negative" in current marital functioning, "it would be a misnomer to attach this label when discussing these variables in a causal or predictive sense" (Smith et al., 1991, p. 17).

Studies using the "negativity/positivity perspective" have shown that there is some evidence to support the idea that premarital communication processes are linked to marital satisfaction. However, these early studies have done little to clarify how, and in what ways, interactional patterns affect couples over time. In many ways, studies utilizing this perspective may have been limited by their micro-level of analysis that observationally measures brief clinically orchestrated discussions with small samples of couples. As demonstrated in this review, more recent studies have begun to show that conceptualizing communication processes as merely negative or positive is overly simplistic and does not tap into the more complex cognitive and emotional workings of couple dynamics.

A Model for Constructive Marital Conflict

As couple communication research has progressed, the validity of the concept of negative communication and its use as a general predictor of later marital distress has been called into question. In an innovative study, Gottman and Krokoff (1989) found that some features of communication previously deemed detrimental to marriages (i.e., negativity, anger exchanges) were actually related to *improved* marital functioning at a 3 year follow-up. In particular, they found that the wife's tendencies to respond to her husband angrily or with disgust/contempt, which were associated with lower levels of current marital happiness, predicted improvements in the wife's marital satisfaction over time. These results suggest that the wife's strong negative affect could be functional for a relationship in a longitudinal sense. It is important to note however, that the data for this study came from couples married for approximately 24 years and were therefore in a different stage of married life than the other studies reviewed here.

Sparked by Gottman and Krokoff's (1989) findings, several studies have been done that have taken a new look at how negativity in communication is defined and how negativity works as a predictor of future marital quality. In a critical reappraisal of longitudinal studies that investigate "negativity" in couple communication, Smith et al. (1991) found that while "negativity is a robust cross-sectional correlate of (poor) marital adjustment, the longitudinal significance of these cross-sectional correlates is surprisingly meager" (p. 7). This finding supports their previous longitudinal research (Smith et al., 1990). Based on these findings, the authors suggest that negativity in couple communication, as it has been traditionally conceptualized, may be a "misnomer" (Smith et al., 1991).

In a similar line of research and commentary, Sher and Weiss (1991) have raised the possibility that negative communication in marital interaction may at times be "functionally negative" or in other words, communication patterns that have previously been classified as destructive to relationships may benefit at least some types of couples. Exploring this idea, Krokoff (1991) analyzed the data from 52 married couples who participated in a 3-year longitudinal study that allowed him to measure their communication orientation (e.g., conflict-avoider and conflict-engagers) and if this orientation acted as a moderator of the positive or negative effects of communication. Specifically, this study showed that while conflict-engaging couples conformed to the traditional view that negative communication is dysfunctional, expression of negative affect may actually be beneficial for conflict-avoiding couples. These findings were, however, only significant for wives' marital satisfaction. In summary, Krokoff(1991) concluded that "strong negative affect of a specific kind may be either functional or dysfunctional, depending on the couple's communication orientation" (p. 61).

In a very recent study, Gottman, Coan, Carrere, and Swanson (1998) analyzed seven different types of "process models" that have been used to conceptualize marital interactions in an effort to evaluate which of these models are able to predict later marital stability and satisfaction. The seven models evaluated were: (1) anger as a destructive emotion, (2) active listening, (3) negative affect reciprocity, (4) negative start-up by the wife, (5) de-escalation, (6) positive affect, and (7) physiological soothing of the male. This study utilized a two-stage longitudinal design to follow 130 newly married couples (i.e., within 6 months of their marriage) over a 6-year period in cohorts of approximately 40 couples per cohort. The follow-up period (Time 2) varied from 3 to 6 years for each couple, depending on the cohort to which they were assigned. At the end of the 6-year period, three comparison groups were selected to conduct the study: (1) couples who had divorced ($n = 17$), (2) couples with high marital satisfaction ($n = 20$), and (3) couples with low marital satisfaction ($n = 20$). At the time of initial contact (Time 1), all of the couples participated in a "marital interaction assessment" session in which they engaged in a 15-minute discussion of an ongoing disagreement in their marriage. This session was followed by two "recall sessions" in which each partner reviewed a videotape of their discussion and rated their own and their partner's affect. Physiological measures (e.g., heart rate) were collected during the couple interactions. These sessions were also behaviorally observed and coded using a coding system that focuses solely on the affect expressed (e.g., vocal tone, facial expression, speech content).

In summary, Gottman et al. (1998) found little evidence to support the conceptual idea that all types of negative expressivity in couple interactions are detrimental to later relationship satisfaction and stability. In fact, the only variable that was found to predict both marital stability and satisfaction was the amount of positive affect couples could maintain in their conflictual interactions. It was also found that gender and power issues play a large part in how couples interact and respond to conflictual exchanges. Gottman and his colleagues (1998) noted,

> We conclude that the marriages that wound up happy and stable had a softened start-up by the wife, that the husband accepted influence from her, that he de-escalated low-intensity negative affect, that she was likely to use humor to effectively soothe him, and that he was likely to use positive affect and de-escalation to effectively soothe himself. (p. 17)

It is clear from these findings that traditional methods of conceptualizing positivity and negativity in couple interactions have been overly simplistic and new theoretical models are needed to get at the intricacies of how couple communication processes affect relationship happiness over time.

In recent years, marriage prediction scholars have started to integrate new findings in couple communication research into the beginning threads of more complex theories of negative expressivity in premarital and marital relationships (Gottman et al., 1998; Markman, 1991). Many of these new theoretical models are being developed from asking new questions about negative and positive affect in relationships. Summarizing this idea, Krokoff (1991) noted, "The relevant questions to ask may not be whether negative affect is functional or dysfunctional for a marriage, but rather, what type of negative affect is functional/dysfunctional for what type of couple under *what temporal condition* [emphasis added]?" (p. 63). Markman (1991) added to this new line of investigation by proposing that the question left to be answered is: "*Under what conditions* [emphasis added] does negativity predict positive or negative outcomes?" (p. 90). It appears that much of the emphasis of the "under what conditions" approach to investigating negative and positive affect will include: (1) how couples manage conflict and (2) the role of the gender differences in affective communication processes. In particular, the idea that the expression of negativity can be enhancing or diminishing in a couple's relationship depending on how it is expressed and received, may prove to be a beneficial line of investigation. This theoretical concept of "constructive marital conflict" expands earlier models of negativity and positivity in couple communication patterns and looks for specific couple styles or variables that may explain why negativity predicts low marital satisfaction in some cases but not in others.

Other Communication Studies

While most of the recent premarital/marital prediction studies done on couple communication processes have focused on conflict management, some research has been done that conceptualizes communication in other ways. In a study using questionnaire data from 174 premarital couples, Brooks (1988) conceptualized quality of communications as "the degree to which one partner confides in the other partner and shares feeling and concern about the relationship" (p. 20). Using path analysis techniques, he found that at a 3-year marriage follow-up, quality of communication was a moderate yet significant predictor of marital satisfaction. In another study using a multivariate model to explore premarital predictors of marital quality and stability, Rhoades (1994) found that a global measure of premarital couple communication was related to marital quality 3 years later. Of special note, this relationship was twice as strong for females than for the males.

Summary

In many ways, premarital couple communication research appears to be in a transitional era of theory and model development. Marital prediction research has stretched beyond the explanatory limits of the theoretical models previously used to conceptualize communication process and has left us with the need to develop more complex models of how various components of couple interactional processes predict and influence marital quality over time (Gottman et al., 1998; Markman, 1991; Wamboldt & Reiss, 1989). However, despite the current call for new directions in research and theory, there are several conclusions from past research that should guide future efforts. These guidelines include:

- *Distinguish between Cross-Sectional and Longitudinal Studies.* Scholars should be careful to distinguish between models of couple communication that are based on cross-sectional research versus models developed using longitudinal findings. Several studies have shown that the effects of communication processes on marital quality are not necessarily the same longitudinally as they are cross-sectionally (Gottman & Krokoff, 1989; Markman, 1984; Smith et al., 1990, 1991). Since most people see their marriages as ongoing relationships that they want to last over considerable periods of time, premarital communication research needs to continue to make efforts to implement longitudinal designs that follow couples from pre- to postmarriage (Krokoff, 1991; Larson & Holman, 1994; Smith et al., 1991).
- *Build More Complex Models of Marital Functioning.* The last 20 years of research have highlighted the need for more diverse and complex theoretical models for explaining couple communication processes. Communication is a multilayered, complex process that is open to multiple meanings and interpretations by the people involved. Theoretical models need to respect this complexity and strive to identify variables that act to modify or mediate negative expressivity in couple communication (Gottman et al., 1998; Krokoff, 1991). Particular emphasis needs to be given to couple communication styles or orientations, rather than lumping all couples together as responding similarly to generically defined interactions and/or processes (Krokoff, 1991).
- *Incorporate Gender Differences in Model Development.* One of the most consistent findings of premarital communication research to date is that there

are gender differences in communication styles and how conflict is handled (Gottman et al., 1998; Markman, 1991). Future research models need to explore how gender impacts communication processes and how men and women are similar and different from one another when it comes to how communication is expressed and received (Larson & Holman, 1994). How couples define and deal with issues of power related to gender may also prove to be a crucial factor in the prediction of marital success or failure (Gottman et al., 1998).

• *There Is More to Communication Than Resolving Conflicts.* Several marriage scholars have highlighted that elements of communication other than conflict management are related to marital quality over time (Wamboldt & Reiss, 1989). Positive communication processes, empathetic communication, and consensus building communication are all examples of different constructs of communication that have proven to predict marital quality (Gottman et al., 1998; Wamboldt & Reiss, 1989). In fact, in multivariate models that have included measures of both positive and negative communication, positivity has been shown to have more impact on later marital satisfaction and stability (Gottman et al., 1998). Future models of marital functioning need to incorporate elements of communication that broaden our perspective beyond conflict management and problem solving.

As noted previously, most of the research studies completed to date that investigate how premarital couple processes affect later marital quality have been grounded in a behavioral or social learning perspective of interpersonal relationships. While this theoretical position has proven to be beneficial in helping family professionals define and recognize the overt *process* component of couple communication, it offers few conceptual tools for exploring the *meaning* individuals give to their interactions with their partners. In other words, while behavioral models of marriage are quite adept at detailing *how* couples communicate and manage conflict, they offer little explanatory power as to *why* partners ascribe certain meanings to their interactional processes. These ideas are of particular significance given Gottman and colleagues' (1998) recent finding that issues of power and gender often play a crucial role in how couples interpret and react to conflictual interactions in their relationships. These findings suggest that, in order for future models of marital functioning to prove beneficial, they will need not only to address the observable, behavioral processes of couple communication, but also to explore how people's internal perceptions and meaning structures influence, and are influenced by, interactions with their partners.

Similarity

Similarity has long been viewed as   important in the establishment and maintenance of relationships (White & Hatcher, 1984). Mate selection has been seen largely as a process of responding to perceived similarities, and then of building a relationship as similarity is perceived or created (Adams, 1979; Burr, 1973; Byrne, 1997; Kerckhoff & Davis, 1962; Murstein, 1986). Correspondingly, similarity is seen as a component of high quality and stable marriages (Lewis & Spanier, 1979; Spanier, 1976). However, whether premarital similarity is related to later marital quality has not been nearly as well addressed. Also, what *type* of similarity, and similarity on *what*, has not been adequately addressed. In this section we review the research on the relationship between premarital similarity and later marital quality, noting what research in the personal relationships area has to add to our understanding of similarity, and showing how theory suggests similarity is related to marital quality.

Before reviewing the research on premarital similarity and marital quality, we will make a distinction between three *types* of similarity based on the work of Acitelli, Douvan, and Veroff (1993). Acitelli et al. (1993) focus on three types of similarity, or perceptual congruence, in intimate interpersonal relationships: *actual similarity*, which is the congruence of both partners' self-perceptions; *perceived similarity*, which is the congruence between persons' perceptions of themselves and their perceptions of their partners on the same issue; and *understanding*, which is the congruence between persons' perceptions of their partners and the partners' self-perceptions. We distinguish between these types of similarity in the following literature wherever possible.

Of the classic studies, only Burgess and Wallin (1953) studied the relationship between premarital similarity and marital quality. They found that premarital actual similarity on attitudes and beliefs about marriage was related to marital success 3 to 5 years into marriage. Bentler and Newcomb (1978) collected premarital data from newly married couples and then 4 years later collected "marital success" data. They found that couples still married after 4 years were significantly more similar (actual similarity) than separated and divorced couples on a number of personality features, including art interest, attractiveness, and extroversion.

Fowers and Olson (1986) and Larsen and Olson (1989) studied the predictive validity of the premarital assessment tool, PREPARE. They created "couple positive agreement" (CPA) scores from scales measuring beliefs and attitudes about marriage, and perceptions of self and partner behaviors. These CPA scores appear to be measuring actual similarity of responses. In the Fowers and Olson study, they report that the "married-satisfied" group has significantly higher premarital CPA scores than the "married-dissatisfied" group on communication, conflict resolution, leisure activities, financial management, sexuality, equalitarian roles, and their overall average CPA score. The couples had been married on average just under 2 years. In the second longitudinal study of PREPARE's predictive validity, Larsen and Olson (1989) do not provide statistical tests of the difference between the married-satisfied group and the married-dissatisfied group, but the mean differences are similar to the Fowers and Olson study.

Wamboldt and Reiss (1989) measured the actual similarity of their premarital couples' perceptions of important relationship issues, the actual similarity of each of their families of origin, and their "understanding" of the males' and females' families of origin. The study found that a couple's similarity of attitudes and beliefs about relationships premaritally was significantly and positively correlated with the females' relationship satisfaction 1 year later, but not with the males' relationship satisfaction. The actual similarity of families of origin was not related to either the males' or females' later relationship satisfaction. However, the greater the males' agreement with their partners concerning the females' family of origin, the greater was the males' later relationship satisfaction. Interestingly, the greater the understanding females had with their partners concerning the males' family of origin, the lower was the relationship satisfaction of both males and females. Wamboldt and Reiss offer no explanation of this finding.

Rhoades (1994) included a measure of actual similarity of attitudes and beliefs, and also a type of "perceived similarity" in his longitudinal study. His perceived similarity was different from that of Acitelli et al. (1993) in that it was each person's perception of how much agreement they, as a couple, have on seven issues such as time together, finances, and dealing with parents/in-laws. His actual similarity is unrelated to marital quality 1 year into the marriage, but the perceived similarity (agreement) was significantly and positively related to marital quality for both the husbands and wives.

Holman et al. (1994) also studied the predictive validity of PREP-M. They measured the actual similarity of couples premaritally on their attitudes about money and possessions, religion, moral/ethical behavior, premarital sex, wife/mother employment, family planning and contraception, privacy, and marital role expectation. They found that the greater the premarital actual similarity in values, the higher was the marital satisfaction of husbands 1 year into marriage. However, premarital actual similarity in values was not related to wives' marital satisfaction.

Another kind of similarity that has been investigated in previous research is social similarity, or homogamy. Earlier studies have shown some relationship between homogamy and marital quality (Burr, 1973; Lewis & Spanier, 1979). Research on homogamy since 1970 has been limited, but those studies that have been done have given some support for greater marital quality for couples who are similar in race, socioeconomic background, religious affiliation, intelligence, and age (Antill, 1983; Birtchnell & Kennard, 1984; Kurdek, 1991). Some research, however, finds no support for homogamy influencing later marital quality (Whyte, 1990).

In summary, studies of premarital similarity and later marital quality have shown that similarity of attitudes and values appear to have some relationship to later marital quality. Premarital personality similarity and similarity of perceptions of each other's families of origin may also relate to later marital quality. The type of similarity studied has generally been actual similarity.

Couple Identity Formation

Viewing marriage with a developmental-constructivist perspective, Wamboldt and Reiss (1989) propose that much of the stability and satisfaction of a couple's marriage is linked to how well they were able to create a strong *couple identity* during the early years of courtship and marriage. Expounding this idea, they note,

> During this phase of the family life cycle, the couple has to struggle with the entwined tasks of defining themselves with regard to the families in which they were raised and the relationship they are forming. In other words, the couple has to accomplish two related definitions: (a) their heritage, that is what they will emulate and what they will change from each origin family, and (b) their relationship identity, that is how will they take themselves as two individuals and create a couple, a "we." (p. 330)

Wamboldt and Reiss have theorized that much of a couple's sense of identity comes from their ability to reach a certain level of consensus or agreement about key issues within their relationship. Using measures of agreement on relationship beliefs and family-of-origin processes as indicators of a couple's identity formation, they found that their respondents' actual similarity on values and attitudes was significantly correlated to later dyadic adjustment for the females, but not the males. The actual similarity of their families of origin is not related to dyadic adjustment for either the females or males. However, greater understanding (accuracy of perceptions) of the females' family of origin is positively related to the males' later dyadic adjustment, but not to that of the females. Understanding (perceptual accuracy) of the males' family of origin is negatively and significantly related to both the males' and females' dyadic adjustment. We suggest that another indicator of couple identity formation is the perceived permanence of the relationship premaritally. We postulate that the more individuals wonder about and talk about the viability of the relationship, the less of a sense of "coupleness" they have. Therefore, we include a measure of couple identity formation, or couple permanence, in the model.

Hypotheses

Previous research and theorizing indicates that at least three aspects of premarital couple interactional processes are related to later marital quality—communication, similarity, and couple identity formation.

Given the potential for "negative" communication to have a positive effect on marital quality over time, we have tried to distinguish between what we call "relationship-enhancing communication" and "relationship-diminishing communication." Rather than being measures of specific types of communication processes, both of these latent variables are measures of how partners experience the larger "communication environment" in their relationship. Relationship-enhancing communication primarily gets at perceived levels of understanding and empathy in the relationship, while relationship-diminishing communication measures levels of perceived criticism and withdrawal. Therefore, these latent variables should not be thought of as processes of "positivity" and "negativity," rather they are measures of how general communication patterns have resulted in being perceived as either "enhancing" (perceptions of listening or being listened to and/or understanding or being understood) or "diminishing" (perceptions of withdrawing or being withdrawn from and/or criticizing or being criticized) to the relationship. We also have a latent variable represented by indicators of perceived agreement or similarity which we call "consensus on relationship issues." Our last latent predictor variable is called "similarity on values and personality characteristics" and has indicators of actual similarity, perceived similarity, and understanding (perceptual accuracy).

Our hypothesis is that there is a relationship between one or more of the couple interactional factors and later marital satisfaction even when controlling for the effect of the other couple interactional factors. Given the paucity of multivariate research, we are not able to suggest which factors have a stronger relationship with later marital quality than others.

Results

There are several noteworthy innovations in the following analyses worth mentioning. First, our analysis, except for unpublished studies by Rhoades (1994) and Linford (1997), is the only analysis that simultaneously tests the effects of multiple latent variable indicators of various components of couple interactional processes. Other studies have looked at communication, consensus, or similarity, but none have studied the simultaneous effect of multiple couple interactional processes. Second, our measures of relationship-enhancing communication and relationship-diminishing communication not only have an indicator of how ego perceives his/her own communication styles, but also how ego perceives his/her partner's relationship-enhancing and -diminishing communication. While survey data may not provide a "videotape" of couple processes, our indicators come as close to measuring a perceived pattern in process as survey data are able to come. Third, in light of some research and theoretical speculation, it is deemed appropriate to get at different "types" of similarity. Our purpose is not to see which type is "best," but rather to increase the predictive power of similarity by having indicators of three types of similarity. Our premarital measurement tool, the PREP-M questionnaire, is unique in that it asks respondents their perceptions about their

Table 7.1. Means (with Standard Deviations) for Relationship-Enhancing Communication, Relationship-Diminishing Communication, Couple Identity Formation, Perceived Consensus, and Couple Similarity

	Females	Males
Relationship-Enhancing Communication		
Perception of self's enhancing communication	3.53 (0.40)	3.78 (0.45)*
Perception of partner's enhancing communication	3.53 (0.45)	3.45 (0.47)*
Relationship-Diminishing Communication		
Perception of self's diminishing communication	1.25 (0.55)	1.12 (0.56)*
Perception of partner's diminishing communication	0.75 (0.56)	0.92 (0.63)*
Couple Identity Formation		
Thought relationship in trouble	1.39 (1.14)	1.55 (1.18)*
Thought of breaking off	0.81 (1.02)	0.89 (1.08)
Discuss terminating with partner	0.66 (0.92)	0.76 (0.95)*
Perceived Consensus on Relationship Issues		
Agreement on leisure activities	3.18 (0.52)	3.11 (0.45)*
Agreement on handling finances	2.67 (1.15)	2.71 (1.11)
Agreement on affection/intimacy	3.39 (0.60)	3.30 (0.58)*
Agreement on ways of dealing with parents/in-laws	2.70 (1.17)	2.78 (1.08)
Agreement on amount of time spent together	3.37 (0.63)	3.25 (0.59)*
Couple Similarity		
Actual similarity of values	19.65 (6.79)	
Actual similarity of personality	5.17 (3.02)	
Perceived similarity of personality	4.04 (2.87)	4.51 (3.50)*
Understanding (accuracy) of personality	4.52 (2.66)	4.69 (2.78)

* Difference significant at .05 level.

own *and* their partner's attitudes, behaviors, and personality characteristics. This allows us to compute three types of similarity on personality constructs.

The measures of the various interactional process variables used in the analyses are described in Chapter 2. Table 7.1 shows the means and standard deviations for the indicators of the five latent predictor variables. The means and standard deviations of the indicators of the latent criterion variable, marital satisfaction, are found in Table 4.1 and are not repeated here. It should be noted that "homogamy" was dropped as an indicator of couple similarity because of very poor reliability and validity found in the test of the measurement model and therefore is not included in the descriptive and bivariate reports in Tables 7.1 and 7.2.

There are several informative differences between the males and females. The males perceive themselves and their partners to have more relationship-enhancing communication than do the females. The males perceive themselves as engaging in less relationship-diminishing communication compared with their partners, but believe their partner to engage in more relationship-diminishing communication than the females believe their partners do. The females think the relationship is in trouble less often than do their partners, and also think they discussed it less often together. Males are more likely to believe they have consensus on leisure activities than the females, but less likely to believe they have consensus on affection/intimacy and time spent together with the females. The males also perceive greater personality similarity than the females.

Table 7.2 reports the bivariate correlations of the latent variables used in these analyses. For the males, all five of the aspects of the premarital couple

Table 7.2. Bivariate Correlations between Latent Variables[a]

	1	2	3	4	5	6
1. Marital Satisfaction	1.00	.29*	-.17*	.08	.13	.17*
2. Relationship-Enhancing Communication	.28*	1.00	-.49*	.37*	.60*	.59*
3. Relationship-Diminishing Communication	-.15*	-.53*	1.00	-.64*	-.76*	-.59*
4. Couple Identity	.13*	.34*	-.46*	1.00	.57*	.30*
5. Perceived Consensus	.18*	.58*	-.67*	.47*	1.00	.56*
6. Couple Similarity	.20*	.55*	-.62*	.33*	.44*	1.00

[a] Coefficients above the diagonal are for wives ($N = 336$), those below the diagonal are for husbands ($N = 336$)
* $p < .05$.

interactional processes are correlated to their marital satisfaction 6 years later. For the females, only premarital relationship-enhancing communication, relationship-diminishing communication, and similarity are correlated to marital satisfaction. Perceived consensus is related at $p < .10$. Having established that the premarital predictors relate as expected to the criterion variable of marital satisfaction, we proceed to our multivariate model test. Structural equation modeling (SEM) using LISREL 8 (Jöreskog & Sörbom, 1996) is used to perform the analyses.

We began the SEM analyses by specifying the measurement models for the wives and husbands separately, thus specifying which observed variables in each model assess our latent variables. All of the factor loads on constructs are statistically significant in both models and the squared multiple correlations are at an acceptable level except for the homogamy latent variable. Therefore, it was dropped from further analysis. Having established acceptable reliability and validity with the measurement model, we specified the structural model and estimated its parameters. The wives' base model is depicted in Figure 7.1 and the husbands' base model is depicted in Figure 7.2. The χ^2 for both models approach nonsignificance, and other goodness-of-fit statistics suggest that the models provide reasonable fits to the data. Additional modifications suggested by the LISREL 8 program to lower the χ^2 were deemed inappropriate since they did not make

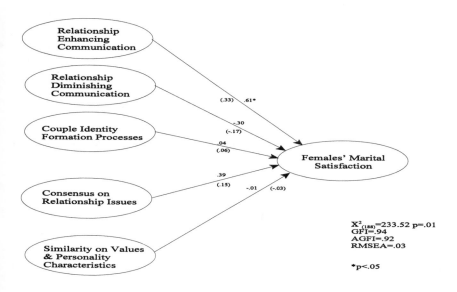

Figure 7.1. Females' perceptions of couple interactional processes and marital satisfaction, unstandardized (and standardized) coefficients ($N = 336$).

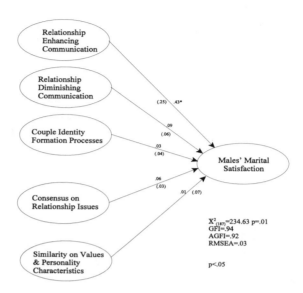

Figure 7.2. Males' perceptions of couple interactional processes and marital satisfaction, with unstandardized (and standardized) coefficients ($N = 336$).

theoretical sense and since all of the other goodness-of-fit indices were strong. Both the wives' and husbands' models, premarital relationship-enhancing commu-nication is the only premarital variable to retain a significant relationship with later marital satisfaction when controlling for the other couple interactional variables. This is a positive relationship in both models and indicates that the greater the perceived premarital relationship-enhancing communication by self and partner, the greater is the marital satisfaction several years into marriage. Using the unstandardized path coefficients to compare across models, we see that the premarital couple interactional processes predict the wives' later marital satisfaction better than that of the husbands. Within-model comparisons of predictor latent variables using the standardized path coefficients show that the magnitude of the association between the relationship-enhancing communication variable and marital satisfaction is twice that of any other predictor variable for the wives and four times the magnitude for the husbands.

Similarity's Indirect Effect

While the possibility of similarity having an indirect relationship to marital quality through communication is not discussed or tested in the premarital prediction literature, there is speculation of such a relationship in theoretical writings and there is a hint of such a possibility in Rhoades (1994) and our results reported above. In their chapter on symbolic interaction and the family, Burr, Leigh, et al. (1979) proposed that many premarital factors are indications of the general construct quality of role enactment. They presented a theory of role enactment in which they suggested that the amount of consensus (or dissensus) about role expectations is related to the quality of role enactment. Role enactment was defined as "how well a person performs a role relative to the expectations for the role" (p. 58). If our "perceived consensus" and "similarity" are indicators of their "amount of consensus about role expectations," and if our "relationship-enhancing communication" is an indicator of their "quality of role enactment" (and we believe they are), then a symbolic interactionist argument supports the indirect relationship from similarity through communication to marital satisfaction. Trost (1964) provides the argument from a symbolic interactionist perspective for this relationship. He suggests that couples with similar "symbolic environments," that is, with shared symbols or mental representations derived from the environment, will tend to communicate more effectively.

More recently, Duck (1994) has also proposed that similarity could be related to factors like communication. He suggests that the more levels on which one is similar with a partner, the greater is the likelihood of understanding and the easier the communication becomes.

Rhoades (1994) studied three premarital constructs of importance to this discussion—actual similarity of couple values, communication, and perceived agreement on relationship issues—using structural equation modeling to test the relationship between these three "latent" predictor variables and two "latent" marital criterion variables: marital quality and marital stability. The sample couples had been married an average of 1 year when the marital data were collected. Although Rhoades does not specify relationships between the predictor variables, his presentation of the measurement model shows a small positive correlation between the indicators of actual similarity and communication (mostly for the females), but essentially no relationship between similarity and agreement. Rhoades tests the structural model separately for males and females. When other premarital factors are taken into account, premarital communication has a significant relationship to marital quality, but neither values similarity or perceived agreement are significantly related to marital quality for the males or females.

Also, as is shown in Table 7.2, all five of the interactional process variables are related to one another. In the structural equation model, only relationship-enhancing communication retains a statistically significant relationship to marital satisfaction. Thus, the lack of a direct effect by the similarity variables on marital satisfaction, but their bivariate relationship to the communication variable, opens the possibility for similarity to be related indirectly to marital satisfaction through communication. To test this idea, we retain only relationship-enhancing communication as an endogenous predictor variable and the two similarity variables—

perceived consensus and similarity of values and personality—as the exogenous variables.

Figures 7.3 and 7.4 show the model we tested and the results of the SEM analysis. For both wives and husbands, the greater the perceived consensus, the greater is the relationship-enhancing communication. Greater similarity of values and personality (actual, perceived, and understanding similarity) is significantly and positively related to relationship-enhancing communication for the wives, but only marginally related for the husbands ($p < .10$).

We conclude that while similarity may have a bivariate relationship with later marital quality, it is most consistent with our data and theory to suggest that similarity's greatest contribution is in its effect of increasing relationship-enhancing communication, which then predicts later marital satisfaction.

Discussion

Our primary purpose in this chapter was to test the direct relationship between aspects of premarital couple interactional processes and the marital quality of

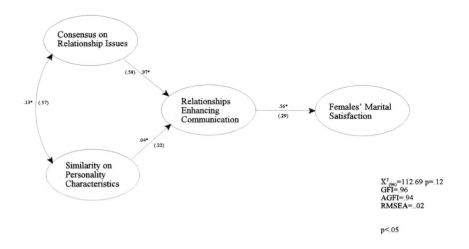

Figure 7.3. Females' premarital similarity and communication, and later marital satisfaction; unstandardized (and standardized) coefficients, *$p < .05$ ($N = 346$).

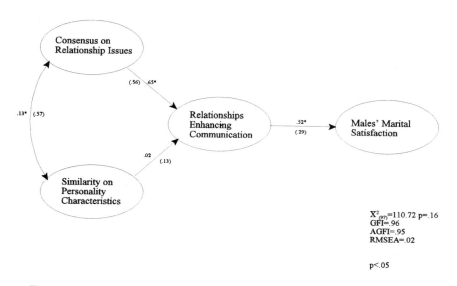

Figure 7.4. Male's premarital similarity and communication, and later marital satisfaction; unstandardized (and standardized) coefficients, *$p < .05$ ($N = 346$).

individuals several years into marriage. We identified several important conceptual aspects of couple interactional processes including relationship-enhancing communication, relationship-diminishing communication, sense of couple identity formation, and similarity/consensus. Each couple interactional process variable was bivariately related to marital satisfaction 6 years (on average) into marriage, although some were only marginally related for the wives. The structural equation analyses, however, demonstrated that only relationship-enhancing communication was significantly related when all of the couple interactional processes were included in the analyses. It is clear that the association all of these other variables have with marital satisfaction is largely due to the overlap of these factors with relationship-enhancing communication.

The strong bivariate relationship of the five couple interactional process variables with each other and their relationship with the criterion variable, marital satisfaction, suggested the possibility of indirect relationships. While no research we are aware of has investigated similarity's indirect effect on marital quality through communication, theoretical speculations suggest that similarity should be related directly to communication. Therefore, we tested models that showed that perceived consensus was strongly related to relationship-enhancing communication for both husbands and wives, and that similarity of values and personality was also related although of a lesser magnitude than perceived consensus.

Our most fundamental conclusion is that premarital couple interactional processes are able to predict marital satisfaction, up to at least 6 years into marriage, and of particular importance are those processes that "enhance" feelings of receptiveness and understanding. Persons who perceive both themselves and their partners as using a high level of this type of relationship-enhancing communication are significantly more likely to have highly satisfying marriages. However, just because the other aspects of couple interactional processes were not significantly related to later marital quality when relationship-enhancing communication was present, does not mean they were not important. An analysis of similarity's indirect effect through relationship-enhancing communication demonstrated that the greater is the similarity and consensus, the greater the relationship-enhancing communication, and consequently, the greater the marital quality.

Implications

We save most of our discussion of research, theoretical, and practical implication until we have seen, in Chapter 8, the role couple interactional processes play as intervening variables, since they are the conduits for the indirect effects of all of the other premarital factors' indirect effects on marital quality (see Figure 1.1). However, a few things are already clear.

Research and Theory

It is clear that what we have called relationship-enhancing communication processes in a premarital relationship translate into marital processes that establish, maintain, and enrich the quality of marriage. How this happens is not yet clear and awaits greater theoretical specificity and research.

Practice

From a practical point of view, it is clear that couples who desire long-term, high quality marital relationships can benefit from strengthening their ability to carry on relationship-enhancing communication with one another while in the courtship stage. It would also be helpful for couples to increase consensus and similarity as a mechanism for increasing their ability to have relationship-enhancing communication.

8

Putting It All Together: Four Longitudinal, Multivariate Models of Premarital Prediction of Marital Quality

Thomas B. Holman, Steven T. Linford, Kent R. Brooks, Suzanne F. Olsen, Clifford Jay Rhoades, and Jason S. Carroll

> *Marriage is a lot harder than you realize. It takes two people willing to compromise and work together. I thought because we are of the same religion and beliefs it would just work out that way. I was too idealistic about marriage, and I hate conflict. Wish there were ways to change our relationship so that I felt more at ease with it.*
>
> —Female respondent

> *We have a good relationship most of the time, she could be more to me and vice versa. But we are committed to succeed. Both of our parents were divorced while we were kids. We're going to succeed. When it's good, it's good, when it's bad we talk over it, make adjustments and then talk some more. Ha! We're going to make it.*
>
> —Male respondent

This chapter is unique among the chapters in this volume. It is unique because we present the findings of three previously unpublished longitudinal studies of models of premarital prediction of marital quality, along with the test of a model derived from the data set used in the rest of this book and based on the research reported on in Chapters 4–7. We then conclude the chapter with a summary of all of the research, including the research reported here, on premarital prediction of marital quality. We present it in table format so readers can quickly get a comprehensive overview of what has been done, when it was done, how it was done, and what the findings were. This table is based on a thorough and comprehensive review of the literature. For the benefit of researchers and other interested readers, we include the written description of Table 8.1 in a comprehensive in-depth review of the research in Appendix C. Unlike typical reviews (like we have done in the previous chapters in this book) that usually review and report only the *findings* of a study, the review in Appendix C reports the purpose, theoretical grounding, and methods of each study, along with the findings. We believe the multiple studies and the tabled review (along with the comprehensive review in Appendix C) reported below make this a very useful chapter and lead us to extremely useful implications in Chapter 9.

Four Longitudinal, Multivariate Studies of Premarital Predictors of Marital Quality

Before presenting four studies, a word of introduction seems in order, since all of these studies are interconnected. It all began with the formation of the Marriage Study Consortium in 1979 at the annual meeting of the National Council on Family Relations. The consortium was organized by a group of family scholars, researchers, and practitioners who were interested in the twofold mission of (1) strengthening premarital and marital relationships and (2) doing research on premarital and marital relationships. The consortium is housed at Brigham Young University, although its members include researchers and practitioners from universities and private practice settings. The major task of the Marriage Study Consortium is to develop instruments that are used by practitioners and teachers in classroom, workshop, and counseling settings to help couples evaluate and strengthen their relationships, and which are used simultaneously to gather research data. The first instrument was developed by Burr, Yorgason, and Baker (1979) and was called the Marital Inventories for LDS Couples, or MIL. The MIL was only in use for 1 year and was replaced by a nondenominational version simply called the Marital Inventories, or M.I. (Yorgason et al.,1980). The M.I. was in use until 1989, and was administered to over 15,000 people in the United States and Canada. In 1989, it was replaced by the PREParation for Marriage Questionnaire, or PREP-M (Holman et al., 1989). The PREP-M was taken by 13,000 people at various universities, clinics, churches, and elsewhere in the 8 years it was used. Most recently, the PREP-M has been replaced by the RELATionship Evaluation, or RELATE (Holman, Busby, Doxey, Klein, & Loyer-Carlson, 1997). These instruments were designed to provide a comprehensive evaluation of the premarital relationship based on the best available research and theory in premarital prediction of marital outcomes. RELATE is designed to evaluate marital as well as premarital relationships.

Since 1980, four different longitudinal, multivariate studies of premarital predictors of marital quality were conducted using data from either the MIL, M.I., or PREP-M, of which the study reported thus far in this book is the most recent. All four studies were published as dissertations (Brooks, 1988; Holman, 1981; Linford, 1997; Rhoades, 1994). Although numerous studies using those data sets have been published in professional journals, none of the dissertations were published in journal or book (chapter) form.[1]

The first three studies are reported here for the first time. Our reports of the first three studies are summaries of the purpose, methods, results, and conclusion as they were reported in three dissertations. The fourth study, as noted above, is a test of a "total model" based on the results reported in Chapters 4–7 of this monograph. The four studies are presented chronologically.

Study Number One

Purpose

The purpose of the first study (Holman, 1981) was both to test a part of Lewis and Spanier's (1979) theory of marital quality and stability and to expand and refine their theoretical model. Based on Lewis and Spanier's propositional inventory and on the symbolic interaction perspective, a path model with three premarital variables and five marital variables was proposed. Lewis and Spanier's model hypothesized a direct relationship between a number of premarital factors and marital quality. This study was designed to test some of these relationships. Lewis and Spanier further hypothesized that a number of marital factors were related to marital quality, and this study investigated some of these relationships also. The study expanded Lewis and Spanier's model by hypothesizing relationships between the premarital variables and the intervening marital variables.

Methods

Fifty-seven couples comprised the study sample. All 57 couples had been engaged or steady dating when they completed a premarital questionnaire in 1979, and were married when they completed a marital questionnaire approximately 1 year later. The lengths of marriage ranged from 4 to 14 months with the mean length being 10 months. The mean age at marriage of the wives was 20.7 years and that of the husbands was 22.4 years. The couples were engaged an average of 5.4 months with the range being from 2 to 15 months. All 114 husbands and wives were members of the LDS Church and had been married in an LDS temple. All but one were Caucasians, the one exception being of Mexican extraction.

The premarital data were obtained from the respondents' answers on the Marital Inventories for LDS Couples (Burr, Yorgason, et al., 1979), or MIL. The MIL contained over 380 items measuring premarital values, marital role expectations, family background, and couple interactional processes. Respondents generally completed the MIL as part of preparation for a marriage course at Brigham Young University.

The premarital variables in this study were adequacy of role models, emotional health, perceived consensus on values and roles, and actual consensus on values and roles. The adequacy of role models variable was a scale created by summing the answers to five questions about the happiness of parents' marriage, attitude toward each parent as a child, and level of childhood happiness. Emotional health was a scale derived from the summed scores of 13 items asking about such things as the respondent's moodiness, depression, impulsivity, anxiety, and loneliness. Perceived consensus was also a scale composed of the summed responses on 5 items measuring the respondent's perceptions of his/her consensus with the partner on issues of religion, purpose of marriage, physical affection, and leisure time. Actual consensus was created by summing the absolute differences between partners' responses to items measuring values and attitudes. There were either four or five responses to the items used to create these three premarital scales.

The marital data were gathered by means of a marriage questionnaire that was either delivered to the respondents or mailed to them if they no longer lived in the same community as the university. The marriage questionnaire consisted of items measuring demographics, companionship, agreement, communication, marital role enactment, and marital satisfaction.

The four marital variables were frequency of marital companionate activities, frequency of effective marital communication, quality of marital role enactment, and degree of satisfaction with the marriage. Marital companionship was a scale created from summing responses to 12 items asking how frequently the couple did things together, had enjoyable times together, and were affectionate toward each other. Marital communication effectiveness was a scale based on the summed responses to 15 items measuring such areas as communicating, understanding, listening, and complaining. A scale of marital role enactment was created from the summed response to 7 items asking about how well the spouse enacted activities such as housekeeping, keeping in touch with relatives, and earning a living. Marital satisfaction was a scale based on the summed responses to 11 items measuring such things as current happiness with the marriage, whether they would marry the same person again, and the personal satisfaction they have derived from marriage.

Given issues of multicollinearity in the use of path analysis, only one type of consensus variable could be included in the model. Therefore, zero-order correlations were performed with perceived consensus, actual consensus, and marital satisfaction. The analyses showed only perceived consensus to be significantly related to marital satisfaction. Therefore, only perceived consensus was used in the test of the path model.

Results

For the husbands, at the bivariate level, premarital emotional health positively relates to marital satisfaction and quality of marital role enactment. Adequacy of role models is not significantly related to any of the marital variables. Perceived consensus, on the other hand, is significantly and positively related to frequency of marital companionship, frequency of effective marital communication, quality of marital role enactment, and marital satisfaction.

For the wives, at the bivariate level, premarital level of emotional health is significantly and positively related to frequency of effective marital communication. Adequacy of role models is not significantly related to any of the marital variables. Premarital perceived consensus on values and roles is significantly and positively related to frequency of companionate activities, frequency of effective communication, and marital satisfaction.

The results of the test of the multivariate path model are shown in Figure 8.1. While Holman (1981) was interested in theoretically important direct and indirect relationships among marital variables, our only interest here is the direct and indirect effects of premarital variables on the various marital variables.

For the husbands, when controlling for other premarital factors, only perceived consensus retains a significant relationship with a marital quality variable and then only with frequency of effective communication. Adequacy of role models is positively related to premarital emotional health, but not to marital satisfaction as hypothesized. Premarital emotional health was not significantly related to any of the marital variables in the path model.

For the wives, premarital emotional health and perceived consensus on values and roles are both positively related to the marital quality outcome of frequency of effective marital communication. Perceived consensus is also positively related to frequency of marital companionate activities. Adequacy of role models is significantly and positively related to emotional health, but is not related to marital satisfaction.

This first study demonstrates a number of things about the premarital prediction of later marital quality. Like previous studies, this research shows that premarital factors can predict later marital quality. However, this study is the first

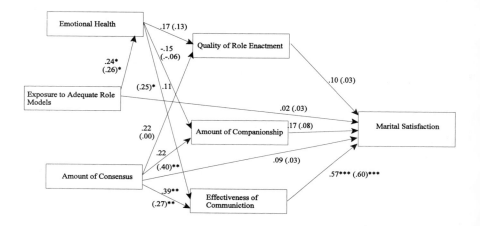

Figure 8.1. Holman study path model. Standardized path coefficients (females in parentheses); * = p < .05; ** = p < .01; *** = p < .001.

to simultaneously test a multivariate model with both direct and indirect relationships. From the findings, we conclude that some premarital factors are better predictors of early marital quality than others, and that the premarital factors predict some aspects of marital quality better than others. In this instance, premarital perceived consensus on values and roles is the best predictor of marital quality variables, and frequency of effective communication is the marital quality indicator that the premarital factors are most consistently related to.

Furthermore, some premarital factors have more influence on marital quality indirectly than directly. That is, some premarital factors have statistically significant relationships with (and possible effects on) other premarital factors that then predict marital quality. For example, adequacy of role models for wives is positively related to their emotional health, which in turn is positively related to effectiveness of communication.

The last important point this study demonstrates is that different aspects of the premarital circumstances have important direct or indirect effects on marital quality. The theoretical model posited in Figure 1.1 suggests that premarital influences should come from four main sources—the family of origin, the individual him/herself, the social context in which the developing relationship is embedded, and the couple interactional processes. Holman's three premarital variables are indicators of three of these sources. (He had no indicator of social context.)

Study Number Two

Purpose

The second study (Brooks, 1988), undertaken in 1987, noted that the two major reviews of research and theory on marital satisfaction and quality in the 1970s (Burr, 1973; Lewis & Spanier, 1979), and Holman and Burr's (1980) review of family theory development in the 1970s, call for improved theory and research that tests theoretically derived propositions. To this end, several of the propositions derived by Burr, and Lewis and Spanier, and from symbolic interaction, social exchange, and balance theories are integrated in order to study their influence on marital satisfaction. Specifically, the purpose of this study was to investigate the relationship that the premarital factors of homogamy, actual similarity, love, perceived similarity, and communication have on marital satisfaction. Both direct and indirect effects were hypothesized.

Methods

The sample consisted of 87 couples who completed a premarital assessment instrument in 1980–1981. The couples all completed the Time 2 Questionnaire in 1984. At the time of completing the initial premarital instrument the mean age of the males was 22.5 and that of the females was 20.6. Eighty-three percent of the males and 88% of the females were college students. Nine percent of the males and 3% of the females were college graduates, while 8% of the males and 7% of the females had attained only a high school diploma. Twenty-two percent of both the males and females were Protestants. Thirty percent of the males and 13% of the females were Catholics, while 46% of the males and 47% of the females were Mormons. Two percent of the males and 6% of the females were members of other religions. Ninety-seven percent of the sample was white, 2% Oriental, and 1% Hispanic.

The premarital data were gathered using the Marital Inventories (M.I.), a 383-item paper-and-pencil questionnaire developed to study premarital factors thought to be predictive of later marital quality. At the time they completed the M.I., most of the respondents were students at Arizona State University, Brigham Young

University, University of Iowa, University of Wisconsin-Stout, University of Notre Dame, Southwest Texas State University, Texas Tech University, or University of New Mexico, and completed the M.I. as part of a marriage and family course. Those respondents who were not students were partners of students. The addresses of the respondents were obtained from the universities they had attended. The respondents were sent a cover letter, two Marriage and Family Life follow-up questionnaires, two answer sheets, and a return envelope. A second mailing was sent approximately 4 weeks later.

The premarital variables of interest in this study are homogamy, actual similarity, perceived similarity, love, and quality of communication. Homogamy is operationalized with 11 items measuring race, education, age, and social class. A difference score is created for each person. The actual similarity variable is computed by creating a difference score between partners on 46 family role expectation items. Perceived similarity is a scale computed from summing each respondent's answers to 9 items on how similar the respondent thinks she or he and the partner are on values, roles, and expectations. The love variable is a scale created from summing the responses on 6 items that reflect the Greek and Roman philosophies of love. Quality of communication is derived from the summed scores of 6 items.

The primary marital variable of interest is marital satisfaction. It is a scale computed from the summed score of seven items. The hypothesized model was tested using path analysis. Separate models for males and females were not hypothesized or tested.

Results

The results are seen in Figure 8.2. The most important finding of this study is that the premarital factor of quality of communication predicted later marital satisfaction even when other premarital variables are held constant. Two indirect relationships are of interest. There is a strong relationship between premarital feelings of love and premarital quality of communication, and a weaker but significant relationship between actual similarity and quality of communication. However, neither love nor actual similarity is directly related to marital satisfaction.

Also important are the nonfindings. Except for quality of communication, none of the other premarital factors predicts marital satisfaction. Post hoc analyses were performed in an attempt to understand these nonfindings better. Based on the results, it is concluded that the nonfindings are not a result of measurement error for marital satisfaction, as the measure of marital satisfaction is both reliable and valid. Rather, the nonfindings are partly the result of measurement error for the Time 1 premarital factors and partly the result of faulty theory. For the premarital factors of actual similarity and perceived similarity, measurement error is present because some of the items making up these scales are not related to marital

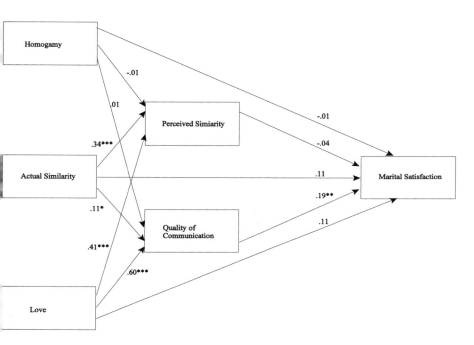

Figure 8.2. Brook's path model. Standardized path coefficients. *p = < .10; **p = < .05; ***p = < .001.

satisfaction, while some of the items are related. Moreover the results do not support the use of perceived similarity as an intervening variable.

Study Number Three

Purpose

This study was done in 1994 (Rhoades, 1994). It is different from the first two studies in that it does not test indirect relationships. However, it tests more predictor variables simultaneously than either of the two previous studies, and it uses a structural equation modeling procedure. This allows for considerably more flexibility in the model testing process than either of the previous studies, which use path analysis.

The purpose of this research was to identify premarital factors that are related to marital satisfaction and stability. More specifically, this study tests a longitudinal, multivariate model of the premarital predictors of later marital satisfaction and stability. Larson and Holman's (1994) review of premarital predictors of marital quality and stability was used as a conceptual starting point for this study and provides a theoretical model for testing. In their review of the literature, Larson and Holman (1994) gather the findings into three categories. These categories are family background and contextual factors, individual traits and behaviors, and couple interactional processes. An ecological, or ecosystemic, perspective, as recently conceptualized by Bubolz and Sontag (1993), provides Larson and Holman (1994) with an overarching theoretical scheme for organizing the findings of the premarital predictors of marital outcomes. Their theory suggests that a couple in the mate selection stage of the life course can be seen as a developing system that responds to inputs from within and without the system. The relationship develops at a number of levels, including the individual, couple, and contextual levels. To fully understand the mate selection process and probable intervention effects, an understanding is necessary in many of the levels of environments or ecosystems with which the couple system comes in contact.

Larson and Holman further conceptualize the couple's system as being composed of both individuals and a relationship, and these parts and the whole are interdependent. They summarized research on the individual members of the couple system that have generally been conceptualized in terms of psychological traits, the couple interactional processes, and the contexts or environments in which the couple system was or is embedded.

Methods

The subjects in this study were 208 individuals (104 couples) who completed a premarital assessment questionnaire in late 1989 or early 1990 while engaged, and then completed information concerning marital quality 1-½ or 2 years later. At the time of the follow-up, 91 of the couples had married and 18 had either canceled or delayed their marriage. The married couples had been married for a mean of 12 months.

The majority of the subjects (68%) grew up in the western United States. The educational level ranged from having completed high school to graduate work, with the majority of the subjects having completed some college (72%). The ages of the subjects ranged from 17 to 48 years with a mean age of 22 years. The predominant race was Caucasian (95%). The respondents were mostly students (69%), with 12% being professionals and 8% being service employees. The reported religious preferences of the subjects were Latter-day Saint, commonly referred to as Mormon (80%), Protestant (9%), and Catholic (5%). The couples who participated in this project completed the PREParation for Marriage

Questionnaire or PREP-M (Holman et al., 1989). The PREP-M contains 204 self-report assessment items that are divided into four sections. These four sections measure attitudes about marriage and related areas, demographic and background variables, individual perception of readiness for marriage, and partner's perception of the other's readiness for marriage.

Those who were engaged at the time of taking the PREP-M in late 1989 or early 1990 were contacted by phone in early 1991. Initial questions were asked over the phone to determine the marital status of the couple. Marital status was categorized as married, canceled, delayed, or legally separated or divorced. None of the couples contacted were separated or divorced. Only the married couples were sent the follow-up questionnaire. Data were obtained from 85 of the married couples for a 93% response rate.

In testing the theoretical model, latent variables are selected that best represented each category and for which there are measures available. Four latent predictor variables were used from the family background/contextual category. These variables are family structure, parents' marital quality, quality of the parent–child relationship in the family of origin, and approval of parents and friends for the marriage. In the category of individual traits and behaviors, two predictor latent variables are used. They are emotional health and impulsivity. The couple interactional processes category includes three latent predictor variables. These latent variables are attitudes and beliefs about issues important to marriage and family life, couple communication skills, and couple agreement.

Two latent criterion variables were investigated—marital satisfaction and marital stability. The satisfaction variable is a summed scale of 32 items about marital satisfaction based on Sabatelli's (1984) Marital Expectations Scale. The measurement of marital stability was based on the definition of Booth, Johnson, and Edwards (1983), which involves thoughts about and discussion of marital separation or divorce. This is different from Lewis and Spanier's (1979) definition of marital stability as whether a person is married, or divorced or separated. The Booth et al. (1983) Marital Instability Scale measures marital stability, using three items asking about thoughts of the marriage being in trouble, thoughts about divorce, and discussion of divorce with the spouse.

Two structural models were tested, one for males and one for females. The statistical analyses used to test the structural equation models is Latent Variable Path Analysis with Partial Least Squares (PLS). This method is also referred to as soft modeling. PLS was used in this study because (1) there was more than one outcome variable, (2) constructs had multiple indicators, (3) the sample size for this project was small and PLS handles smaller sample sizes well, (4) the goal of the project was more predictive than causal in nature, (5) PLS uses less restrictive assumptions than maximum likelihood procedures such as LISREL, and (6) PLS can utilize categorical variables (Falk & Miller, 1992).

In soft modeling the latent variable construct accounts for as much of the variance in the manifest variables as possible. PLS uses a series of interdependent ordinary least-squares regressions while seeking to maximize variances and the prediction of all raw scores in the manifest variables by minimizing the residual variances of all variables, manifest and latent (Fornell & Bookstein, 1982). Preference is given to the manifest variables. With this procedure, the highest percentage of common variance among the measured variables is extracted. As a result, the component maximally predicts the variance of the individual manifest variables. Therefore, PLS is attempting to reproduce observed variances using principle component functions with few restrictions on the data.

Results

Bivariate analyses revealed that few of the predictor variables were very highly related to one another but that many of them are highly related to the criterion variables. The most important conclusion is that constructs in all three of the general categories are correlated with marital satisfaction and to a lesser extent, marital stability. This suggests the feasibility and advisability of a multivariate test.

The measurement models for the males and females were tested to determine how well the indicator variables chosen for this study loaded onto the latent constructs. Factor loadings of .55 level were considered acceptable (Falk & Miller, 1992). It was necessary to delete a number of indicators from the measurement model because they did not reach the .55 cutoff level. There was inadequate variability in other indicators, so they were also deleted due to the small homogeneous sample from which the data were obtained.

In testing the full models, both the measurement and structural models were analyzed together. Because of this, changes may result in the measurement model. The communality coefficient, or how well the indicators loaded onto the constructs, was .72 for the males, and for females, .69. A level below .30 is unacceptable, signifying poor loading of the indicators. The closer to 1.00 the communality coefficient is, the stronger the loading of the indicators onto the constructs (Falk & Miller, 1992). Thus, for both models, indicators loaded adequately. The structural path coefficients for the males and females are shown in Figure 8.3. These path coefficients may be interpreted as betas. The .10 level is the minimum acceptance level.

To be a reliable predictor variable, a variable should account for at least 1.5% of the variance in the outcome variable. This is accomplished by multiplying the path by its corresponding latent variable correlation which provides an estimate of the percentage of variance explained by that variable (Falk & Miller, 1992). Paths shown in Figure 8.3 met this criterion.

The strongest predictor variables of marital satisfaction for males from highest to lowest are parent–child relationship ($\beta = .23$), other approval ($\beta = .19$), couple communication ($\beta = .18$), and emotional health ($\beta = .18$). The higher the values in these areas, the higher is the marital satisfaction.

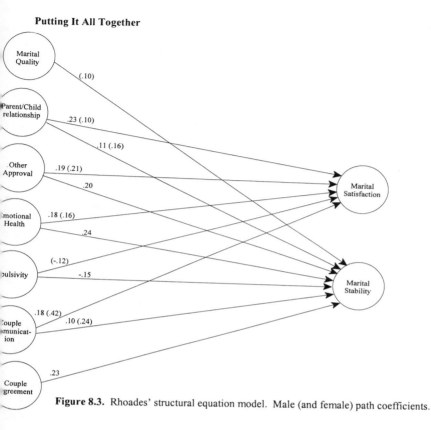

Figure 8.3. Rhoades' structural equation model. Male (and female) path coefficients.

For marital stability, emotional health is the highest predictor (β = .24), followed by couple agreement (β = .23), other approval (β = .20), impulsivity (β = -.15), parent–child relationship (β = .11), and couple communication (β = .10). This suggests that for males, good premarital emotional health (lack of depression) is the strongest predictor of marital stability. Having strong couple agreement, other approval, lack of impulsivity, and strong premarital couple communication are also important to creating a sense of stability in the marriage.

The model for females appears to be weaker in the prediction of stability, but stronger in the prediction of marital satisfaction than for males. For marital satisfaction, the strongest predictor is couple communication (β = .42). This is followed by other approval (β = .21), emotional health (β = .16), impulsivity (β = -.12), and parent–child relationship (β = .10). Marital stability had only three predictors. The strongest of the three is parents' marital quality (β = .24) followed by parent–child relationship (β = .16) and couple communication (β = .10).

Several differences between the male/female models are noteworthy. One important difference is that premarital predictors predict marital satisfaction better for females than for males, but marital stability was better predicted for males than for females. The R^2 for females' marital satisfaction is .42 and that for males is .31. For marital stability, the R^2 for males is .23 whereas that for females is .08. This may indicate that the PREP-M measurement tool and the variables used for this study measure marital satisfaction and stability differently by gender. Or it may also suggest the need for more diversity in measurement of these two constructs.

Couple communication is the best predictor for females' marital satisfaction and is twice as strong as the next best predictor, approval. Couple communication was also the strongest predictor of marital stability for females. It appears that for females, background and contextual factors, as well as individual traits and behaviors, provided more predictors of marital satisfaction, however, relations were only moderately strong. Other approval and parent–child relationship for females prove to be as important as the personality predictors of emotional health (lack of depression) and impulsivity. Parental marriage satisfaction was a predictor for female marital stability, but failed to remain in the model for males.

Males have a slightly different model in predicting marital satisfaction and stability. As stated earlier, marital satisfaction is not predicted as well in the male model as it is for females. However, this model also shows that background and contextual factors, as well as personality factors are viable and valid predictors of marital satisfaction. Again, variables in each of the three major categories predict marital satisfaction in the areas of parent–child relationship, emotional health (lack of depression), and couple communication. This suggests that for males, the stronger the parent–child relationship is, the higher the males' marital satisfaction and stability. Emotional health, or lack of depression, positively affects the satisfaction of the marriage, as does the ability to communicate with the males' partner. Although the male marital satisfaction predictors are few, they are strong.

The strength of the male model is its ability to predict marital stability. Each of the three categories again provides a predictor, with the strongest being couple agreement. Couple communication proves to be a significant predictor for males in both marital satisfaction and stability. A difference between males and females is where approval, emotional health (lack of depression), impulsivity, and couple agreement all are notable predictors for males but fail to predict marital stability for females. This would seem to indicate that for males, the social interaction of others and couple interaction, has a greater predictive ability than for females for later marital stability.

Study Number Four

Purpose

The last longitudinal multivariate study of premarital predictors of marital quality sponsored by the Marriage Study Consortium is the one reported in

Chapters 4–7 of this book. An initial exploratory study was done with those data by Linford (1997). His study only investigated direct relationships (replicating Rhoades, 1994) and the results informed the models created in this and earlier chapters.

Using the results of Chapters 4–7, we created final models that test, as far as is possible, the totality of the model presented in Figure 1.1. Because the theoretical and empirical rationale for this model was given in Chapter 1 and in succeeding chapters, we will not repeat it here. Also, Chapter 2 describes all of the variables to be used in the following models and that description need not be repeated here.

We begin with the females' model. Based on the findings of Chapters 4–7, we hypothesized that only two aspects of the four premarital factors in Figure 1.1 would retain a direct effect on marital satisfaction after 6 years of marriage. These are family of origin, represented by the parent–child relationship quality, and couple interactional processes, represented by relationship-enhancing communication. However, the other two conceptual areas of individual characteristics and social contexts are both represented in the females' model (see Figure 8.4). Based on the earlier findings, both self-esteem (an individual characteristic) and social network connection (an aspect of social context) were hypothesized to have an indirect effect on marital satisfaction. They are both conceptualized to be intervening variables coming between the parent–child relationship quality and relationship-enhancing communication. Social network connection is also hypothesized to affect self-esteem.

The males' model is slightly more complicated. One additional family-of-origin variable is included—the partners' parent–child relationship quality—and two additional direct paths are specified—a direct relationship from the female's parent–child relationship quality to marital satisfaction, and a direct relationship from self-esteem to marital satisfaction. Since the females' parents' approval is part of the social network, a path from females' parent–child relationship quality and social network support is hypothesized.

Results

The covariance matrices were analyzed with structural equation modeling procedures using the LISREL 8 program. The path models are shown in Figures 8.4 and 8.5. We report not only the direct effects as seen in the figures, but also the results of tests of the indirect and total effects. The standardized coefficients (in parentheses on the path models) allow us to compare the strength of relationships within each model and the unstandardized coefficients allow us to compare the relationships across the two models.

Good fit of the model is indicated in goodness-of-fit indices well above .90. In the female model, we suggested that there would be two direct paths from

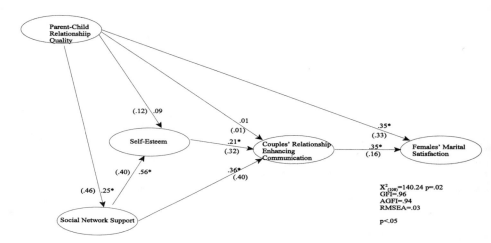

Figure 8.4. Study Number Four female model; unstandardized (and standardized) coefficients
(*N* = 351).

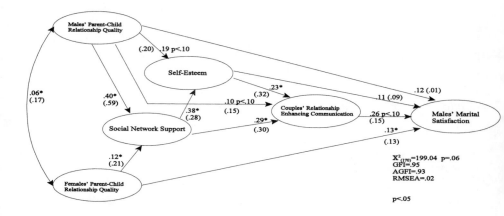

Figure 8.5. Study Number Four male model; unstandardized (and standardized) coefficients (*N*
= 352).

premarital variables to marital satisfaction. Both of the premarital variables—the quality of the females' childhood parent–child relationships ($\gamma = .33$) and the amount of premarital relationship-enhancing communication ($\gamma = .16$)—are positively and significantly related to marital quality an average of 6 years into the marriages. It is noteworthy that the childhood relationship between parent and child, as remembered premaritally, has twice as strong a relationship to marital quality several years later as premarital couples' communication does.

The females' parent–child relationship quality variable is also indirectly related to their marital satisfaction through social network support, but not through the individual characteristic self-esteem, or through couples' relationship-enhancing communication. Even so, the parent–child relationship quality variable has a significant indirect relationship to marital satisfaction ($.05, p < .05$). It also has a statistically significant total effect ($.38, p < .05$) on marital satisfaction.

Two premarital variables were not hypothesized to have a direct relationship to marital satisfaction, but both variables were hypothesized to play an important indirect role. The results support the hypothesis. Social network support has a statistically significant positive relationship with couples' relationship-enhancing communication, and is also positively related to premarital self-esteem. Premarital self-esteem is also positively related to couples' relationship-enhancing communication. Social network support has a statistically significant indirect and total effect ($.08, p < .05$) on marital satisfaction, as does self-esteem ($.05, p < .05$).

Good fit of the model is indicated in goodness-of-fit indices well above .90. We hypothesized that four premarital variables would be directly related to males' marital quality. Of those four, only the *females'* parent–child relationship quality was significantly related ($\gamma = .13, p < .05$). The amount of premarital relationship-enhancing communication was positively related ($\gamma = .15$). Neither self-esteem ($\gamma = .09$) nor the males' parent–child relationship quality ($\gamma = .10$) is significantly related to marital quality when controlling for the other variables.

The females' parent–child relationship quality is also indirectly related to marital satisfaction through social network support and then through couples' relationship-enhancing communication. The indirect effect is nonsignificant ($.02$), but the total effect ($.14$) is at a statistically significant level.

Even though males' parent–child relationship quality is not significantly related to marital satisfaction directly, it does have a statistically significant total effect ($.20$) on marital quality primarily because of the significant direct relationship it has with social network support and social network support's direct relationships with self-esteem and couples' relationship-enhancing communication.

While social network support and self-esteem were not hypothesized to have direct effects on marital quality, they were hypothesized to have important indirect effects. This hypothesis is supported with social network support, which had a statistically significant indirect and total effect ($.08$). Self-esteem's total effect ($.14$) is just below the .05 level of significance ($t = 1.93$).

A comparison of the male and female models (using the unstandardized path coefficients) leads to some interesting conclusions. The females' parent–child relationship has a considerably larger effect on females' marital satisfaction than males' parent–child relationship quality has on males' marital satisfaction. Also, the females' report of the couples' premarital relationship-enhancing communication has a greater effect on females' marital satisfaction than males' report of their premarital relationship-enhancing communication has on males' marital satisfaction. In both models the parent–child relationship variables have greater total effects on marital satisfaction than any other premarital variables. Interestingly, parent–child relationship quality in both models does not have a direct effect on couples' relationship-enhancing communication when other premarital variables are in the equation. But parent–child relationship quality, again in both models, has indirect effects on couples' relationship-enhancing communication through its relationships with social network support and self-esteem.

What We Learn from the Four Longitudinal, Multivariate Studies

The results of these four longitudinal, multivariate studies of premarital predictors of aspects of marital quality lead to several conclusions. They are: (1) premarital factors continue to influence marital quality after several years of marriage, (2) several premarital factors are prominent in influencing later marital quality, not just one, (3) some premarital variables have more lasting influence than do others; (4) some premarital variables are more important for their indirect effects on later marital quality, than for their direct effects, (5) some aspects of the marriage are more likely to be influenced than others, and (6) there are differences by gender. We discuss each point in turn.

Continuing Influence of Premarital Variables

The results reported above show continued relationship of premarital variables and marital quality variables. We reported two 1-year follow-up studies, one 3-year follow-up study, and one 6-year follow-up study, all from different samples. These results are important for several reasons. First, the results demonstrate continuity in behavior of individuals and couples over several years. There are at least two reasons why these individuals and couples could be expected to be changing; they are in a period of life—late adolescence and young adulthood—when change is likely to occur and they are entering into one of the most change-inducing statuses—marriage—in the life course.

There are methodological factors that also contribute to our confidence that premarital factors continue to affect the (marital) relationship over time. These data were collected using paper-and-pencil survey methods and there was not a great deal of control over the administration of the instruments. Furthermore, the individuals were all in serious, committed premarital relationships when those involved tend to see themselves, their partners, and their relationships in a "rosy" light. Given all of these measurement error-producing factors, the fact that we can still discern effects increases our confidence that premarital factors have on ongoing influence on marital functioning at least several years into the marriages. In fact, the methodological limits of such data would suggest that the influence of the premarital variables is probably more pronounced than we were able to demonstrate. Our results only showed the "tip of the iceberg" of effects that premarital factors have on the consequent marriages.

Several Premarital Factors Are Important

Earlier theorizing often suggested that a single premarital factor was the "cause" of later marital function or dysfunction. Freud spoke of the psychological needs individuals had because of their family backgrounds. Psychoanalytically oriented theorists continue to stress this point (Napier & Whitaker, 1978). Winch discussed complementary needs and the problems couples would have if needs were not met. Others have emphasized similarity, homogamy, and the exchange of rewards (Murstein, 1986). Most recently, the emphasis has been on couple communication as the predictor (e.g., Markman, 1979). Indeed, most early research was only able to test the relationship of a single premarital variable on a later marital outcome, and even later research seldom included a second factor in their research (Larson & Holman, 1994).

Our research, however, shows that multiple factors are involved, either directly or indirectly. Clearly, multiple premarital factors from all four of the areas we hypothesized—family of origin, characteristics of the individual, social connections, and couple interactional processes—have an ongoing influence on marriages.

Some Predictors Are More Important Than Others

While predictors from all four areas are important, apparently some are more important than others. Our four longitudinal, multivariate studies show that family-of-origin background factors are perhaps most important (Studies # 3 and 4). Furthermore, couple processes such as similarity and communication are also more important than other factors (Studies # 2, 3, and 4).

Some Factors' Importance Is through Their Indirect Effects

Family-of-origin factors had strong direct and indirect effects, making them the most important predictor in the models. Other factors that had only small direct effects on later marital quality, like similarity and social support, made important contributions indirectly, through their relationships with other premarital variables.

Our current study (Chapters 4–7 and Study # 4 in this chapter) shows the utility of hypothesizing indirect effects among the premarital variables. However, what we did not do, and what most studies do not do, is hypothesize indirect paths between different variables on the *marital* side of the equation. Study #1, reported in this chapter, shows the advantage of this — the premarital variables were related to various marital variables, which in turn were related among themselves.

Some Aspects of Marriage Are More Influenced by Premarital Factors than Others

The most frequently used marital outcome variable is marital satisfaction. But marriage is certainly more than just satisfaction. The two studies reported here that used marital outcome variables other than marital satisfaction—Studies # 1 and 3 (as well as Linford's [1997] unpublished study of the same data set used for Study #4)—suggest that other marital variables may be more highly related to premarital factors, and that these marital variables are highly related to marital satisfaction. Therefore, premarital factors probably have a greater impact on marriage than is shown by research that uses only a single indicator of marital quality or that does not allow for indirect relationships among the marital outcome variables.

There Are Gender Differences

Studies # 1, 3, and 4 show differences in effects for males and females. But Study # 4 is the only one that created different models for males and females. These studies make it clear that the same premarital variable often has distinct effects on the males' versus the females' marital outcomes. Study # 4 in particular shows that even different variables may be involved in predicting the females' versus the males' marital satisfaction.

Summary Table of Previous and Current Research

Table 8.1summarizes all previous research on premarital predictors of marital quality outcomes. We have divided the table based on three research designs. First

Table 8.1. Longitudinal Studies of Premarital-to-Marital Couples (Divided by Design and Chronologically Arranged)

Design	Study	Sample characteristics at Time 1	Sample size			Independent variables	Measurement[a]	Dependent variables[b]	Number of assessments/ total duration	Method of analysis[c]	Comments[d]
			Initial	Final	Attrition (%)						
Longitudinal/ premarital to marital	Adams (1946)	Students recruited at college and through invitation	—	100	—	Background Personality Attitudes	SR SR SR	MS(TER, B&C)	2/ variable	COR	1, 2, 3, 4, 6, 7, 10, 12, 15, 16
	Terman & Oden (1947)	Gifted individuals and their spouses	661	643	3	Background Personality	SR SR	MS(TER) STAB	2/ 7 yrs	TT	1, 2, 5, 6, 7, 10, 15
	Burgess & Wallin (1953)	Engaged couples, from metropolitan Chicago, 90% college students	1000	666	33	Family of origin Demographics Sexual attitudes Neuroticism	SR SR SR SR	MS(B&W)	2/ 3–5 yrs	COR	1, 2, 4, 6, 10, 14, 15, 16
	Vaillant (1978)	Men, age 18–20, recruited at Harvard	102	95	7	Background Family of origin	SR SR	MS(CR)	3/ 25 yrs	ANOVA	2, 5, 7, 9, 13, 15
	Fowers & Olson (1986)	Engaged couples, selected by clergy	—	164	—	Attitude homogamy	SR	MS(ENR) STAB	2/ 2–3 yrs	ANOVA	1, 2, 8, 13, 15
	Kelly & Conley (1987)	Engaged couples, age 20–30, recruited through media	300	249	17	Background Personality	SR PR	MS(1 ITEM)	3/ 45 yrs	TT COR DFA MR	1, 5, 10
	Filsinger & Thoma (1988)	First-time premarital couples, recruited through media	31	21	32	Conflict behavior	OB	MS(DAS) STAB	5/ 5 yrs	COR ANOVA	1, 2, 3, 13, 15

Table 8.1. (continued)

Study	Sample	N	N	N	Variables	Method	Measure	Design	Analysis	Findings
Larsen & Olson (1989)	Engaged couples, selected by clergy	1204	179	85	Attitude homogamy	SR	MS(ENR)	2/ 2 yrs	ANOVA	1, 2, 3, 8, 13, 15
Smith, Vivian, & O'Leary (1990)	First-time engaged couples	91	72	21	Conflict behavior	OB	MS(MAT)	4/ 2.5 yrs	MR	1, 4, 8
Holman, Larson & Harmer (1994)	First-time engaged couples, recruited through churches and schools, mostly LDS	224	208	16	Attitudes Background	SR SR	MS(MCL)	2/ 1 yr	COR	1, 2, 10, 13, 15
Fowers, Montel, & Olson (1996)	Engaged couples selected by clergy	1368	393	70	Attitude homogamy	SR	MS(ENR) STAB	2/ 2–3 yrs	LLA	1, 2, 3, 8, 13, 15
Holman, Linford, Brooks, Olsen, Rhoades, & Carroll #1 (Chapter 8, this volume)	University students & partners who were engaged, all LDS	114	114	0	Family of origin Emotional health Consensus	SR SR SR	MS(12) COMM ROLE COMPAN	2/ 1 yr	PATH	2, 7
Holman, Linford, Brooks, Olsen, Rhoades, & Carroll #2 (Chapter 8, this volume)	University students & partners from 8 universities	—	174	—	Homogamy Actual similarity Perceived similarity Love Communication	SR SR SR SR SR	MS(7)	2/ 3–4 yrs	PATH	2, 7, 8

Table 8.1. (continued)

Study	Sample				Variables		Measure	Design	Analysis	Findings
Holman, Linford, Brooks, Olsen, Rhoades, & Carroll #3 (Chapter 8, this volume)	First-time engaged couples, recruited through churches and schools, mostly LDS	224	208	16	Family of origin Background Individual traits Couple processes	SR SR SR SR	$MS_{(MCL)}$ STAB	2/ 1 yr	SEM	2, 7
Holman, Linford, Brooks, Olsen, Rhoades, & Carroll #4 (Chapter 8, this volume)	University students & partners from across United States	2176	1016	53	Family of origin Demographics Individual traits Couple processes	SR SR SR SR	$MS_{(6)}$ STAB	2/ 6 yrs	ANOVA SEM	2, 3
Longitudinal/ ambiguous relationship status										
Markman (1979)	Engaged couples, recruited in college and through media	26	14	46	Conflict behavior	SR	$MS_{(MRI)}$	3/ 2.5 yrs	COR MANOVA	3, 4, 6, 8, 11,13, 15, 16
Markman (1981)	Engaged couples, recruited in college and through media	26	9	65	Conflict behavior	SR	$MS_{(MRI)}$	4/ 5.5 yrs	COR	3, 4, 6, 8, 13, 15, 16
Markman, Duncan, Storaasli, & Howes (1987)	First-time engaged couples, recruited through media	135	125	7	Conflict behavior Relationship attitudes	SR SR	$MS_{(MAT)}$	4/ 3 yrs	COR	4, 6, 8, 10, 15

Table 8.1. (continued)

	Wamboldt & Reiss (1989)	Engaged couples, recruited through media	16	14	13	Demographics / Family of origin	SR / SR	MS(DAS)	2/ 1 yr	COR	1, 4, 6, 15
Longitudinal/ premarital data collected retrospectively	Bentler & Newcomb (1978)	Newlywed couples, aged 18–60, recruited through licenses	162	77	52	Background / Demographics / Personality	SR / SR / SR	MS(MAT) STAB	2/ 4 yrs	COR MR	1, 3, 5, 6, 16
	Kelly, Huston, & Cate (1985)	Newlywed couples, recruited through licenses	50	21	58	Courtship history / Perceptions of courtship	SR / SR	MS(DAS, B&K)	2/ 2yrs	COR	3, 4, 5, 6, 15

Note. Dashes indicate information that was unavailable or not reported.

a: Measurement: OB = observational coding; PR = peer rating; SR = self-report.

b: Dependent variables: The subscript refers to the measures used to assess marital satisfaction (MS). When unpublished measures were used, the number of items in the measure is reported. B&C = Burgess & Cottrell (1939) Marital Adjustment Scale; B&K = Braiker & Kelley (1979); B&W = Burgess & Wallin (1953) Marital Adjustment Scale; CR = clinical rating; DAS = Dyadic Adjustment Scale (Spanier, 1976); ENR = Enrich (Olson, Fournier, & Druckman, 1986); MAT = Marital Adjustment Test (Locke & Wallace, 1959); MCL = Marital Comparison Level Index (Sabatelli, 1984); MRI = Marital Relationship Inventory (Burgess, Locke, & Thomes, 1971); TER = Terman (1938) Marital Happiness Test; STAB = marital stability; COMM = quality of communication; COMPAN = amount of marital companionship; ROLE = quality of role enactment.

c: Method of analysis: ANOVA = analysis of variance; COR = correlation; DFA = discriminant function analysis; LLA = log linear analysis; MR = multiple regression; PATH = path analysis; SEM = structural equation modeling; TT = *t*-test

d: Comments: 1. Incomplete longitudinal design; 2. Biased or unusual sample; 3. High attrition rate. 4. Divorced couples omitted from analyses; 5. No distinctions between first-married and remarried couples; 6. No distinction between childless couples and parents; 7. No controls for variations in duration of marriage; 8. Males and females not analyzed separately; 9. No distinction between quality and stability as criterion; 10. Invalidated measure used; 11. No report on longitudinal stability of variables; 12. No longitudinal analyses of longitudinal data; 13. Categorized continuous data. 14. Inappropriate statistics; 15. No controls for correlations between Time 1 variables.

are the truly premarital-to-marital longitudinal designs where the premarital data were collected premaritally and the marital data were collected at some point after the couples had married. Second are what we call the "ambiguous" designs. The premarital data were collected premaritally, but it is unclear whether the Time 2 data were collected after the couples were married, or if they were still unmarried at the second data collection. Third are the studies where the "premarital" data were collected retrospectively shortly after the couples were married, and then marital quality data were collected at some second point in the marriage. We hope this tabled information will help practitioners and researchers alike to get a quick sense of what we know at the present time. This book provides more detailed reviews of the *findings* of all of these studies in one or more of the chapters. For the serious student of this area of study, we present an extensive review of each of these studies including the purpose of each study, the theoretical perspective (if any) taken by the researchers, the methods used, and the results and implications. This should be especially useful for some of the older studies that are difficult to find. This extensive review is found in Appendix C.

In sum, the research reported in this chapter suggests that the study of premarital predictors of marital quality is a worthwhile endeavor. Undoubtedly, understanding the continued influence of things that happened to the individuals and the couples before their marriages has implications for practice, for research, and for theory. Chapter 9 presents these implications.

Endnote

1.   For example, the data set used by Rhoades in his study was also used to assess the predictive validity of the PREP-M instrument. The results of the predictive validity study have been published (Holman et al., 1994).

9

General Principles, Implications, and Future Directions

Thomas B. Holman, Jeffry H. Larson, Robert F. Stahmann, and Jason S. Carroll

> *My husband and I recently faced a very difficult experience. I was extremely ill and our fourth child was born prematurely (at 5 months gestational age). Our little son lived for 1½ hours. We've grown closer through this experience. I saw a strength and wisdom surface in my husband which I had only sensed before. I knew he was a good man when we married, but my esteem and admiration have grown a great deal in 6 years. I think that all couples need to give themselves time to grow through life's experiences (hopefully closer and not apart). I know that we are amazed at how much we've learned in just 6 years. We've passed through some difficult times which have challenged our relationship. We do not consider our marriage a temporary commitment so we seek to find ways to make it better because separation is not an option.*

> — Female respondent

> *I have learned that marriage is not always easy and does take work. However, I feel that there is great honor in staying with your commitments. I believe that love is not enough to hold a family together. It is natural for love to waiver from time to time but it is religion, family, friends, and honoring commitments that help to keep you going through any hardships. I'm lucky I married my best friend and I thank God for him and my son every day.*

> — Female respondent

In each of the data chapters, we concluded with a short section on implications (except for Chapter 8). In the current chapter we bring together all of these implications and organize them around the areas of practice, theory, and research. We are especially keen on presenting what we call "Principles for Practice" and other information for practitioners. We suspect that many practitioners find our discussion in earlier chapters (on theory, methods, and statistical models) uninspiring. Therefore, we first present a discussion of how the research from the earlier chapters leads to Principles for Practice, and how practitioners can use these ideas in workshops, classrooms, and premarital counseling. We conclude the chapter with implications for theory development and future research.

Principles for Practice

When most researchers present practical implications of their research, they simply give what Burr and Klein (1994, p. 26) call "descriptive generalizations, which are descriptions of patterns in the processes in family systems. They describe what is happening, but they do not give us information about why or how to intervene to make things better." Authors often then say something to the effect that policymakers, family life educators, therapists, and others ought to implement these recommendations into their policies, therapies, or lesson plans.

We do not find this approach very useful, and as applied social scientists ourselves, we find that this approach does not lead to many helpful interventions. Instead, we present "general principles" (Burr, 1976; Burr et al., 1977; Burr & Klein, 1994) based on research. These general statements typically follow an *if—then* format; that is, *if* interventions can inspire change in one aspect of the process, *then* fairly predictable outcomes will result. In our case, we are suggesting principles stating that *if* changes can be encouraged in the premarital period, *then* marital quality outcomes can be improved.

Our Most General Principles

Do premarital factors continue to influence the unfolding marital relationship? Our review of the research and our own research confirm the idea that premarital background, beliefs, and behaviors do indeed have a continuing influence on marital functioning. While marriage is a "fresh start" in many ways, we do not start marriage with a "clean slate." We bring many attitudes, perceptions, biases, and patterns of behavior into the new relationship. Some of those come from who we are as individuals, some from our families of origin, and some develop in our interaction with our partner(s). Therefore, this fundamental concept can be stated as a principle as follows:

PRINCIPLE: *Premarital attitudes, perceptions, events, and patterns of behavior continue to influence the dynamics of marital functioning several years into the marriage. Therefore, if we are to help couples establish and maintain stable, high quality marriages, then we need to begin teaching and intervening before the marriage.*

A second general principle comes out of our research and our review of over 60 years of research on premarital prediction of marital quality. This research suggests that the pathways to successful marriage are much more complex than most of the early theories and research indicated. Early theories, often based on Freudian psychology, usually saw the process of mate selection, and the consequent success of a marital union, to be grounded in the adult child's relationship with a parent, usually the opposite-sex parent. This early theorizing and research also focused on the premarital mental health of the partners as preeminent in the success or failure of marriage. Later research and theory proposed that mate selection was based primarily on complementarity and/or similarity, and that the resultant marital quality was maintained by strengthening similarity between spouses. More recently, research and theory from a behavioral perspective has focused on the behaviors, particularly the communicative behaviors, of couples before marriage as the foremost predictor of later marital quality. While all of this theory and research has been helpful, most of it has not captured the complexity of the developing premarital relationship and how multiple factors play out in later marital quality. This leads to our second general principle.

PRINCIPLE: *If efforts are made to address the complexity of relationship development premaritally, then the probability of high marital quality increases.*

Our studies reported here are the first not only to attempt to explicate more fully the relationship between a premarital variable and later marital quality, but also to demonstrate which of these variables are most highly related to marital quality when taking the other factors into account. Also, our studies in this book are the first to attempt to clarify the relationship between the major predictors of marital quality.

While most earlier research paid little attention to sex and gender differences, we did in our studies for this book. Basically, we found that some of the factors predicting marital quality were different for men than they were for women, and even when they were the same, they influenced men's marital satisfaction differently than they did women's marital satisfaction. Therefore, the following principle results:

PRINCIPLE: *Gender differences need to be taken into account in premarital interventions if later marital quality is to be optimally strengthened.*

One example of this is found in our results about family of origin. Family-of-origin factors play a greater role in predicting females' marital satisfaction 6 years into marriage, than they do for males. Also, spouse's family of origin has more impact on males' marital satisfaction than does their own family of origin. It is just the opposite for females—their own family of origin influences their marital satisfaction, but their husbands' family of origin has no significant effect on females' marital satisfaction.

One last general principle needs to be stated. Generally speaking, researchers have only looked at one or at most two predictor variables, and only one criterion variable. Our research demonstrates the utility of models containing multiple predictor variables. But our multivariate models reported in Chapter 8 show what few theorists or researchers have noticed—the premarital predictors are differentially related to different aspects of the marriage. Therefore:

PRINCIPLE: *Changes in premarital beliefs and behaviors can impact various aspects of the later marital relationship differently.*

This suggests that practitioners need to know that even if their interventions are successful in changing some aspect of the couples premaritally, these changes may affect some aspects of the marriage more (or less) than others. For example, from our research, it appears that marital satisfaction may be affected indirectly by premarital factors as much or more than it is affected directly. However, further theory and research is needed to more fully understand which premarital factors are directly or indirectly related to which marital factors and why.

Principles Specific to Particular Premarital Factors—Family of Origin

We now look for principles from each of the four major premarital factors starting with the family of origin. Larson and Holman (1994) concluded that family-of-origin background characteristics were an important predictor of marital quality, but that it was the least important of the predictors. Our recent research is showing otherwise. Our bivariate group comparisons in Chapter 3 showed that those who were most satisfied with their marriages 6 years into marriage had better relationships with both mothers and fathers as children and youth, and had better home environments than the other groups (i.e., broken up premaritally, divorced, and married-low satisfaction). They also generally had parents with better marital quality than did members of the other three groups.

Although the importance of family of origin varied from model to model in the multivariate studies reported here, the general conclusion we must reach is that family-of-origin factors, especially parent–child relationship quality, are the most important premarital predictors of later marital quality. In Chapter 4 we noted that parent–child relationship quality is positively and significantly related to marital satisfaction and that, at least for the males, their female partners' parent–child relationship quality is related to their marital satisfaction. Even when other premarital variables are taken into account, parent–child relationship quality generally remains the most powerful premarital predictor of later marital quality. We were surprised at these findings, especially given our review of earlier research (Larson & Holman, 1994) showing family-of-origin factors to be the weakest premarital predictor. We believe that the problem with previous findings is twofold: first, relatively poor measurement of family-of-origin processes in past research, and second, the lack of understanding of family-of-origin processes' indirect effects on marriage through more proximal factors (e.g., social network support). Given our findings, then, we suggest the following:

PRINCIPLE: *Of all the family-of-origin issues that could be addressed, interventions that specifically improve the parent–child relationship, the parents' marriage, the parents' mental health and/or dysfunctional behavior will tend to lead to the most improvement in the probability of adult children's marital success.*

The most important things parents can do for the future marital happiness of their children are to maintain a strong marriage, create a pleasant, happy home environment, and be involved in their children's lives. Practitioners need to help parents understand that what is happening in their marriage, in their home, and in their relationship with their (young and adolescent) children matters.

On the other hand, this is a difficult principle to implement if one is working with young adult couples—their parents' marriages and their childhood relationships with parents have already happened. Because the family background "can't be changed," some practitioners recommend targeting premarital factors that are more "amenable to intervention" (Stanley, Markman, St. Peters, & Leber, 1995). However, these practitioners and researchers are making assumptions based on traditional positivist science and philosophy. As we noted in Chapter 2, we are persuaded by postmodern writers that the past is not an unchanging "entity." Rather, the past is "alive" and "changeable," especially in the sense of how we "remember" the past and how we allow the past to influence present goals, attitudes, and behaviors. This thinking, combined with our findings, leads to a corollary principle to the one above.

PRINCIPLE: *Restructuring, "restorying," "coming to terms with," or "letting go of" unpleasant issues from the family-of-origin experiences will tend to lead to higher-quality marriages for adult children.*

Premarital Counseling Interventions for Family-of-Origin Issues

Several family-of-origin background factors that should be assessed as part of premarital counseling include the following:

Parental marital quality. For adult children of divorce, assess their appraisal of the divorce and its effect on them emotionally and interpersonally. It is common for young adults from divorced families to still experience some depression, anger, or have trust or commitment issues as a result of the trauma of divorce (Amato, 1996). They were likely exposed to poor models of communication and conflict resolution. These problems may be carried into their own marriage unless awareness and commitment to change are first established. Interventions may include cognitive restructuring (e.g., Bedrosian & Bozicas, 1994; Burns, 1980; Epstein, 1982) to deal with emotional problems, and communication and conflict resolution training (e.g., Miller & Olson, 1998; Stanley et al., 1995) to help overcome the effects of poor parental modeling of these skills.

Family functioning and parent–child relationship quality. There are a variety of short, valid, and reliable self-report methods for measuring various aspects of family-of-origin functioning (see Yingling, Miller, McDonald, & Galewaler, 1998). More specifically, parent–child attachment and adult attachment styles can be assessed (Collins & Read, 1990; Hazan & Shaver, 1987). Individuals from families that were emotionally cold and distant, chaotic, dangerous, unpredictable, detached, conflictual, or where addictions or violence were chronic problems, will need therapeutic assistance overcoming the legacy of such an upbringing. Individual therapy (e.g., Bedrosian & Bozicas, 1994), focused on awareness of how the family environment has affected the grown child and how to overcome resulting emotional and interpersonal problems, will help individuals overcome the legacy of family dysfunction. Bedrosian and Bozicas (1994) offer a model for treating the current signs of family-of-origin problems so that, despite a historical focus, treatment can be geared toward an individual's present-day complaints. Family-of-origin groups, focusing on intergenerational influences in the context of adult therapy groups or couples' groups, are also recommended (Framo, 1976; Ginsberg, 1997). Individuals should be encouraged to make peace with their family history and adopt a new working model of healthy relationships. Self-help books (e.g.,

Blevins, 1993; Bloomfield, 1983) may also be useful. (See Santrock, Minnett, & Campbell, 1994, for an evaluation of the best self-help books on this topic.)

Premarital Education Interventions for Family-of-Origin Issues

Premarital educators (e.g., teachers, clergy, professors) can assist individuals from dysfunctional families by first increasing their awareness of the relationship between family-of-origin processes (especially attachment) and later marital quality. Group discussions and writing assignments on the effects of divorce, alcoholism, abuse, and other types of family dysfunction on children will help individuals to seriously consider how these processes may have negatively affected their attitudes about marriage and readiness for marriage. (See list of discussion questions in Table 9.1.) In addition, educators should expose individuals to healthy models of marriage, through reading assignments, group discussions, live interviews with happily married couples, case studies, and viewing videos of constructive conflict management in marriage. Students should be encouraged to clarify their attitudes toward the subjects of marriage, divorce, conflict, trust, and commitment.

Some individuals will need to be referred for more in-depth assessment and therapy. Reassure them that the negative effects of growing up in a dysfunctional family do not have to be permanent, and can be overcome through education and therapy.

Table 9.1. Family-of-Origin Discussion Questions for Use in Marriage Preparation Courses

Ask yourself and your partner:
- Describe your family of origin and its effects on your personality. Focus on emotional closeness, communication, patterns, family rules, roles, and rituals.
- Describe your relationship with each parent and how it has affected your personality and your interpersonal relationships.
- If there was a divorce or an unhappy parental marriage, explain what happened and your short-term and long-term reactions to it.
- Which family-of-origin interaction patterns and rules will you transfer to your own relationships? Which will you avoid transferring? Why?
- Describe how your parents handled conflict or disagreements in their marriage. How has this affected how you deal with disagreements or conflict?
- Discuss the characteristics you like/dislike in your parents' marriage. Which will you transfer to your own marriage?

Principles Specific to Particular Premarital Factors—Individual Characteristics

Our literature reviews (Larson & Holman, 1994; Stahmann & Hiebert, 1997) and research reported in this book demonstrate the importance of good emotional health and self-esteem, and the importance of valuing marriage and family life for a successful marriage. These factors increase the likelihood that an individual will not distort or overreact to negative relationship events. They will contribute to the individual being someone with whom it is easier to live (Kurdek, 1993) as they will be more likely to handle stress effectively, be more cooperative and flexible, be less impulsive and more sociable, and be more committed to the marriage. Based on these conclusions, we propose the following principles:

PRINCIPLE: *Interventions that improve an individual's emotional health and self-esteem and his/her valuing of marriage and family life, will increase the probability of marital success.*

PRINCIPLE: *Interventions that help an individual revise negative values, attitudes, and beliefs about marriage, will increase the probability of marital success.*

Premarital Counseling Interventions for Emotional Health/Self-Esteem Issues and Negative Beliefs

Emotional health and self-esteem may be assessed with a variety of short, self-report self-report instruments that serve as an initial screening. Depending on the results of such screening, more intense personality assessment may be warranted (e.g., MMPI). The instruments suggested here do not require licensure as a psychologist to administer, score, and interpret them. However, test administrators first should be trained in evaluating tests and test usage (see Hood & Johnson, 1997).

- *NEO Personality Inventory* (Costa and McCrae, 1992) assesses 10 specific emotional health and personality traits that have been shown in one or more studies to be related to marital success (see Table 9.2). Norm scores for each trait are available so the assessor can compare the client's scores with a norm group to determine problems in certain traits.
- *Taylor-Johnson Temperament Analysis (TJTA)* (Taylor & Johnson, 1984) measures many important traits and delineates scores on traits that are considered to be in the "clinical range." This popular premarital counseling test also allows the counselor to compare both

partners' personalities on one protocol and to compare individuals' ratings of self to their partners' ratings of them. This is called the Criss-Cross method and is unique to the TJTA.

- *Sixteen Personality Factor Questionnaire* (Russell, 1995) measures a number of personality traits and provides an extensive couple's counseling report to aid in personality and relationship assessment.
- *Tennessee Self-Concept Scale* (Fitts & Warren, 1996) is a popular measure of several dimensions of self-esteem (e.g., physical and social).

The above instruments should be considered first-line assessments. If a client's scores appear in the clinical range on any scale, more in-depth interviewing, history taking, and assessment with instruments like the MMPI (Butcher, Dahlstrom, Graham, Tellegen, & Kaemmer, 1989) and the Beck Depression Inventory (Beck, 1996) should be considered.

Individuals with emotional or self-esteem problems will likely require individual or group psychotherapy in addition to premarital counseling. Counselors should emphasize to clients the importance of correcting psychological

Table 9.2. Personality Traits and Instruments

Personality traits	Suggested instruments[a]
1. *Neuroticism*	• *NEO Personality Inventory*(NEO-PI-R; Costa & McCrae, 1992) (Traits 1–5)
a. Anxiety	
b. Hostility	• *Taylor—Johnson Temperament Analysis* (TJTA) (Taylor & Johnson, 1984)
c. Depression	(Traits 1a–1e, 2, 4)
d. Self-consciousness	
e. Impulsiveness	• *Sixteen Personality Factor Couple's Counseling Report* (5th ed.) (Russell, 1995)
f. Vulnerability to stress	(Traits 1, 2, 4)
2. *Sociability*	• *Tennessee Self-Concept Scale* (2nd ed.) (Fitts & Warren, 1996)
3. *Conventionality*	(Trait 5, Physical Esteem, Moral Esteem, Social Esteem, Work Esteem)
4. *Interpersonal Skills*	
5. *Self-Esteem*	

[a] Norm scores are available.

problems *before* marriage. As Warren (1992) emphasizes, marriage is *not* a cure for personal problems; rather, it makes personal problems worse: "The stress of marriage, the vulnerability of living with someone day in and day out, the weight of responsibility, the fear of failure, the realization that marriage isn't a cure-all—all these combine to thrust existing problems to the forefront" (p. 66).

Our findings reported in Chapter 5 and in Study #2 of Chapter 8, show that premarital values, attitudes, and beliefs can have long-term effects on marital quality. Thus, highly valuing marriage and family life and having marriage and children as important goals can lead to a sense of satisfaction with marriage. Thus, it is crucial to help partners explore their attitudes, beliefs, and values concerning the importance of marriage and family life, their commitment to marriage and family, and their beliefs about the role each will play in their adult lives. Given the link between family-of-origin relationships and later attitudes/values about family life (see Chapter 5), counselors can help couples explore the origin of their attitudes and values and find ways to change how they think about marriage and family life.

Premarital Education Interventions for Emotional Health/Self-Esteem Issues and Negative Beliefs

Premarital educators should know how to recognize symptoms of emotional and self-esteem problems, such as abnormally high anxiety or irritability, hostility, depression, and interpersonal sensitivity (Derogatis, 1983). The American Psychiatric Association publishes public information pamphlets that can be ordered for a small fee and that describe depression, anxiety disorders, and other mental disorders. (Address: APA Division of Public Affairs, 1400 K Street, NW, Washington, DC 20005.)

The educator's task is to teach couples the relationship between good mental health and later marital functioning and how to recognize symptoms of emotional problems in themselves and others. Educators can help students understand that most of these mental health problems can be successfully treated in short-term psychotherapy and/or with psychotropic medications (Burns, 1980). Many self-help books may also be useful (see Santrock et al., 1994). Referrals for psychological assessment and treatment often may be necessary. Thus, the educator should have a list of qualified therapists for referrals.

Furthermore, educators can discuss the implications of having negative attitudes and beliefs about marriage and family life on the likely success of marriage. They can also help students understand that attitudes can be changed through thoughtful consideration of the genesis of the attitudes, largely from experiences in the family of origin, and through discussing the concerns behind the attitudes (e.g., my parents are so miserable together, why should I think I can be happy in marriage?). Examples can be shared of couples with troubled backgrounds and with initial reservations about how marriage fits in with their fundamental life goals, yet who have gone on to find happiness and success in long-term marriage and family life.

Principles Specific to Particular Premarital Factors—Social Contexts and Networks

Our comprehensive review of the literature (Larson & Holman, 1994) and our more recent multivariate studies on premarital predictors discussed in this book, emphasize the importance of premarital support of one's marriage from parents and friends in order to create a successful marriage. Our findings reported in Chapter 6 could be taken to suggest that once family-of-origin processes are taken into account, social network support is of minor importance in the prediction of later marital quality. However, Study # 4 in Chapter 8 shows otherwise. That study shows, first, that the parent–child relationship is of continuing importance. How well parents and children got along when the child was young is related to how supportive parents are of their adult child's premarital relationship. Second, our research shows that this support of the relationship by parents and also by friends, while not directly related to later marital quality when other factors are taken into account, is related to premarital self-esteem and to the quality of premarital couple interactional processes. Furthermore, our results in Chapter 3 showed that the married with high satisfaction group had had significantly more support from parents and friends premaritally than did any of the other groups. Thus, the social network's support should not be overlooked when preparing couples for marriage.

Social network support provides a safety net for tough times in marriage. Lack of support from parents and friends removes the net. In addition, lack of support also may lead to a form of isolation of the couple by the network. Warren (1992) suggests that this isolation may take the form of not including the couple in extended family events. The network may do this in response to their perception that the relationship is not good, and they may begin early to prepare for its demise. Thus, we propose the following principle:

PRINCIPLE: *Interventions that increase social network support will increase the probability of marital success.*

The results in Chapter 3 demonstrate one other aspect of the social network support issue. The couples who broke up before marrying had the lowest support from family and friends. Also, they were more like the divorced/separated and married-low satisfaction groups than like the married-high satisfaction group in most other comparisons. Therefore, we concluded that the breakup couples were probably wise to have broken up, since they would probably not have ended up in the married-high satisfaction group. The parents and friends may have seen this, and perhaps that was the reason they were giving less support to the relationship than were the parents and friends of other couples. Thus, garnering support from the network for the relationship may not be what is best. What may be more appropriate is for the couples to listen to the concerns of parents and friends. When parents and friends have no ulterior motive for breaking the couple up, the couple would do well to listen closely to their concerns. This leads to another principle:

PRINCIPLE: Interventions that increase couples' ability to discern the legitimate concerns of parents and friends about the relationship, increase the probability of later marital quality, even if the marriage is not to the current partner.

Our finding that the time-honored advice not to marry young, poor, or uneducated was not highly related to later marital quality must be taken with caution. The amount of variation in these factors in our research studies was so small as to make it difficult to adequately test the relationship between these premarital sociocultural variables and later marital satisfaction. Hence, although we do not state it as a principle, we cautiously suggest that the advice mentioned earlier is still good. Common sense dictates that not having those resources necessary for optimal marital success in our society—older age, finances, and education—serve as "deficits in the marriage account."

Premarital Counseling for Social Network Support Issues

The following premarital interventions are suggested:

Assess the support level of parents and friends for the couple's relationship and eventual marriage. Stress to couples that these individuals who know them very well and care for them a great deal may have opinions that are more accurate than their own. Thus, they should be respected. Frequently these people can see important "red flags" in a relationship or person that need to be considered. If these individuals find themselves unable to support a couple's decision, they at least need to be listened to carefully (Warren, 1992).

If a couple cannot get this social network support, advise the couple to proceed with the marriage *slowly*. This gives the objecting individuals more time to become acquainted with a partner. Tell the couple to find time to discuss their objections. Encourage objectors to tell the couple everything they can think of that has entered into their conclusions (Warren, 1992). Have the couple compare the objectors' observations with their own. Seek help from other friends, relatives, or professionals who can provide objective viewpoints. The bottom line with social support is, make every possible effort to bring each person on board (Warren, 1992).

Regarding age, income and education at the time of marriage, advise couples to stock up on all three before marrying! It is like "putting deposits in the marriage account." Discourage marriage if one or both partners are teenagers, since the divorce rate for teens is nearly double the national average (Martin & Bumpass, 1989). Discuss the ramifications of limited education and income to the fulfillment of marital roles and the ability to "survive" as a marital couple without these resources. In some situations, referrals to community educational and career counseling services for personal assessment, planning, and placement may be appropriate.

Premarital Education Interventions for Social Network Support Issues

Premarital educators can demonstrate the negative effects of parental disapproval and lack of support by discussing case studies or showing video clips of couples who struggled with this issue. Examples of the stressors placed on a couple who lack social network support before and after marriage can be illustrated by using Shakespeare's classic play *Romeo and Juliet* (now available in movie formats that may appeal to young adults) or by using the movie *Love Story*. After viewing these couples' struggles, class members may be asked to suggest ways the couple could have been more sensitive to parental input. Couples should brainstorm ways in which the couple could have eased their parents' premarital anxieties. A more humorous example of the effects of lack of parental support on marriage can be seen in the movie *She's Having a Baby.*

Such classroom exercises can prepare couples better for dealing with social network support problems if they should arise later. Couples with more serious social support problems (e.g., a parent who threatens to never speak to them again if they marry) should be referred to premarital counseling.

Principles Specific to Particular Premarital Factors—Couple Interactional Processes Issues

Several premarital couple interactional processes have been shown to affect marital success. Relationship-enhancing communication styles, perceived similarity, and consensus appear to be marriage-enhancing premarital factors. If we add to these findings the recent research on the prevention of marital distress through premarital communication and conflict resolution skills training (e.g., Hahlweg, Markman, Thurmaier, Engl, & Eckert, 1998; Markman, Stanley & Blumberg, 1994), we can confidently state the following principle:

PRINCIPLE: *Interventions that improve a couple's communication and*
                 conflict resolution skills and increase perceived similarity and
                 consensus will increase the probability of marital success.

Premarital Counseling Interventions for Communication Processes Issues

Premarital counselors should assess couples' communication skills, similarity
and consensus. Three psychometrically sound premarital counseling instruments
are especially suited for a comprehensive examination of communication skills,
similarities, and consensus and are readily usable in premarital counseling:
PREPARE (Olson, Fournier, & Druckman, 1986), *RELATE* (Holman et al., 1997),
and *FOCCUS* (Markey, Micheletto, & Becker, 1997). A review of these
instruments is given later in this chapter.

Premarital counselors should assess communication, conflict management, and
consensus-building skills by using both self-report and direct observational
techniques. For in session observational assessment of couple communication
skills we suggest using the *Communication Rapid Assessment Scale (CRAS)*
(Joanning, Brewster, & Koval, 1984). This dual approach is superior to using self-
report measures alone (Cromwell, Olson, & Fournier, 1976). Teach skills or refer
to skills training programs such as the *Prevention and Relationship Enhancement*
Program (PREP) (Renick, Blumberg, & Markman, 1992), the *Premarital*
Relationship Enhancement Program (Ginsberg, 1997), or Miller and Olson's
(1998) *Great Start* program, which have demonstrated validity and long-term
positive effects.

Premarital Education Interventions for Couple Interactional Processes Issues

Of the three comprehensive premarital assessment instruments noted above,
the most appropriate one to use in an educational group or classroom is RELATE
(Holman et al., 1997; Larson, 1998). Educators can focus students on reviewing
their similarities/dissimilarities on a variety of topics (e.g., spiritual values, money,
children, sex.) in a classroom or group setting and make assignments to discuss the
ramifications of these similarities or dissimilarities in their relationship and future
marriage. For example, if partners differ greatly on the importance or value of
money in marriage, what conflicts are they likely to have later in marriage? How
will they deal with these conflicts?

The educator should also direct couples to study their perceived
communication strengths and weaknesses and ability to reach consensus by
examining their subscale scores on the RELATE or other questionnaires that assess
empathy, assertiveness, clarity, and other dimensions of couple communication
(see Touliatos, Perlmutter, & Straus, 1990, for a listing of instruments). The
RELATE *Instructor's Manual* contains many educational activities the educator

can utilize in a group or classroom to increase awareness of couple interaction processes, similarities, and consensus.

Educators are strongly encouraged to provide communication and conflict resolution skills training to couples as part of their programs or classes. Larson, Harper, Wampler, and Sprenkle (1995) have demonstrated how to teach these skills to a large group of couples in a college classroom setting using the *Couple Communication* program (Miller, Miller, Nunnally, & Wackman, 1992). Miller and Miller's (1997) new *Core Communication* skills training program is designed for individuals to learn basic communication and conflict resolution skills that they can use in any intimate relationship. Miller's programs and the others suggested here are especially recommended because of their impressive theoretical and research base.

Implementing Our Principles for Practice

Implementing our principles means several additional important points. First, we suggest that premarital education begin at the earliest possible time in families and in organizations like schools and churches. Parents need to understand that their children's later marital success depends to some extent on things that happen while children are young or in their teens, and living at home.

As youth in their mid-teens approach marrying age, efforts should be increased in the schools, churches, and community organizations to teach about successful marriage. This information needs to be taught not only to the youth, but also to their parents, since parents are the primary teachers of children for most of their childhood. Parents need to be taught the basic principles we have identified, taught how to teach them to their children, and taught how to "practice what they preach."

Youth should be taught these principles and how to implement them in their lives. This effort should be done primarily in the home by parents who are themselves emotionally healthy and in high-quality marriages. If this is not the case, assistance should be directed to help parents so they can better help their children. But it should also be done in institutions that work with adolescents, such as schools, churches, and community organizations (e.g., YMCAs, YWCAs, Boys and Girls Clubs, 4-H, Boy Scouts, Girl Scouts). These principles can be used to counteract the misinformation propagated in the media that teach marital myths. These marital myths include ideas such as "love is all you need," "sex is love," and the idea that "other people and other things won't make a difference if we are in love." Also included is the myth of naturalism (Mace, 1983), which states that individuals just *naturally* learn how to have healthy relationships with the opposite sex as they grow up without any special efforts by parents, teachers, clergy, and the like.

There are a variety of methods for teaching these principles to parents, youth, and young adults. Examples of some of the best programs and materials that teach about marital preparation have been catalogued by the Coalition of Marriage, Family, and Couples Education. A description of these programs and materials can be found on the Internet at the following address: http://www.smartmarriages.com. We cannot elaborate on each of the programs and the materials that can be used with them here, but we will recommend an assessment inventory, briefly describe the content of a workshop we have used successfully, and suggest a textbook to go with it.

Comprehensive Premarital Assessment Questionnaires: Bringing Science to Premarital Counseling

An important component of premarital counseling is assessment. Until recently, premarital assessment has suffered from the lack of scientifically valid and reliable measures of premarital predictors of marital satisfaction and stability. However, today, therapists and educators conducting premarital assessment and counseling may choose from three scientifically sound, comprehensive premarital assessment questionnaires (PAQs): *PREmarital Preparation And Relationship Enhancement* (PREPARE; Olson, Fournier, & Druckman, 1996), *Facilitating Open Couple Communication, Understanding, and Study* (FOCCUS; Markey et al., 1997) and the *RELATionship Evaluation* (RELATE; Holman et al., 1997).

Each of these PAQs has solid evidence for validity, reliability, comprehensiveness, ease in administration and scoring, and practicality. Most importantly, they all have evidence of predictive validity. Using these questionnaires as part of premarital counseling increases the couple's interest and investment in the process, provides a convenient and concise way to provide a couple with feedback on the strengths and weaknesses of their relationship, themselves as individuals, and their social context, and provides a way for couples to set goals for improvement before they marry.

The three PAQs are both similar and different in important ways (see Table 9.3). They are similar in that they all assess about 90% of the premarital predictors of marital satisfaction and stability (see Larson & Holman, 1994). The differences are discussed in the following pages. The differences are important to understand before choosing a PAQ to use in premarital counseling or education. The descriptions below will assist the counselor or educator in making the best choice.

PREPARE

PREPARE (Olson et al., 1996) is a 195-item inventory designed to identify and measure premarital "relationship strengths" and "work areas" in 11 categories.

Table 9.3. Psychometric Properties of Comprehensive PAQs

Instruments	Number of items	Time to administer	Cost per couple	Scoring	Supporting materials	Validity	Reliability	Instructor training
FOCCUS	156	45–60 min.	$10.00	Hand or computer	Facilitator's Notebook, Couple Profile, Goalsetting Form	Content, construct, predictive	Internal consistency .86—.98	Optional 1-day seminar or video
RELATE	271	60–90 min.	$10.00	Computer	Couple Report, Instructor's/ Counselor's Manual	Content, construct, predictive	Internal consistency .70–higher	Self-study
PREPARE	195	30–40 min.	$30.00	Computer	Counselor's Manual, Counselor Feedback Guide, Computer Report, Couple Workbook	Content, construct, concurrent, predictive	Internal consistency .73–.85 Test–retest .74–.93	One-day workshop required

In addition to the standard form, the PREPARE-MC (Marriage with Children) version is available for use when one or both of the premarital partners have children.

The 11 relationship areas assessed by PREPARE comprise: marriage expectations, personality issues, communication, conflict resolution, financial management, leisure activities, sexual relationship, children and parenting, family and friends, role relationship, and spiritual beliefs. A separate Idealistic Distortion scale serves as a correction score for idealism.

Four additional scales on PREPARE assess cohesion and adaptability in the current couple relationship and each individual's family of origin. PREPARE also assesses four personality traits: assertiveness, self-confidence, avoidance of problems, and partner dominance.

The therapist or counselor receives a Computer Report that summarizes and analyzes the couple's responses to the PREPARE items. The *Counselor's Manual* (Olson, 1996) contains detailed information on organizing feedback to the couple. During feedback sessions the couple uses a 25-page workbook called *Building a Strong Marriage,* which contains communication exercises (e.g., assertiveness and active-listening) that can be used with the couple to help them discuss their PREPARE results. A unique feature of PREPARE is the required day-long training workshops for users.

Strengths. PREPARE's strengths include its relatively short length and comprehensiveness. Excellent supplemental counseling materials are available. There is a version for couples who are remarrying.

Concerns. PREPARE is the most expensive of the three instruments reviewed here ($30/couple). In spite of the workbook and counselor guide, it is relatively difficult to interpret the results to couples because the inventory results are not shown to or given to the couple. Counselors must complete an instructor training workshop before using PREPARE.

FOCCUS

FOCCUS is a 156-item instrument with an additional 33 optional items for interfaith couples, cohabiting couples, and remarriage. Its design reflects the values and ideals of marriage as sacred including issues of permanency, fidelity, openness to children, forgiveness, shared faith in God, and unconditional love (Markey & Micheletto, 1997). The nondenominational edition of the questionnaire contains the same items, but with specific references to the Catholic church omitted. The 19 premarital factors assessed by FOCCUS include lifestyle expectations, personality match, personal issues, communication, sexuality issues, family of origin, and religion and values.

The FOCCUS computer printout lists all of the statements for each of the 19 scales and shows on which items the partners agree both with each other and with the preferred responses. A preferred response is the ideal or optimum response that the authors believe to be most advantageous to the couple. Responses to items that are key problem indicators are also listed for each scale.

A useful way to examine a couple's scores is to use the Patterns for Couple Study. Patterns are determined from observing the couple's scores on several related items on the test. Counselor Aids on Individual Items also help the therapist and the couple look more in-depth at statements that may seem to be especially significant, sensitive, or troublesome; for example, "I am uncomfortable with the amount my future spouse drinks." The facilitator's job is to (1) facilitate couple communication about the results and (2) teach the couple more effective behaviors as necessary. The Facilitator's Notebook gives details on how to do this.

On completion of the questionnaire, the couple may purchase and complete an additional 14-item form called FOCCUS for the Future, which helps them consolidate what they learned about their relationship as a result of completing FOCCUS and helps them plan how to use this information in improving their future relationship.

Strengths. FOCCUS's strengths include the availability of several versions for couples who do not speak English or have reading problems. Key problem areas are conveniently listed on one scale. Patterns for couple study and counselor aids on especially important individual items are very helpful in interpreting the results. Remarriage, cohabitation, and interfaith items are included. Cost is $10/couple.

Concerns. Objective evidence for the validity of preferred responses is missing. Interpretation is moderately difficult.

RELATE

RELATE is a 271-item instrument. Two unique characteristics of RELATE are its possible use with non-dating individuals (e.g., friends or strangers), as well as dating, engaged, cohabiting, and married couples; and its adaptability for use in the classroom. Non-dating individuals can complete the test by skipping sections that refer only to serious dating or engaged couples. Before taking the test, a non-dating person is encouraged to pair off with a partner in the class or outside of the class whose responses to the items he or she can compare with his or her own.

RELATE items measure factors in four broad areas: (1) personality characteristics; (2) values, attitudes, and beliefs; (3) family background; and (4) relationship experiences. RELATE results are sent to the therapist or educator in the form of a computer printout that is self-interpretive. The printout can also be sent directly to a couple. The first section of the printout includes bar graphs that demonstrate how each partner rated *the other* and *self* in eight different personality areas including kindness, sociability, calmness, organization, flexibility, emotional maturity, happiness, and self-esteem. The second section compares partner agreement on values and attitudes in areas such as marriage roles, employment, sexuality, children, and religiosity. In the third section, a comparison is made of partner perceptions of family background experiences including family processes, parental marital satisfaction, relationship with parents, family stressors, and parental and couple conflict resolution styles. The fourth section summarizes relationship experiences including couple communication styles, conflict styles based on John Gottman's (1994a, b) research, and relationship satisfaction and stability. An assessment of problem areas in the relationship (e.g., who's in charge, alcohol or drug problems, money problems) is also included.

RELATE also can be used in a variety of ways in a classroom or group setting. One possibility is the didactic use of the concepts and empirical findings. For example, the notion of couple unity can be introduced and its significance discussed. Students who complete RELATE as part of a couple (this can include students matched by the instructor) can discuss their results in small discussion groups. Areas where there is a lack of unity (e.g., money management) can be discussed. Also, students or couples can role-play using communication and problem-solving skills learned in class. The role-play is more effective because they can discuss "real" differences or similarities found on RELATE.

Strengths. RELATE is the easiest instrument to interpret, because the respondents are given their actual responses to the inventory questions in the RELATE Report, and it is the easiest to use in large groups and teaching settings. RELATE is available in English or Spanish, and in paper-and-pencil format or online (http://relate.byu.edu). The paper form (like both PREPARE and FOCCUS) are mailed in and scored. The online versions are scored and the RELATE Report is returned electronically within minutes after both partners complete RELATE. Online versions only of several other cultural/language versions are contemplated including Portuguese, French, German, English-UK, English-Australia, and Japanese. Other language versions will follow as needed. RELATE costs $5/person or $10/couple. It can be used in a variety of settings and with individuals in a number of nonmarital statuses.

Concerns. There currently are no remarriage items, and the instrument is the longest of the three. Remarriage items are currently in development.

Guidelines for Selecting a PAQ

- Decide what your priorities are in assessment—e.g., cost, length, how you intend to use the results, the nature of your clientele.

- For couples who want to know how prepared they are for marriage but prefer not to go to a therapist, use RELATE (easiest to interpret).
- For premarital education and group use with a heterogeneous population of single individuals (e.g., non-dating, dating, engaged), use RELATE.
- For populations with limited financial resources, RELATE or FOCCUS is about one-third the cost of PREPARE.
- For more intense premarital counseling when the therapist has three or more sessions to work with the couple, all three are useful.
- For counselors preferring several structured exercises to use with the results, use PREPARE (best supporting materials).
- PAQs should not be used for prediction purposes; however, the therapist has an ethical responsibility to adequately counsel couples who are a poor marriage risk (i.e., have "low marital aptitude") (Larson, 1998).

Our preference is to use RELATE, as it was designed with the research and principles discussed in this book in mind and covers all of the important premarital predictors of marital quality. The educational program and the textbook we recommend below are based on this work, on Larson and Holman's (1994) review of premarital predictors of marital quality, and on Stahmann and Hiebert's (1997) work on premarital counseling. Both incorporate RELATE in their presentations.

Using RELATE in Education and Counseling for Marriage Preparation and Enrichment

It has been found that the use of an inventory such as the newly developed RELATE (which stands for RELATionship Evaluation) can be an important and useful part of the marital preparation process. Participants and marriage preparation providers can both benefit from the information provided by the RELATE Report. This is true whether the setting is educational or counseling and whether the participants are one couple, a group of four to eight couples, or a larger group in a larger classroom.

While each marriage preparation provider will have specific goals and bring a particular background, training, and experience to the process offered, the following are some ideas and suggestions that will assist in presenting a quality marital preparation experience using RELATE (Stahmann & Hiebert, 1997). First, there is research and clinical evidence that those who benefit most from a marriage preparation program must voluntarily seek it, rather than be forced into it. The key is to have a good program that is made widely available and where the couple is encouraged to participate together in the process.

Second, persons seeking premarital counseling or education expect to learn about themselves to some extent, but primarily about their relationship and each other. The event of both partners taking RELATE together gives them a shared experience of responding to similar questions about their marital attitudes, perceptions, and expectations.

Third, marriage preparation, rather than being a screening process, is designed to help the couple evaluate and enhance their relationship. It is up to the individuals to screen themselves out of the relationship if they choose to do so. The RELATE Report contains important information for couples to use in this process.

Fourth, another purpose of premarital counseling and education is to help the couple become more aware of their expectations, issues, and patterns, giving them a new understanding and some skills to deal with them. Therefore, skills such as decision making, conflict resolution, communication, value clarification, budgeting, and so forth, may be taught. Since these are skills, even those with competence in these areas can sharpen or increase those abilities in the premarital setting.

Fifth, it is known that premarital counseling is most beneficial if obtained early in the relationship and several months before the wedding. While the number of sessions or meetings depends on many factors, there should be adequate time spent in the process, and it must be spread across a sufficient time span so that the partners can learn and integrate the information into their lives and relationship. RELATE can be administered as the meetings begin, when there will be enough time to have it scored and the RELATE Report returned to be used in later meetings (if using a paper-and-pencil version of RELATE; the online version results are returned almost immediately).

Sixth, those responsible for providing marriage preparation programs should have training that includes such areas as relationship enhancement and skill building, marital interaction, marital quality and stability, family interaction, and the use of assessment inventories. Marriage preparation teams, including persons trained in the above areas and laypersons or marriage mentors, can be helpful and do have good validity for some populations.

Seventh, it has been found that bringing both sets of parents (or stepparents) into the last session with the couple can be a very dynamic and useful option. The focus here is to involve the two generations in discussing their changing relationship(s) now that a marriage is occurring. This meeting also allows for the passing on of marital and family "wisdom" from the parents to their adult children. A speaker telephone conference call can be used if geographical distance is a problem in arranging a meeting together.

Lastly, a postwedding follow-up session is an important conclusion to premarital counseling or education. This can be scheduled to be held about 6 months or so after the wedding when the couple has experienced living together as a married couple long enough to have confronted some of the differences that appear during day-to-day married life. Often, as the counselor and couple(s) discuss, "how has it been to be married these 6 months?" the focus for this session emerges. At the conclusion of the session, the counselor can suggest that, at some future date, the couple participate in a marriage enrichment program or retreat as a means of keeping their marriage alive and in tune.

Session-by-Session Outline Using RELATE in Marriage Preparation

The following outline is just one possibility for using the RELATE inventory in a premarital counseling process that integrates skill building, relationship enhancement, personal and couple information, and topical information through an interactional couple experience. Details of this outline are in the book *Premarital and Remarital Counseling* (Stahmann & Hiebert, 1997). RELATE can be used in individual and group counseling as well as educational and enrichment settings. Additionally, it can be used for first marriages, remarriages, and already-married couples.

Session 1

Get acquainted; agree on goals and expectations of premarital counseling; discuss couple's relationship history; assess couple strengths; participants complete the RELATE inventory (counselor mails in the RELATE inventory for scoring if using the paper-and-pencil version).

Session 2

Continue with relationship history; discuss family backgrounds and family-of-origin similarities/differences; introduce genogram and have couple(s) complete it as a between-session activity.

Session 3

Follow up on genogram assignment and discuss family-of-origin influences on this relationship; give the couple their copy of the RELATE Report; discuss guidelines of interpreting the Report; discuss the "Family Background" section of the RELATE Report (pp. 5–6); introduce the topic of communication; discuss the "Couple Communication Styles," "Other Relationship Scales," and "Relationship Satisfaction and Stability" sections of the RELATE Report, (pp. 8–10); introduce communication skills exercise(s) as needed; assign the couple(s) to review and discuss the RELATE Report together and to bring the Report with them to the next session.

Session 4

Follow up on questions/reactions to the RELATE Report; discuss couple's and parents' "Marital Conflict Resolution Types" (pp. 6–7); introduce and/or review conflict resolution skills; discuss "Personality Characteristics" and "Values" from the Report (pp. 2–5); introduce information on finances/budgeting; assign couple(s) to make a budget to bring, along with their RELATE Report, to the next session.

Session 5

Follow up on questions from the RELATE Report; discuss budget; provide and discuss information on other topics, such as sexuality, marital roles and expectations, and parenting; discuss the possibility of inviting parents to next session (in person or via speaker phone).

Session 6

Conduct session with couple and parents to foster positive interaction and allow parents to pass on advice and wisdom (methods vary and this can work well with one parent also—see Stahmann & Hiebert, 1997, pp. 103–105); if parents are not included, this can become Session 7 or can be used to follow up on earlier material/topics and skill-building exercises.

Session 7

This is an integrative session to reinforce couple strengths identified in previous session and from the RELATE Report; discuss wedding plans and arrangements; set a date for a post-wedding session about 6 months after the wedding.

A new self-help book entitled *Should We Stay Together? A Scientifically Proven Method for Evaluating Your Relationship and Improving Its Chances for Long-term Success* (Larson, 200) uses the theory and research results of the present book combined with short assessments of the factors that predict marital satisfaction from the RELATE instrument, to educate the reader about the important predictors of marital success. The reader thus becomes both more informed and more aware of his/her strengths and weaknesses as a future spouse. The book also contains thought-provoking guidelines on whom not to marry and unrealistic beliefs about choosing a mate (e.g., "You're my one and only!"). This book is most appropriate for single young adults, aged 18–30, as they prepare themselves for marriage.

Finally, in terms of premarital interventions, we support the views of several prominent marriage researchers who have emphasized the following: "These results suggest the sobering conclusion that, for many couples, the seeds of divorce are there premaritally—ironically, at a time of great commitment and satisfaction" (Stanley et al., 1995, p. 394). Jacobson and Addis (1993) emphasized: "Given the promising findings from the enrichment and prevention literatures, it seems clear that such efforts should be encouraged.... It makes sense that the problems would be easier to prevent than to modify after the fact. Newlyweds or couples in a premarried state are much more amenable to change-oriented programs, in part because they are younger, happier, and emotionally engaged. We think that prevention efforts should be expanded" (p. 90).

Implications for Research and Theory

In 1964, Bowerman asserted that premarital prediction research could not advance without advances in theory. We believe that as we enter the new millennium, the opposite is true. There have been advances in theory such as the development and refinement of perspectives like attachment theory, family systems theory, and ecological theory which were unknown or in their infancy when Bowerman made his comments. But the premarital prediction research has not kept up with these theoretical advances.

Furthermore, research design, research methods, and analytic tools have improved considerably since 1964, and especially since the last large longitudinal study of premarital prediction was published in 1953 by Burgess and Wallin. For example, all of the analyses in this book were done using statistical programs—SPSS 7.0/8.0 for Windows and LISREL 8.14 for Windows—on desktop personal computers. Such would have been impossible only a few years ago. Also, the use of structural equation modeling was comparatively rare as a research design even just a decade ago.

And yet, despite advances in theory, research capabilities, and statistical analysis, ours is the first attempt since Burgess and Wallin's to do a large sample, truly longitudinal, premarital to marital study of the predictors of marital quality. Why is this? Certainly the cost of a large, longitudinal study is prohibitive. But we believe that the major reason is because the prediction of marital quality from premarital data is no longer fashionable among many researchers and funding agencies. Interest has shifted from establishing and maintaining heterosexual legal marriage to nonmarital cohabitation, issues of power and gender in relationships, and the study of generic "personal relationships." Many researchers, it seems to us, agree with Scanzoni, Polonko, Teachman, and Thompson (1989) that *marriage* and *family* are terms only useful for communicating with the masses, but that researchers and theorists should concentrate on the more general category of SBPRs, sexually based personal relationships. This elitist mentality does little to help the "masses" who continue to want to marry in overwhelming numbers and who prefer long-term, stable marriages.

We believe the time is right to call for a more careful study of the factors leading to the establishment and maintenance of long-term, stable, high-quality marriages. This call makes sense, since, despite the naysayers, marriage is and will continue to be a part of the human experience for the foreseeable future. But, as we noted in Chapter 2, we also believe in the desirability of stable, long-term, high-quality marriages. Our call, however, should not be misconstrued as a call for a return to the "traditional" marriages of the 1950s. A call for studying and supporting stability in marriage cannot automatically be presumed to call with it any of the inequalities and abuses of some of the stable marriages of the 1950s. But happiness is the end goal of all human beings, and we believe that long-term, stable, high quality marriage is clearly one of the most important means for humans to achieve real and lasting contentment and joy. Thus, we see our study described in this book as an attempt to "jump-start" the further development of research and theory in the area of premarital prediction of later marital quality and stability.

Our lament may be overstated. There are several indications that a number of people have sensed the same need we have. First, it is probably no coincidence that four major reviews of premarital prediction have been done in the last decade (this volume; Cate & Lloyd, 1992; Larson & Holman, 1994; Wamboldt & Reiss, 1989). Furthermore, Karney and Bradbury (1995) have done a thorough review of all longitudinal research on the course leading to marital quality and stability, including premarital-to-marital studies. Lastly, the explosion of grass-roots organizations and legislative interest in preventing divorce and strengthening marriage is indicative of changes that are in the wind. With these things in mind, we proceed to make recommendations for future research and theorizing.

Research

From our in-depth review of over 60 years of research, it is clear that predicting marital satisfaction and stability prior to marriage has long been an interest of family researchers and clinicians. However, despite its long tradition and history, this type of research can still be considered to be in its adolescence. Much of the marital prediction research to date has been atheoretical and has lacked a cumulative process of building on previous findings. Perhaps we are at a point as family professionals where we have recognized a need to regroup and take a look at our progress before we push forward in new and productive ways. The reviews noted above are an indication of an attempt to regroup, to see what we know, and then to see where we need to be headed. In light of the current status of premarital/marital prediction research, we echo two recommendations that others have made for future research. First, we concur with other researchers in their call for the development of more diverse and complex theoretical models in the area of marital prediction (Gottman et al., 1998; Markman, 1991; Wamboldt & Reiss, 1989). In particular, we believe that future models need to focus on detailing the specific *processes* by which variables influence marital quality and stability. This type of approach will likely lead us to expand our definition of "predictive research" and endeavor to develop models of *explanation*. While we concur with Lewis and Spanier's (1979) perspective shared 20 years ago that "the study of prediction is a worthy endeavor, but the explanation of the influence of premarital factors on marital quality is a necessary part of theory development" (p. 274), we also suggest that theoretically driven prediction research *does* provide explanation. We will discuss this issue in the next section.

Second, we agree with Larson and Holman's (1994) conclusion that for future research to be useful and productive, certain "methodological shortcomings" of past premarital/marital prediction research must be addressed. We restate and expand on Larson and Holman's (1994) six recommendations for future premarital/marital prediction research.

Recommendation #1

"The practice of utilizing secondary analyses of data from surveys not designed to study how family of origin, current contexts, personality traits, interactional processes, etc. are related to marital satisfaction or stability should be avoided" (p. 233).

With much of the past research in the field relying on secondary data sets, we know more about demographic variables than we do about couple and family variables (Larson & Holman, 1994; White, 1990). The complexity of this type of research demands that we design studies with the particular purpose of investigating specific elements of couple development and change.

Recommendation #2

"Future studies need to include more family process measures that are valid, reliable, and multidimensional" (p. 233).

In conjunction with our call for additional process-oriented work in theoretical models, future studies need to move beyond demographic and background indicators and attempt to define and explain couple and family processes.

Recommendation #3

"Efforts should be made to use large, representative samples that gather data from both premarital/martial partners" (p. 233).

Past research has been hindered in its utility by several frequently occurring sample problems, including use of small sample sizes, use of large samples that were atypical in some way, and the use of only one marital partner. Because premarital prediction research to date has generally used Caucasian, middle-class college students, it is extremely limited in its ability to be generalized to other populations or groups. This becomes a significant shortcoming in that it is currently predicted that, within the next 30 years, ethnic minority groups will become the numerical majority of the U.S. population (Henry, 1990; Ponterotto & Casas, 1991; Sue, 1991). Consequently, we believe that an important direction for future research will be to include couples from diverse ethnic and racial populations so that these groups can be better understood and served in our collective intervention efforts.

Recommendation #4

"Future research should include more longitudinal studies that begin with partners' first acquaintance and follow the couples through several decades of marriage" (p. 233).

Several studies have shown that the effects of some types of predictors of marital quality are not necessarily the same longitudinally as they are cross-sectionally (Markman, 1984; Smith et al.,1990, 1991). In other words, there is evidence to suggest that some predictors of *current* levels of marital quality do not generalize to the prediction of changes in marital quality *over time*. Therefore, since most people see their marriages as ongoing relationships that they want to last over considerable periods of time, premarital prediction research needs to continue to make efforts to implement longitudinal designs that follow couples from pre to postmarriage. We concur with Smith et al. (1991) who admonish that marriage prediction researchers "must simply be prepared to face the task of doing the difficult longitudinal studies, fortified by the certainty that there is much left to be learned" (p. 22).

Recommendation #5

"Future research should study predictors of marital quality by gender" (p. 233).

While much of the previous premarital prediction research has not dealt substantially with differences between men and women, our research reported here shows that in some cases different premarital variables influence later marital quality and stability for men than for women. In the areas where similarities have been found, predictors have often been found to vary in their degree or level of influence. Because of this, we concur with Larson and Holman (1994) in that "there may be a 'his and hers' set of premarital factors that predict marital quality and stability" (p. 233). Future research needs to continue to identify and study sex/gender-linked variables and processes.

Recommendation #6

"Caution should be taken in how we apply prediction research to specific couples" (p. 233).

Prediction research only provides probability estimates that are accurate for groups of couples, rather than for an individual couple. While we may know general domains of variables that influence marital quality and stability, we do not yet fully understand their relative importance or the specific process by which certain variables affect later marital outcomes. Therefore, we concur with Larson and Holman (1994) that "without better designs, specific data, and more sophisticated analytical procedures that will allow us to more accurately classify couples as high and low risk, ethical considerations should preclude us from labeling them as such. Rather than labeling couples, we should educate, counsel, and teach decision-making skills, so that they can apply this research to their own individual, unique relationships" (p. 234). The reader may wonder how we can say this after presenting the cases of four couples in Chapter 1 and in Chapter 10. Our case studies were given to demonstrate that "risk factors" can indeed be identified in couples premaritally. Knowledge of these risk factors can help professionals structure interventions, but not predict with total accuracy whether the couples will "make it" or not.

Theory

We began planning this research in 1987–88, created the instrument to collect the premarital data in 1988–89, and began collecting data in September of 1989. We conducted a thorough review of the premarital prediction research and theory in 1993 (Larson & Holman, 1994). This was done both to help us begin redesigning our premarital data collection instrument, and to help us start this present book and the follow-up study that is part of it. We designed the follow-up study and located our sample in 1996, and collected the marital (or breakup) data in early 1997. Interestingly, at the time we were planning our follow-up study, Karney and Bradbury (1995) published their benchmark review of the longitudinal course leading to marital quality and stability. We were not aware of this publication until sometime in 1998.

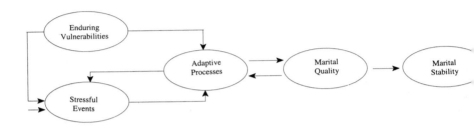

Figure 9.1. Karney and Bradbury's (1995) vulnerability-stress-adaption model of marriage.

We give this background to set up what we want to note in this section. The main point we want to make is that two sets of scholars, independent of each other, came to many of the same conclusions. We note first the similarity of the models we both developed and then we discuss the theoretical perspectives both sets of scholars used, noting differences and similarities. We conclude with comments about the interplay of theory and research for the future.

Karney and Bradbury (1995) hypothesize a four-category model of marital quality. These four categories, or what they call domains of marriage (Bradbury, 1995), are enduring vulnerabilities, stressful events, adaptive processes, and marital outcomes (including marital quality and marital stability). Their model is shown in Figure 9.1. "Enduring vulnerabilities" includes the personal characteristics a person brings to marriage, including family-of-origin experience, social background, personality, and attitudes toward marriage; "stressor events" includes circumstances external to the couple that put stress on the relationship; and "adaptive processes" includes behavioral exchanges in problem-solving such as communication behaviors and conflict resolution skills. They reviewed 115 longitudinal studies of marital quality and stability; we reviewed all of the same premarital-to-marital studies they did, plus we reviewed a number of other longitudinal studies and cross-sectional studies just about the premarital-to-marital case. Comparing their model in Figure 9.1 with our model in Figure 1.1 shows that we came to essentially the same conclusions. Our model is less abstract than theirs, but has many of the same elements. For example, our family-of-origin background and personal characteristics represent the same domain they call enduring vulnerabilities. Our social contextual factors are similar to their stressor events, and their adaptive processes includes all of what we call couple interactional processes. Our connection of the variables is similar to theirs, except we do not hypothesize reciprocal relationships and we connected all of our variables to marital quality, whereas they have all of the effect going through adaptive processes. In essence, the models we tested in this book can be seen as a test of their more general ideas. Indeed, our tests essentially support their theoretical model.

For example, Karney and Bradbury (1995, p. 25) suggest that "one implication of this framework is that the relationship between any two of these three dimensions (as they relate to marital quality) will be imperfectly understood without information on the other dimension." We also suggested that a full understanding of premarital prediction of marital quality requires an understanding of all four of our premarital dimensions. Our resulting research demonstrated the validity of our claim and theirs.

Karney and Bradbury (1995) produced a developmental model of marriage with behavioral theory tenets given a central role. They also used tenets from crisis theory and attachment theory. Our model is a developmental model that uses ideas from family process/systems theory and the ecological theory of human development. We also depend on attachment theory notions in our model. While Karney and Bradbury see little value in social exchange theory or symbolic interactionist ideas, we found them useful for our model building. This seems to indicate several things. First, no one theoretical perspective is sufficient to explain continuity and change in marriage over time. Second, a number of different perspectives are helpful in elucidating the development of marriages. These theories need to explain why some marriages appear to remain stable and have high quality, while others deteriorate from high quality and stability to low quality with either high stability or low stability, and still others may improve from low quality and low stability to high quality and stability. Karney and Bradbury believe that behavioral theory does the best job of explaining change in marriage quality and stability.

> A strength of [a behavioral] approach is that it suggests a mechanism to explain how judgments of marital satisfaction change over time. Specifically, "spouses learn on the basis of their interactions and the appraisals that follow from them whether or not they are in a rewarding relationship" (Bradbury & Fincham, 1991, p. 134). For satisfied couples, each satisfying interaction justifies continued satisfaction, which in turn makes further satisfying interaction more likely. Marital distress, on the other hand, may be largely a consequence of a couple's difficulty dealing with conflict. (Karney & Bradbury, 1995, p. 5)

However, other theoretical perspectives also suggest mechanisms for change in levels of marital satisfaction over time. Karney and Bradbury claim that the social exchange perspective does not address how change happens in marriages. However, we suggest that social exchange does indeed show how relationships can change over time. For example, social exchange includes the concept of satiation. Satiation suggests that interactions that were rewarding at one point in time tend to lose their reward ability, or that it takes considerably more of the behavior to be rewarding. Thus, a rose given as a symbol of love during courtship may be perceived as highly rewarding, but single roses given over time tend to lose their reward value as the receiver becomes satiated with that particular behavior. Thus, a spouse who understands this idea will increase the rewarding behavior over time (send more roses) or do alternative behaviors to retain the rewarded-ness of interactions (e.g., take the spouse to dinner at a nice restaurant). Furthermore, a symbolic interactionist approach suggests that satiation may or may not occur because of the reward in and of itself, but because of the meaning attached to the exchange of the reward. A single rose, exchanged in such a way as to convey continued or growing love and satisfaction, will not lead to satiation, and satisfaction or love will not decline; rather it will grow.

While the previous discussion does not lead to any modification of the Karney and Bradbury model, it does deepen our understanding of change over time in marital outcomes, and suggest alternatives to a purely behavioral explanation of change. Karney and Bradbury say that marital distress, from a behavioral perspective, is the result of conflict in couple interaction. But we propose that the addition of social exchange and symbolic interactionist perspectives suggests another alternative. That alternative is that rewarding behaviors can decrease in value because of satiation and because of the meaning attached to the (previously rewarding) behavior. Marital satisfaction can also increase over time as the meaning of the behavior of the spouse is perceived as more rewarding. The reward does not necessarily have to change (it can still be a single rose, for example), but the perception of caring, remembering "after all these years" can increase its reward value.

Karney and Bradbury's work and our work in this book suggest a need to continue to clarify conditions under which change and continuity take place in marriages over time. The theorizing of Karney and Bradbury as well as our own theorizing suggest models, relationships, and variables to be tested in the future.

10

Epilogue and Invitation

Thomas B. Holman

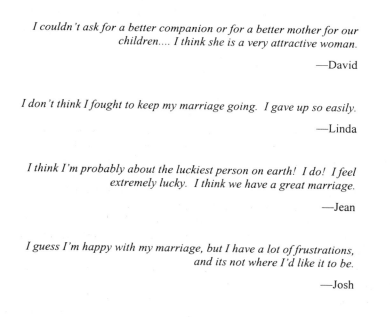

I couldn't ask for a better companion or for a better mother for our children.... I think she is a very attractive woman.

—David

I don't think I fought to keep my marriage going. I gave up so easily.

—Linda

I think I'm probably about the luckiest person on earth! I do! I feel extremely lucky. I think we have a great marriage.

—Jean

I guess I'm happy with my marriage, but I have a lot of frustrations, and its not where I'd like it to be.

—Josh

In Chapter 1 we introduced you to four couples and let them tell you about their courtships. Then, in the following chapters, we took you through our research on premarital predictors of breakup or marital quality. In this chapter we want to update how the four couples were doing 8 years after their marriages. We also want to tell you about the latest version of our premarital assessment instrument and invite you to participate with us in using that instrument to strengthen relationships and gather data about relationships. First, let's look at the four couples.

Four Vignettes Concluded

In Chapter 1 we introduced you to Heidi and David, Linda and Steve, Jean and Bob, and Becky and Josh. We challenged you to use the premarital history of each couple and the research information that followed, and predict which couples were happily married, which couple was married (but rather unhappy), and which couple had divorced. We understand very well the dangers of using statistical results from survey research to predict how well any particular couple is going to fare. But based on what the couples told us and on what we have learned from over 60 years of research, including our own research reported in this book, might we notice some "red flags," or lack thereof, that could give us hints of the kind of marriages these couples were going to have? We believe those hints were there. We conclude this book, then, with a brief look at each of the couples 8 years after their courtships and how their marriages turned out.

Heidi and David

Our research has demonstrated the importance of family-of-origin relationships for the eventual well-being of a marital relationship. Both Heidi and David remember their childhoods as "very happy," and their relationships with their parents as close and loving. Again, our research shows that relationships with parents during the courtship are important predictors of marital quality. Now, 8 years into their marriage, Heidi and David acknowledge the importance of families in the quality of their relationship. Heidi notes, "Both of us come from pretty strong families. Families that are close to us and keep pretty strong contact with us by letters or phone calls."

During their courtship, David demonstrated his capacity to recognize when he had taken Heidi for granted and he had responded sensitively to her concerns and changed his behavior. They were able to communicate about the problem, and David, rather than becoming defensive, had acknowledged Heidi's feelings and responded by spending more time with her. This ability to communicate openly, to share concerns, and to respond non-defensively resulted in an engagement period that was "pretty smooth sailing," in Heidi's words.

The "smooth sailing" continued into their first year of marriage, about which Heidi said: "Things pretty much went as we expected. It really was a very good year for us."

Especially interesting is the pattern of communication and conflict resolution we see in their marriage. First, Heidi recognizes that David has the personality traits that "set up" good communication. "David is very patient, he is very patient." Then about their communication, she says,

> David is really ... easy to talk to and I know that he concedes a lot more than I do.... We do have disagreements, we do have them, but they don't seem to be fiery and stormy and drug out over days or weeks or months and those kinds of things. I am very lucky.

Furthermore, Heidi notes this about their communication:

> For the most part, I think that we are able to communicate very well. I am certainly not afraid to say to him the things that I am feeling.... I feel like David is a good listener.

David's report of their communication show s us something of his personality and style of conflict resolution.

> I hate conflict ... I try to avoid it usually. If I think I am in the right and I think she is in the wrong, then I will just try to avoid the conflict for a while and just try to see if it will, I don't know, lose significance or go away or something. Eventually, if it is something that persists, then we have to talk about it and we have to let it go. I hate to ever leave and go anywhere, and I hate to even go to sleep, on a conflict.

This pattern of communication and conflict management reminds us of the recent findings of Gottman et al. (1998) regarding newlywed couples, namely, that "data suggest that only newlywed men who accept influence from their wives are winding up in happy and stable marriages" (p. 19). Furthermore, "gentleness, soothing, and de-escalation of negativity" were characteristics of stable and happy newlywed couples' conflict resolution styles. Heidi and David have such a conflict style and clearly have a stable and happy marriage.

Linda and Steve

A reading of Linda and Steve's courtship story in Chapter 1 alerts us to several "red flags" based on the research we have presented in this book. Steve was "very shy" around girls and had a hard time meeting them (low sociability) and Linda was "really young [19]." Furthermore, they had, according to Linda, "a lot of differences" including "different backgrounds." Linda's was a "wild family background" and she had little support from her mother to marry Steve. Also, neither of them was "really good at communicating."

On the other hand, they seemed to have several things going for them—Linda saw Steve as a "gentle, stable, even-tempered man" and Steve described Linda as a "nice person, vivacious, fun, and pretty." Yet after 3 years of marriage, they were separated and eventually divorced. Steve has since remarried and had one additional child (he and Linda had a little boy), but Linda has not remarried. The question is: Did the premarital issues of family background and poor communication continue into the marriage? They did, according to both Steve's and Linda's reports.

First, Steve's comments about the dating and engagement period demonstrate the difficulty of "getting through" to seriously involved couples. This may also serve to suggest how premarital interventions will need to find ways to get past the defenses people create to avoid dealing with the issues that could negatively impact their marriages.

> I think I understand things about myself and things about Linda that I didn't understand then and probably couldn't understand then. Things that I remember reading about that were important and yet not feeling their importance and not giving as much heed to them as I should have.... I guess I always had a feeling that problems can always be worked out. So I guess I kind of glossed over [possible problems].

Linda's comments about her marriage show the same kind of "looking back and wishing" attitude.

> I think now, looking back, I think that I should have come back and we should have gone through marriage counseling and sexual counseling or whatever. I don't think I fought to keep the marriage together. I left the situation, which was easy. I got on a plane, and I left. When I was out there [with her mother], I discovered a new person. It was me again. And I think if I had come back and said to Steve, 'This is what has happened, this is how I am feeling; if I come home, I want to go to school. I want to do things. I need this,' then he would have realized the importance of it. Then it would have been different. I think I gave up too easily.

One of the things Steve and Linda both came to realize was how much her family-of-origin model, and past and present family-of-origin relationships, continued to affect their marriage. Steve says:

> Linda kind of thought of marriage the way her mom thought of marriage; if you're happy, stick with it, if you're not happy, then find something else.

When Linda become unhappy with her role of wife and mother, when she felt stymied, she left Steve and flew to her mother's with their baby for a "visit" that lasted 18 months. Finally, after some attempts at reconciliation, they divorced after 6½ years of marriage. Steve believed the divorce happened for four reasons: (1) Linda's lack of good role models from her mother and her mother's unhappy marriages, (2) Steve's resistance to Linda's career interests, (3) Linda's resentment to her perceptions of their church's ideas about motherhood and men's and women's roles (she had joined Steve's church about 1 year before they married), and (4) Steve's obliviousness to what she was feeling—her feelings of being trapped at home and feeling "old." Linda independently mentioned similar things: (1) she had just joined the church and did not totally agree with its teachings on motherhood, men, and women, (2) she came from a very unhappy family life from which she was trying to get away, (3) they had inadequate couple interactional processes—their poor communication skills, inability to come to agreement on major issues, and unsatisfactory sexual relationship— and (4) they had differences in family backgrounds (his stable, close-knit Hispanic family and her "wild," unstable, dysfunctional family).

The two major premarital areas our research found to have the strongest direct relationship to later marital quality—family of origin and couple interactional processes—were certainly major issues in Steve and Linda's marital deterioration. Also, individual characteristics such as Steve's rigidity on family roles and Linda's values and attitudes about men, women, careers, and motherhood (what Steve called her "lack of commitment" to the idea of marriage), were factors in the divorce. Social contextual areas such as weak support from family and friends, her age, and a sense of isolation from a supportive community seemed to have also been factors.

Interestingly, the factors mentioned above—like Steve being gentle and even-tempered, and Linda being a nice person—have contributed to an amiable divorce and joint-parenting situation. So, while those factors were not strong enough to overcome the negative factors they brought into the marriage, they are now helping them in their postmarriage relationship.

Jean and Bob

Like Heidi and David, Jean and Bob appeared to have many things going for them premaritally. Both had excellent relationships with each of their parents and had parents with stable, high-quality marriages; they were able to communicate well, share feelings, deal with difficulties, and resolve issues in their relationship; they had excellent support from family and friends, and both had great "environ-mental" (work, education, income) support; additionally, there were no apparent personality or attitudinal deficits.

The report of their current marriage suggests that the strong resource base they brought into the marriage continued to help them—they have a stable, strong, happy marriage. Jean says this about her marriage and Bob:

> I don't think anything, anything I could ever have done would have been more fulfilling [than marriage]. Regardness [sic] of whatever. And I've done a lot of traveling and I've done a lot of working. And I do, I think I've got the best of everything.... Bob is very affectionate, and he tells me he loves me all the time. He is a real help at home.

Of course, Bob and Jean have had ups and downs in the marriage. Bob was the youngest brother in a family-owned and operated business, and sometimes, when family and business things got mixed together, this created problems between them. They acknowledge that during one 2- or 3-week period, when differences about how the family should run the business came up, "it was pretty rocky," and Bob spent a few nights on the couch. Here is part of their conversion about this time period.

> Bob: "She got a little mad at me one night, and I slept on the couch, and [said] 'Here's your pillow!' you know [laughs]."

> Jean: "We had a good fight that night [laughs]! I said I didn't want to sleep ... I mean, I didn't want to even be in the same room [with him]; he was doing things [in the business] I didn't like. And he cannot be mad for very long; it just kills him [laughs]! He can't go to bed mad, and he'd come back and say, 'Now come on, we can't go to bed like this, and da, da, da.... ' And I would say, 'Just let me be mad for a minute!' And he wouldn't do that, so we would have to talk it out and finally I said, 'Okay, okay!'"

Open communication and quick resolution of issues is clearly important to Bob. He says this about what he thinks about communication:

> I think one of the keys to a successful marriage is being able to communicate about whatever it is you can talk about. We've always been able to sit on the bed and talk if there's a problem. There are times, though, we could probably do a better job. But I don't really foresee that as a problem. It's an area that I'm sure could be improved. I mean, we're not perfect, by any means, in any one area, but I don't really foresee it as a problem.

When asked what was most gratifying about his marriage, Bob said this:

> I guess what comes to my mind first is just seeing myself in a situation like right here and now with a lovely wife, four choice children. Having been married in

the temple, hopefully doing the things that we should together and saying, 'Yes, here we are now, we've been married 8 years, and we're doing okay!'

When speaking of business trips, Bob said:

"I can't wait to come home! I'll open up my suitcase and there's a picture of the kids and little candy bars or something. You know, she makes it fun and exciting, I want to be here!"

Becky and Josh

Becky and Josh's premarital relationship revealed that they struggled to solve problems. While he was very attracted to her and she to him, they occasionally struggled with issues that would get out of hand. Some of the worst premarital issues revolved around significant others—her parents' lack of support for the relationship and her roommates' attempts to break them up. These issues tended to lead to tense confrontations with the result that one or the other would demand that they not see each other. They would get back together eventually, but they would be less open with one another for fear of disturbing the stability of the relationship.

This pattern seems to have continued into the marital relationship. About 3 months into the relationship, Josh especially began to feel that they had profound differences in some of their values. Josh was extremely committed to his religious faith, and felt she was not. This led to arguments that never really got resolved. As Josh said:

Whatever fight we had, you know how fights go, you say a lot of stuff you don't mean. In an argument she would go completely the other way, probably even farther than she really felt, but I didn't know that, and so at that point, at that 3-month point, I really wondered fairly seriously whether I had made a big mistake.

Indeed, at 8 years into the marriage the basic issue of the importance of religious observance is still a sore point.

Josh: "[It is] still something that I'm struggling with. She has changed, but there are a lot of things she hasn't changed, a lot of attitudes. I feel like she's saying [negative things about the church] to hurt me. That's just such a sensitive area for me, a hard area for me to deal with; it's much harder for me to deal with when I think that she's trying to hurt my feelings by saying something about the church. It cuts to the quick more than anything [else].

Becky: "Religion comes to my mind again [as an area of conflict]. I don't think my husband understands me as much as I'd like him to. I want to be everything that he wants me to be, and so I'm frustrated that he doesn't place me up on a pedestal, and I want to be there, and I want him to think of me there, but I'm not [up there] in his eyes. So that is frustrating for me."

Their premarital patterns of withdrawing and not resolving problems is still evident. Becky explained how they handle disagreements:

... probably not very well. We talk to each other and we'll start talking about a disagreement, one of us will walk out of the room, or we'll backbite each other and start to find fault and get off on other tangents, and then just pull everything, dirty laundry out of the basket, everything that we can think of and it gets so overwhelming that we finally both just get so tired of it, so that it's never resolved.

Yet, despite continued struggles and disappointments with one another, they are both committed to the marriage. As Becky says:

[I'm] totally committed. I want it to work. I know it can work. I know that it won't work unless I put forth everything that I can, and sometimes I get selfish.

While expressing his basic commitment to his marriage, Josh allows that other alternatives have entered his mind:

I don't think there is any question in my mind that marriage is what I want. So in spite of all the frustrations there is a heck of a lot about it that is satisfying and gratifying and that's what I want. Even with all the frustrations, there is no way I'd want to be single. I can't think of any alternatives. In courtship times, I wondered if I should have waited. Maybe I could have married somebody else and been happier, and yet if I look around me, I've never met anybody that I thought, "Well, I bet I'd be happy with them." I've often thought, "Do you see anybody you'd be happier with?" And I can't think of anybody. Maybe this ideal person doesn't exist, because I've never felt impressed with someone. So I don't think I'd want any alternatives. I just wish we could make things work a little better.

Becky and Josh have a fairly stable marriage, and both seem committed to making it work despite continuing problems. But it is certainly not the quality of marriage we saw with Heidi and David or with Jean and Bob.

We hope this discussion of the four couples and our attempt to show how a knowledge of premarital factors in the areas of family of origin, individual traits and attitudes, couple interactional processes, and social networks and contexts, can help one recognize possible strengths or areas of concern. We believe that early intervention in the premarital stage can help a couple take care of at least some of the things that can disrupt their later marriage. One mechanism for identifying these areas of strength or concern is the in-depth interview that we had with each of the four couples. However, each interview lasted between 2½ to 3 hours. This is a very costly and time-consuming way of getting the information you need. Therefore, we recommend the use of a comprehensive premarital assessment instrument like the ones we discussed in Chapter 9. Indeed, we wish to invite interested researchers and practitioners to join us in our attempts to strengthen as well as better understand premarital relationships.

An Invitation

Most of the research reported in this book was based on data gathered with a premarital assessment tool called PREP-M. Research in which the premarital data were gathered with other instruments—namely, the Marital Inventory for LDS Couples and the Marital Inventories—was reported in Chapter 9. All of these instruments, as we explained in Chapter 9, were created by the Marriage Study Consortium.

Based on the research reported here, our comprehensive review of the literature, and changing demographic trends (i.e., fewer and fewer marriages are between never-married young adults) we revised PREP-M and in the fall of 1997 began using a new instrument called the RELATionship Evaluation, or RELATE. RELATE is a 271-item instrument designed to measure various aspects of the family of origin, individual characteristics, social contexts, and couple interactional processes. Couple who take RELATE receive a 20-page RELATE Report detailing their and their partner's perceptions of over 60 aspects of the premarital or marital relationship.[1]

The Marriage Study Consortium retains all of the data generated by the RELATEs. These data are being used for research and development purposes. We invite practitioners to begin using our instrument in their premarital interventions. We also invite researchers to become involved with using RELATE to gather data. Our policy is that, once a professional has had 100 or more couples use RELATE, that researcher is allowed access to the total RELATE data set for cross-sectional research. Longitudinal research can be undertaken with the permission of the consortium's executive board.

Therefore, we invite practitioners and researchers alike to get involved with us in the important task of understanding and strengthening premarital relationships. Interested individuals can contact the Marriage Study Consortium via mail at: RELATE, P.O. Box 25391, Provo, UT 84602-5391; by email at RELATE@byu.edu; or online at http://relate.byu.edu. RELATE is available in paper-and-pencil format in English and Spanish and also on the Internet in English and Spanish. We anticipate adding other language versions to the Internet as we develop them.

Endnote

1. Unlike its predecessors, RELATE is designed for married couples as well as young adult, never-married couples.

Appendix A

PREParation for Marriage (PREP-M)

Thomas B. Holman, Dean M. Busby, and Jeffry H. Larson

PREP-M is primarily designed for couples who are engaged or seriously considering marriage, although individuals who are currently "unattached" may also learn a great deal about their readiness for a long-term relationship. The questions deal with topics that are useful in evaluating your similarity and degree of readiness for marriage.

Each person who completes the PREP-M should have a booklet and an answer sheet. Complete PREP-M alone, and do not talk to your partner or anyone else while you are answering the questions. Hand the answer sheet in and keep the booklet until you get your computer printout.

PREP-M is not a test. There are no "right" or "wrong" answers—only "your" answers. There is sometimes the temptation to give the "ideal" answers, rather than the cold, hard truth. The more honest you are, even if it hurts a little, the more useful the information from the printout you receive will be.

You should be aware that the information on the answer sheets will become part of the PREP-M data bank. These data will be used to update the norms for people like yourself. In addition, research will be undertaken periodically to improve the quality of the questions. The data will only be analyzed in large groups, thus preserving the anonymity of all respondents.

Follow the instructions on the answer sheet. Complete all the information asked for including your name, sex, social security number, partner's social security number, your age, the user number your instructor or counselor will give you, and the follow-up information requested. Then begin answering the questions on the following pages.

Section I

RESPONSE CHOICES for questions below:
a. Disagree Strongly
b. Disagree
c. Undecided
d. Agree
e. Agree Strongly

1. It is not important to me to be financially well off.
2. I feel emotionally ready to get married.
3. Religion is an important part of my life.
4. Having a large family is important to me.
5. I believe that full sexual relations are acceptable for me before marriage even if I don't feel particularly affectionate toward my partner.
6. Even when the child/children are school age a mother's place is in the home not at a job.
7. "Natural family planning" (periodic abstinence from sexual intercourse) i preferable to the use of artificial/chemical birth control methods (the pill spermicide, IUD, condom, etc.).
8. Once married, I believe that it is alright to have sexual relations with someone other than my spouse.
9. It is important to have some private space which is all your own and separate from your spouse.
10. The whole idea of having children and rearing them is not attractive to me.
11. If a goal is important, it is occasionally acceptable to use slightly dishonest means to attain the goal.
12. Having enough money to do whatever I want is one of my life goals.
13. With regard to sexual intimacy, I feel ready to get married.

14. I do <u>not</u> see myself as a religious person.
15. Permanent birth control through surgical operation for either the man or the woman is acceptable for couples who have decided they want no more children.
16. I believe that full sexual relations are acceptable for me before marriage when I am in love with my partner.
17. I expect marriage to give me more real personal satisfaction than just about anything else I am involved in.
18. Husband and children should come before a job or career for a woman.
19. Legal abortion is an acceptable method of birth control.

20. It is O.K. for spouses to go for long periods of time without spending much time together as a couple.
21. Although parenthood requires many sacrifices, the love and enjoyment of children make it worth it all.
22. Sometimes it is O.K. to fudge a little on things like income tax returns, insurance forms, etc.
23. Having the finer things in life is important to me.
24. I feel financially ready to get married.
25. Going to religious services is important to me.
26. My photograph has been on the cover of five magazines.
27. I believe that full sexual relations are acceptable for me when I am engaged to be married.
28. The whole idea of the commitment and sacrifice involved in marriage is <u>not</u> attractive to me.
29. A mother should feel free to pursue a career/job even when there are preschool children in the home.
30. In marriage, privacy is as important as togetherness.
31. My life would be empty if I never had children.
32. It is important to me to be totally honest in all my dealings with others.
33. All things considered, I feel ready to get married.

RESPONSE CHOICES for questions below:
a. Husband entirely
b. Husband more than wife
c. Husband and wife equally
d. Wife more than husband
e. Wife entirely

Some couples like to share different marital duties or roles, others like to split them up between husband and wife. Who do you think should do the following?

34. Housekeeping
35. Yard work
36. Home repairs
37. Earn a living
38. Decide how money is spent
39. Initiate sexual activity
40. Organize and start family recreation
41. Keep in touch with relatives
42. Care for the children
43. Teach and train children
44. Discipline children

Section II

Please answer the following questions about you and your family background. The answers you give will <u>not</u> appear anywhere on the printout you (or your partner) will receive back. Only a summary score will be provided. When questions ask about your father or mother, answer according to the <u>primary caregiver</u> you had, even if that was not your biological mother or father.

RESPONSE CHOICES for questions below:
a.   Very <u>Dis</u>satisfied
b.   <u>Dis</u>satisfied
c.   Neutral
d.   Satisfied
e.   Very Satisfied

While I grew up, how satisfied was I with...

45.   ... my relationship with my father?
46.   ... the way my parents disciplined me?
47.   ... how close I felt to the rest of my family?
48.   ... the way we worked together as a family to solve problems?
49.   ... the number of fun things my family did together?
50.   ... the quality of our communication in my family?

51.   ... my relationship with my mother?
52.   In the home where I grew up, how satisfied was my father in his marriage?
53.   In the home where I grew up, how satisfied was my mother in her marriage?

RESPONSE CHOICES for questions below:
a.   Never
b.   Hardly Ever
c.   Sometimes
d.   Fairly Often
e.   Very Often

While I grew up...
54.   ... my father showed physical affection to me by hugging and/or kissing me.
55.   ... my father participated in enjoyable activities with me.
56.   ... my father and I were able to share our feelings on just about any topic without embarrassment or fear of hurt feelings.
57.   ... my father was consistent when he disciplined me.
58.   ... my father would explain to me why I was being punished.
59.   ... my father was critical about what I did.
60.   ... how frequently did my father use alcohol?
61.   ... my mother showed physical affection by hugging and/or kissing me.
62.   ... my mother participated in enjoyable activities with me.
63.   ... my mother and I were able to share our feelings on just about any topic without embarrassment or fear of hurt feelings.
64.   ... my mother was consistent when she disciplined me.
65.   ... my mother would explain to me why I was being punished.
66.   ... my mother was critical about what I did.
67.   ... how frequently did my mother use alcohol?
68.   ... how often did my mother and father argue with each other?

RESPONSE CHOICES for questions below:
a.   Never
b.   Once
c.   Two to three times
d.   Four to six times
e.   More than six times

In my immediate family, while I grew up...

69.   ... there were transition strains like moving, changing jobs, or changing schools.

70.   ... there were financial strains such as loss of jobs, bankruptcy, large debts, or going on welfare.

71.   ... there were physical strains such as a member(s) being physically handicapped, hospitalized for a serious physical illness or injury, or becoming premaritally pregnant.

72.   ... there were mental strains such as a member(s) being seriously depressed, emotionally unstable, or being hospitalized for a mental disorder.

73.   ... we suffered from significant losses like a family member's death or divorce.

74.   ... there were legal violations such as a member(s) going to jail or being put on probation, using drugs, or dropping out of school.

75. On the average my childhood was:
    a. Very <u>un</u>happy
    b. Moderately <u>un</u>happy
    c. Neutral
    d. Moderately happy
    e. Very happy

76. On the average my teenage years were:
    a. Very <u>un</u>happy
    b. Moderately <u>un</u>happy
    c. Neutral
    d. Moderately happy
    e. Very happy

77. Which best describes the marital status of my father while I was growing up?
    a. Married (first marriage)
    b. Divorced or separated and not remarried
    c. Wife deceased and father not remarried
    d. Remarried after a divorce
    e. Remarried after the death of wife

78. In the last ten years I have not seen an automobile.
    a. True   b. False

79. Which best describes the marital status of my mother while I was growing up?
    a. Married (first marriage)
    b. Divorced or separated and not remarried
    c. Husband deceased and mother not remarried

    d. Remarried after a divorce

    e. Remarried after the death of husband

80. How frequently do I attend religious services?

    a. Regular attendance (weekly)

    b. Frequent attendance (at least monthly)

    c. Occasional attendance (several times a year)

    d. Only on special occasions (once or twice a year)

    e. Never

81. My scholastic average (GPA) is (was):

    a. A- to A (3.7–4.0)

    b. B- to B+ (2.7–3.6)

    c. C- to C+ (1.7–2.6)

    d. D- to D+ (0.7–1.6)

    e. F to F+ (0.0–0.6)

82. The region of the country which best describes where I lived most of the time while I grew up was:

    a. Northeast— ME, NH, NY, VT, MA, RI, CT, NJ, PA

    b. North central— OH, IN, IL, MI, WI, MN, IA, MO, ND, SD, NE, KS

    c. South— DE, MD, DC, VA, WV, NC, SC, GA, FL, KY, TN, AL, MS, AR, LA, OK, TX

    d. West—MT, ID, WY, CO, CA, NM, AZ, UT, NV, WA, OR, AK, HI

    e. Other—foreign country

83. How frequently would I like to have sexual relations in my marriage?

    a. Once a day or more

    b. 4–6 times a week

    c. 1–3 times a week

    d. 2–3 times a month

    e. once a month or less

84. While you grew up, did conflicts which led to physical acts like kicking, hitting hard with a fist, beatings, or hitting with objects happen in your home? [REMEMBER, NONE OF YOUR ANSWERS TO THESE OR OTHER QUESTIONS IN THIS SECTION WILL APPEAR ON THE PRINTOUT YOU OR YOUR PARTNER RECEIVE, SO PLEASE ANSWER THE QUESTIONS HONESTLY.]

    a. No (If "No," skip to question 89)

    b. Yes (If "Yes," answer questions 85–88)

RESPONSE CHOICES for questions below:

a. Very Often (over 50 times)
b. Fairly Often (21–50 times)
c. Sometimes (6–20)
d. Hardly Ever (1–5 times)
e. Never

How often, on the average, did things like kicking, hitting hard with a fist, beatings, and hitting with objects happened to you while you grew up?

85. One of my brothers or sisters did things like this to me or I did it to them.
86. My parents or caretakers did this to me.
87. My parents or caretakers did it to each other.
88. I did it to my parents.
89. At times sexual activities occur in families such as touching children in inappropriate places or performing sexual acts with children. Did these things ever happen to you while you grew up?
    a. No (If "No," skip to question 95)
    b. Yes (If "Yes," answer questions 90–94)

How often, on the average, did things like the above happen to you while you grew up?

90. One of my brothers did things like this to me.
91. One of my sisters did things like this to me.
92. My father did things like this to me.
93. My mother did things like this to me.
94. Another person did things like this to me.
95. Everyone gets into conflicts with other people and sometimes these lead to physical acts like kicking, hitting hard with a fist, beatings, and hitting with objects. On the average, <u>during the last twelve months</u> I did these things to my dating partner(s) or fiancé(e):
    a. More than once a week
    b. Once a week
    c. Once a month
    d. Less than once a month but several times
    e. Never
96. On the average, <u>during the last twelve months</u> my dating partner(s) or fiancé(e) did these to me:
    a. More than once a week
    b. Once a week
    c. Once a month

    d. Less than once a month but several times

    e. Never

97.   In your current relationship how often have you been pressured to participate in intimate behavior (such as petting or intercourse) against your will?

    a. Very often

    b. Fairly often

    c. Sometimes

    d. Hardly ever

    e. Never

    f. I'm not currently in a relationship

98.   I lived most of my life in:

    a. Farm/ranch

    b. Rural—not farm or ranch

    c. Town—2,500 people or less

    d. Town—2,500 to 25,000

    e. Small city—25,000 to 100,000

    f. Large city—over 100,000

99.   My race or ethnic origin is:

    a. African (Black)

    b. Asian

    c. Caucasian (White)

    d. American Indian

    e. Hispanic (Mexican American, Latin American, etc.)

    f. Polynesian

100. My present relationship status is:

    a. Single—not going with anyone (Skip to question 103)

    b. Single—going with one person (but _not_ cohabiting)

    c. Single—after being divorced or widowed and not going with anyone (Skip to question 103)

    d. Single—after being divorced or widowed and going with one person (but _not_ cohabiting)

    e. Engaged

    f. Living with someone of the opposite sex to whom I am not married (cohabiting)

    g. Married

101. How long have my partner and I been going together (dating each other exclusively)?
    a.   Less than 1 month
    b.   1 to 3 months
    c.   More than 3 months but less than 6 months
    d.   More than 6 months but less than 12 months
    e.   1 to 2 years
    f.   More than 2 years
    g.   Don't know or doesn't apply

102. How many months will elapse between our engagement (or the time at which both of us had a definite understanding that we were to be married) and the date of our marriage?
    1.   Less than 1 month
    b.   1 to 3 months
    c.   More than 3 months but less than 6 months
    d.   More than 6 months but less than 12 months
    e.   1 to 2 years
    f.   More than 2 years
    g.   Don't know or doesn't apply

103. Here is a list of things (in alphabetical order) that many people look for in or want out of life. Please study the list carefully, then choose the one that is most important to you.
    a.   Being well-respected
    b.   Fun—enjoyment—excitement
    c.   Security
    d.   Self-fulfillment
    e.   Self-respect
    f.   Sense of accomplishment
    g.   Sense of belonging
    h.   Warm relations with others

104. My religious affiliation is:
    a.   Catholic
    b.   Protestant (Lutheran, Methodist, Episcopalian, Baptist, Presbyterian, etc.)
    c.   Judaism (Jewish)
    d.   Latter-day Saint (Mormon)
    e.   Moslem (Shiite, Sunnite, Druse, etc.)
    f.   Eastern religion (Buddhism, Hinduism, etc.)

    g.   Other

    h.   None

105. For most of my life I was reared by:

    a.   Natural father and mother

    b.   Natural mother only

    c.   Natural father only

    d.   Natural mother and step father

    e.   Natural father and step mother

    f.   Grandparent(s)

    g.   Other relative(s)

    h.   Adopted parent(s)

    i.   Foster parent(s)

106. My birth position in my family is:

    a.   First

    b.   Second

    c.   Third

    d.   Fourth

    e.   Fifth

    f.   Sixth

    g.   Seventh

    h.   Eighth

    i.   Ninth or more

107. How many children (including me) were in my family?

    a.   One

    b.   Two

    c.   Three

    d.   Four

    e.   Five

    f.   Six

    g.   Seven

    h.   Eight

    i.   Nine or more

RESPONSE CHOICES for questions below:

a.   Elementary School

b.   Some High School

c.   High School Diploma

d.   Some College/Technical School
e.   Associate's Degree
f.   Bachelor's Degree
g.   Master's Degree
h.   Doctoral Degree (Ph.D., Ed.D.)
i.   Professional (M.D., J.D., D.D.S.)

108.   How much education have I completed?
109.   How much education has my father completed?
110.   How much education has my mother completed?

RESPONSE CHOICES for questions below:
a.   Trade (plumber, carpenter, electrician, farmer)
b.   Homemaker
c.   Professional (doctor, lawyer, executive)
d.   Sales
e.   Farm worker
f.   Service employee (clerical, custodial, technician)
g.   Other professional (teacher, engineer, manager, nurse, businessperson)

111.   Which best describes my current occupation?
112.   Which comes the closest to describing my father's primary occupation while
       I grew up?
113.   Which comes the closest to describing my mother's primary occupation
       while I grew up?

RESPONSE CHOICES for questions below:
a.   None
b.   Under $5,000
c. $5,000–$9,999
d. $10,000–$14,999
e. $15,000–$24,999
f. $25,000–$34,999
g. $35,000–$49,999
h. $50,000–$69,999
i. $70,000–more

114. My <u>current</u> individual yearly income is:
115. My father's <u>current</u> individual yearly income is:
116. My mother's <u>current</u> individual yearly income is:

Section III

Answer the following items about yourself and about your relationship with a partner such as a boyfriend or girlfriend. If you do not currently have a boyfriend or girlfriend, answer the relationship items according to how you currently interact with an important person in your life.

RESPONSE CHOICES for questions below:
a. Never
b. Hardly Ever
c. Sometimes
d. Fairly Often
e. Very Often

117. I have lived (or will have lived) away from my parents' home before getting married.
118. I get into difficulties because of impulsive acts.
119. I have a tendency to say things to my partner that would be better left unsaid.
120. I feel I have a number of good qualities.
121. In most matters, I understand what my partner is trying to say.
122. How frequently do I use illegal drugs (Marijuana, Cocaine, Heroine, etc.)?
123. I let my partner know when I am displeased with him/her.
124. I feel useless.
125. I sit down with my partner and just talk things over.
126. I feel sad and blue.
127. My parents encourage me to be independent and make my own decisions.
128. I have trouble controlling my temper.
129. I sulk or pout when I'm with my partner.
130. I take a positive attitude toward myself.
131. I understand my partner's feelings.
132. How frequently do I smoke or use chewing tobacco?

133. I fail to express disagreement with my partner because I am afraid she/he will get angry.
134. I think I am no good at all.
135. I talk over pleasant things that happen during the day when I am with my partner.
136. I feel hopeless.
137. My parents try to run my life.
138. I nag my partner.
139. I feel I am a person of worth.
140. I am able to listen to my partner in an understanding way.
141. How frequently do I use alcohol?
142. I have a tendency to keep my feelings to myself when I am with my partner.
143. I'm inclined to feel I am a failure.
144. I discuss my personal problems with my partner.
145. I feel depressed.
146. I get really caught up in my family's problems and concerns.

Section IV

The questions in the next two sections (Section IV and Section V) should only be answered if you are engaged, seriously considering marriage, or living with someone. Those not currently in a serious relationship should skip to Section VI, the optional questions section. If the person you received PREP-M from does not have any optional questions for you to answer, you are finished and should turn in your answer sheet for scoring.

RESPONSE CHOICES for questions below:
a. Never
b. Hardly Ever
c. Sometimes
d. Fairly Often
e. Very Often

147. My partner has lived (or will have lived) away from his/her parents home before we get married.
148. My partner has trouble controlling his/her temper.

149. My partner has a tendency to say things to me that would be better left unsaid.
150. I believe my partner feels he has a number of good qualities.
151. My partner is able to listen to me in an understanding way.
152. How frequently does my partner use illegal drugs (Marijuana, Cocaine, Heroine, etc.)?
153. My partner fails to express disagreements with me because she/he is afraid I will get angry.
154. My partner feels depressed.
155. My partner feels useless at times.
156. My partner sits down with me just to talk things over.
157. My partner gets really caught up in his/her family's problems and concerns.
158. My partner's parents encourage him/her to be independent and make his/her own decisions.
159. My partner sulks or pouts when I'm with him/her.
160. My partner takes a positive attitude toward him/herself.
161. In most matters, my partner understands what I am trying to say.
162. How frequently does my partner smoke or use chewing tobacco?
163. My partner lets me know when she/he is displeased with me.
164. My partner feels hopeless.
165. My partner thinks she/he is no good at all.
166. My partner discusses his/her personal problems with me.
167. My partner's parents try to run his/her life.
168. My partner gets into difficulties because of impulsive acts.
169. My partner nags me.
170. My partner feels she/he is a person of worth.
171. My partner understands my feelings.
172. How frequently does my partner use alcohol?
173. My partner has a tendency to keep his/her feelings to him/herself when with me.
174. My partner feels sad and blue.
175. My partner is inclined to feel she/he is a failure.
176. My partner talks over pleasant things that happen during the day with me.

Section V

RESPONSE CHOICES for questions below:
a.   We've never discussed this
b.   Never agree
c.   Seldom agree
d.   Usually agree
e.   Always agree

Most people have some areas where they agree and others where they disagree.
How much agreement do you and your partner have in the following areas?
177.   Leisure activities
178.   Handling finances
179.   Religious matters
180.   Demonstrations of affection/intimacy
181.   Ways of dealing with parents/in-laws
182.   Amount of time spent together
183.   Number of children to have

RESPONSE CHOICES for questions below:
a.   Never
b.   Once
c.   Two to three times
d.   Four to six times
e.   More than six times

184.   How often have I thought our relationship might be in trouble?
185.   How often have I thought seriously about breaking off our relationship?
186.   How often have my partner and I discussed terminating our relationship?
187.   How often have we broken up and then gotten back together?

RESPONSE CHOICES for questions below:
a.   Disagree Strongly
b.   Disagree
c.   Undecided
d.   Agree
e.   Agree Strongly

188.   I hope marriage will solve some of the major problems in my life.

189. We will never have any problems in our marriage.
190. The male's parents are in favor of the marriage.
191. Time will resolve any problems we have as a couple.
192. The female's parents are in favor of the marriage.
193. Our friends approve of our marriage.
194. We have prayed/meditated about our relationship and deep down we feel good about it.
195. How much do I like my future mother-in-law?
    a. I dislike her very much.
    b. I dislike her.
    c. I have mixed feelings about her, or I don't know her.
    d. I like her.
    e. I like her very much
196. How would I rate my own physical attractiveness?
    a. Very plain looking
    b. Plain looking
    c. Not sure
    d. Good looking
    e. Very good looking
197. How similar are we in our mental abilities (IQ)?
    a. Very dissimilar
    b. Dissimilar
    c. Not sure
    d. Similar
    e. Very similar
198. How satisfied am I with my relationship with my partner?
    a. Very dissatisfied
    b. Dissatisfied
    c. Neutral
    d. Satisfied
    e. Very satisfied
199. How much do I like my future father-in-law?
    a. I dislike him very much.
    b. I dislike him.
    c. I have mixed feelings about him, or I don't know him.
    d. I like him.
    e. I like him very much.

200. How much money will the two of us have saved when we get married?
    a. 0–$500
    b. $501–$1500
    c. $1501–$3000
    d. $3001–$5000
    e. More than $5000

201. How would I rate the physical attractiveness of my partner?
    a. Very plain looking
    b. Plain looking
    c. Not sure
    d. Good looking
    e. Very good looking

202. What will be our combined indebtedness at the time we get married? (Include charge accounts and amount owed on loans.)
    a. 0–$1000
    b. $1001–$3000
    c. $3001–$5000
    d. $5001–$10,000
    e. More than $10,000

203. Am I, or is my partner, currently pregnant?
    a. Yes
    b. No

204. I have personally discussed foreign policy issues with several world leaders.
    a. Yes
    b. No

Appendix B

The Relationship Quality Follow-Up Study

Thomas B. Holman and Steven T. Linford

Section A

YOUR SOCIAL SECURITY # IS: _____

Section B

Please circle the number of the correct response to the following question about your relationship to the person who was your partner when you originally took PREP-M (the person whose name is on the letter that came with this questionnaire). Then go to the section noted after your response and answer those questions about your relationship.

1. WE BROKE UP BEFORE MARRIAGE. Skip to *Section C* and answer questions 1 to 20.
2. WE MARRIED EACH OTHER, BUT ARE NOW DIVORCED OR SEPARATED. Skip to *Section D* and answer questions 1 to 18.

3. WE ARE LIVING TOGETHER (COHABITING), BUT HAVE NOT MARRIED. Skip to *Section E* and answer the remainder of the questions.

4. WE MARRIED EACH OTHER AND ARE STILL MARRIED. Skip to *Section E* and answer the remainder of the questions.

5. WE ARE DATING OR ENGAGED, BUT ARE NOT COHABITING. Skip to *Section F* and answer the five background information questions.

6. NONE OF THE ABOVE RESPONSES DESCRIBES OUR RELATIONSHIP. If this is your response, please describe your relationship in the space below. Then turn to *Section F* and answer the five background information questions.

Section C

If you BROKE UP BEFORE MARRIAGE with the person noted on the letter, you should answer the following 20 questions.

1. Who initiated the breakup? (Circle the number of your answer)
    1. I DID.
    2. MY PARTNER DID.
    3. IT WAS MUTUAL.

From the following list of things that can cause the breakup in a premarital relationship, please indicate how much each one played in your breakup. Use the following scale for your answers:

1 = NOT A FACTOR
2 = A CONTRIBUTING FACTOR
3 = ONE OF THE MOST IMPORTANT FACTORS

2. Becoming bored with the relationship
3. Differences in interests
4. Differences in background
5. Differences in intelligence
6. Conflicting sexual attitudes
7. Conflicting marriage ideas
8. Woman's desire to be more independent
9. Man's desire to be more independent
10. Living too far apart
11. Woman's interest in someone else

12. Man's interest in someone else
13. Pressure from woman's parents
14. Pressure from man's parents
15. Substance abuse (i.e., alcohol, drugs)
16. Differences in religious attitudes and practices
17. Finances
18. Decrease in mutual feelings of love
19. Breakdown in communication
20. Physical abuse

Now turn to Section F and answer the five background information questions.

Section D

If you DIVORCED or SEPARATED from the person noted in the letter, you should answer the following 18 questions.

1. Status (circle answer)
    1. Divorced
    2. Separated
2. Age at marriage (Fill in blanks)
    ___years ___month(s)
3. Length of marriage (Fill in blanks)
    ___year(s) ___month(s)
4. Time since divorce or separation (Fill in blanks)
    ___year(s) ___month(s)

From the following list of things that can cause marital dissolution, please indicate how much each one played in your breakup. Use the following scale for your answer:

   1 = NOT A FACTOR
   2 = A CONTRIBUTING FACTOR
   3 = ONE OF THE MOST IMPORTANT FACTORS

5. Infidelity
6. No longer loved each other
7. Emotional problems
8. Financial problems
9. Physical abuse
10. Alcohol

11. Sexual problems
12. Problems with in-laws
13. Neglect of children
14. Communication problems
15. Married too young
16. Job conflicts
17. Differences in religious attitudes and practices
18. Control/power problems

Now turn to Section F and complete the five background information questions.

Section E

If you are MARRIED to or COHABITING with the person noted on the letter, please answer the following questions.

A. Please answer the following questions about your relationship communication by using the following responses:

1 = NEVER
2 = HARDLY EVER
3 = SOMETIMES
4 = FAIRLY OFTEN
5 = VERY OFTEN

1. In most matters, I understand what my partner is trying to say.
2. I have a tendency to say things to my partner that would be better left unsaid.
3. I sit down with my partner and just talk things over.
4. I let my partner know when I am displeased with him/her.
5. I understand my partner's feelings.
6. I nag my partner.
7. I fail to express disagreement with my partner because I am afraid she/he will get angry.
8. I am able to listen to my partner in an understanding way.
9. I talk over pleasant things that happen during the day when I am with my partner.
10. I discuss my personal problems with my partner.

11. I have a tendency to keep my feelings to myself when I am with my partner.

12. I sulk or pout when I'm with my partner.

B. Most individuals have at least occasional disagreements in their relationships. Please indicate below the approximate extent of agreement or disagreement between you and your partner by using the following responses:

    1 = WE'VE NEVER DISCUSSED THIS
    2 = NEVER AGREE
    3 = SELDOM AGREE
    4 = USUALLY AGREE
    5 = ALWAYS AGREE

1. Leisure activities
2. Handling finances
3. Religious matters
4. Demonstrations of affection/intimacy
5. Ways of dealing with parents/in-laws
6. Amount of time spent together
7. Number of children to have

C. Couples vary a good deal on how they share and divide responsibilities. Please give your estimate of the sharing and dividing of responsibilities in your relationship by using the following responses:

    1 = MAN ENTIRELY
    2 = MAN MORE THAN WOMAN
    3 = MAN AND WOMAN EQUALLY
    4 = WOMAN MORE THAN MAN
    5 = WOMAN ENTIRELY
    6 = DOES NOT APPLY

1. Housekeeping
2. Yard work
3. Home repairs
4. Earn a living
5. Decide how money is spent
6. Initiate sexual activity
7. Organize and start family recreation

    8.   Keep in touch with relatives

    9.   Care for the children

   10. Teach and train children

   11. Discipline children

D.   Please answer the following questions about your relationship with your partner by using the responses below:

        1 = NEVER

        2 = ONCE

        3 = TWO OR THREE TIMES

        4 = FOUR TO SIX TIMES

        5 = MORE THAN SIX TIMES

    1.   How often have I thought our relationship might be in trouble?

    2.   How often have I thought seriously about breaking off our relationship?

    3.   How often have my partner and I discussed terminating our relationship?

    4.   How often have we broken up and then gotten back together?

E.   Please answer the following questions about your religious observance by using the responses below:

        1 = DISAGREE STRONGLY

        2 = DISAGREE

        3 = UNDECIDED

        4 = AGREE

        5 = STRONGLY AGREE

    1.   Religion is an important part of my life

    2.   I do not see myself as a religious person

    3.   Going to religious services is important to me

    4.   How frequently do you attend religious service? (Circle one)

        1 = NEVER

        2 = ONLY ON SPECIAL OCCASIONS (ONCE OR TWICE A YEAR)

        3 = OCCASIONAL ATTENDANCE (SEVERAL TIMES A YEAR)

        4 = FREQUENT ATTENDANCE (AT LEAST MONTHLY)

        5 = REGULAR ATTENDANCE (WEEKLY)

Use the following responses to answer questions 5, 6, and 7.

    1 = NEVER

    2 = RARELY

    3 = SOMETIMES

    4 = OFTEN

    5 = VERY OFTEN

5. Do you pray (commune with a higher power)?

6. Are some doctrines or practices of your church (or religious body) hard for you to accept?

7. Do you read scriptures?

Please rate yourself on the following characteristics, using the scale below.

    1 = LOWEST to 5 = HIGHEST

8. Gentle

9. Humble

10. Kind

11. Loving

12. Patient

13. Unselfish

F. Please answer the following questions about your relationship with your partner by using the responses below:

    1 = VERY DISSATISFIED

    2 = DISSATISFIED

    3 = NEUTRAL

    4 = SATISFIED

    5 = VERY SATISFIED

In your relationship, how satisfied are you with:

1. The physical intimacy you experience

2. The love you experience

3. How conflicts are resolved

4. The amount of relationship equality you experience

5. The amount of time you have together

6. The quality of your communication

7. Your overall relationship with your partner

G. As couples make the transition into marriage (living together), the difficulty or ease of individual adjustments will vary from one area to another. Rate your adjustment in these areas by using the responses below:

> 1 = MUCH HARDER THAN I EXPECTED
> 2 = SOMEWHAT HARDER THAN I EXPECTED
> 3 = ABOUT WHAT I EXPECTED
> 4 = SOMEWHAT EASIER THAN I EXPECTED
> 5 = MUCH EASIER THAN I EXPECTED

1. Finances
2. Sex
3. Career and family
4. Parenthood
5. Religious values and activity
6. Relationship with parents
7. Relationship with in-laws
8. Maintaining or changing friends
9. Demonstration of affection apart from sex
10. Amount of time spent together
11. Decision making
12. Daily household duties and responsibilities
13. Overall transition into marriage (or cohabiting)

H. Please answer the following questions about physical abuse by using the responses below:

> 1 = MORE THAN ONCE A WEEK
> 2 = ONCE A WEEK
> 3 = ONCE A MONTH
> 4 = LESS THAN ONCE A MONTH BUT SEVERAL TIMES
> 5 = NEVER

1 . Everyone gets into conflicts with other people and sometimes these lead to physical acts like kicking, hitting hard with a fist, beatings, and hitting with objects. On the average, <u>during the last twelve months,</u> I did these to my partner...

2. On the average, <u>during the last twelve months,</u> my partner did these to me...

I. Please answer the following questions about sexual abuse by using the responses below.

1 = VERY OFTEN
2 = FAIRLY OFTEN
3 = SOMETIMES
4 = HARDLY EVER
5 = NEVER

1. In our relationship how often have you been pressured to participate in intimate behavior against your will?
2. How often has your partner been pressured against her/his will to participate in sexual behaviors <u>by you?</u>

J. Please answer the following questions about substance use using the responses below:

1 = NEVER
2 = HARDLY EVER
3 = SOMETIMES
4 = FAIRLY OFTEN
5 = VERY OFTEN

1. How often do I smoke or use tobacco?
2. How frequently do I use alcohol?
3. How frequently do I use illegal drugs (Marijuana, Cocaine, Heroine, etc.)?
4. How often does my partner smoke or use tobacco?
5. How frequently does my partner use alcohol?
6. How frequently does my partner use illegal drugs (Marijuana, Cocaine, Heroine, etc.)?

K. Below are descriptions of how people in four different types of relationships handle conflict. We would like to see which type most closely describes how you and your partner deal with conflict in your relationship. Use the following responses:

1 = NEVER
2 = RARELY
3 = SOMETIMES
4 = OFTEN
5 = VERY OFTEN

1. In our relationship, conflicts may be fought on a grand scale, and that is okay, since our making up is even grander. We have volcanic arguments, but they are just a small part of a warm and loving relationship. Although we argue, we are still able to resolve our differences. In fact, our passion and zest for fighting actually leads to a better relationship with a lot of making up, laughing, and affection.

2. In our relationship, conflict is minimized. We think it is better to "agree to disagree" rather than end up in discussions that will result in a deadlock. We don't think there is much to be gained from getting openly angry with each other. In fact, a lot of talking about disagreements seems to make matters worse. We feel that if you just relax about problems, they will have a way of working themselves out.

3. In our relationship, when we are having conflict, we let each other know the other's opinions are valued and their emotions valid, even if we disagree with each other. Even when discussing a hot topic, we display a lot of self-control and are calm. When fighting we spend a lot of time validating each other as well as trying to persuade our partner or try to find a compromise.

4. We argue often and hotly. There are a lot of insults back and forth, name calling, put-downs, and sarcasm. We don't really listen to what the other is saying, nor do we look at each other very much. One or the other of us can be quite detached and emotionally uninvolved, even though there may be brief episodes of attack and defensiveness. There are clearly more negatives than positives in our relationship.

L. Please complete the following sentences by filling in the blanks.

1. How long have you been married (cohabiting)?
   ___year(s) ___month(s)
2. Your age at marriage (or beginning cohabiting).
   ___years ___month(s)
3. How long did you date before marriage (cohabiting)?
   ___year(s) ___month(s)
4. How long were you engaged before you married?
   ___year(s) ___month(s)

Section F

Background Information Questions
Please   answer the following five background information items.
1 . You are: (Circle one)
   1 . Male
   2. Female
2. How much education have you completed? (Circle one)
   1. Less than high school.
   2. High school equivalency (GED).
   3. High school diploma.
   4. Some college, not currently enrolled.
   5. Some college, currently enrolled.
   6. Associate's degree.
   7. Bachelor's degree.
   8. Graduate or professional degree, not completed.
   9. Graduate or professional degree, completed.
3. Your current personal yearly gross income (before taxes and deductions) is: (Circle one)
   1. None.
   2. Under $5,000.
   3. $5,000-$14,999.
   4. 15,000-$24,999.
   5. $25,000-$29,999.
   6. $30,000-$39,999.
   7. $40,000-$49,999.
   8. $50,000-$74,999.
   9. $75,000-$100,000.
   10. Over $100,000.
4. Your race is: (Circle one)
   1. African (Black)
   2. Asian
   3. Caucasian (White)
   4. American Indian
   5. Latino (Mexican-American, Puerto Rican, Cuban, etc.)
   6. Mixed/biracial

       7.   Other

  5. Your religious affiliation is: (Circle one)

       1.   Catholic

       2.   Protestant

       3.   Latter-day Saint (Mormon)

       4.   Jewish

       5.   Islamic

       6.   Eastern religion (Buddhist, Hindu, etc.)

       7.   Other

       8.   None

Appendix C

A Century-End Comprehensive Review of Premarital Predictors of Marital Quality and Stability

Steven T. Linford and Jason S. Carroll

We provided a brief review of the literature of premarital prediction of later marital quality in Chapter 1, and elaborated and extended that review in each of the succeeding data chapters (Chapters 3–7) of the book. Despite this, we believe it is useful to provide a somewhat different type of review here. Most literature reviews simply review the *findings* of previous research without providing a more comprehensive review of the theoretical positions taken (if any), the sample characteristics, the measurement of variables, and the analytic procedures used to conduct the studies. Without this important information it is difficult to analyze and compare findings. Also, this particular area of premarital prediction has a very long history (by social science standards, anyway) and some of the early works are difficult to find, very long, and their results are often "hidden" in various spots throughout them. Therefore, in preparation for testing our final model (Chapter 8) and to help future researchers in this area, it seemed beneficial for us to provide a detailed examination of the literature, particularly of the truly longitudinal premarital-to-marital studies. Also, we believe that the timing of this review is fitting in that it comes at the end of the century that ushered in marital prediction research. It is our hope that this review, along with the other information presented in this book, will provide researchers, educators, and clinicians with a foundation on which to build in helping couples more successfully manage the transition to marriage in the twenty-first century.

The review presented here has been organized so that it can be used in tandem with the literature review table in Chapter 8 (Table 8.1). Therefore, following the structure set forth in that table, we divide our review here according to the research design utilized in each study. First, we review the 11 published longitudinal studies for which data were initially collected premaritally, and then follow-up data collected maritally. After these 11 studies, longitudinal studies with "ambiguous relationship statuses" are reviewed, followed by longitudinal studies wherein *premarital data were collected retrospectively.* Following these reviews of the longitudinal studies, we present a brief review of *cross-sectional studies* of marital quality that retrospectively investigated premarital variables. Next, *four reviews of the research* are summarized. The 11 longitudinal studies that collected data premaritally and then maritally are reviewed in a great amount of depth and detail. However, each successive type of research is less thoroughly reviewed, since each type of research protocol moved further from the ideal of premarital-to-marital longitudinal design. The research is reviewed chronologically within each category. Because we presented our critiques of each study in the table in Chapter 8 (see "Comments" column, Table 8.1), the review presented here is, for the most part, descriptive in nature. Our primary purpose is to present detailed accounts of the studies, so that readers can make their own critique of the research to date. To match the table in Chapter 8, we present our review of each study under three organizational headings: (1) Purpose and Theoretical Perspective, (2) Participants and Methods, and (3) Results and Implications.

Longitudinal Studies: Premarital to Marital

Adams (1946)

Purpose and Theoretical Perspective

One of the earliest longitudinal studies on premarital factors that predict later marital quality and stability was reported by Adams in 1946. The purpose of that study was to "see if information obtained *before* marriage could be used to predict adjustment *after* marriage" (p. 85). No theoretical perspective was explicitly used to guide this study. However, in reviewing the measures used, it is clear that Adams's study focused on identifying the predictive ability of three premarital variables: background, personality, and attitudes about marriage.

Participants and Methods

Between 1939 and 1945, data were collected premaritally on 4000 students at The Pennsylvania State College. The premarital survey used was entitled

"The Prediction Scale for Happiness" (Terman, 1938) and consisted of 143 items divided into four parts. Part I, titled "Interests and Attitudes," included 54 items taken from Bernreuter's (1931) Personality Inventory. Part II, "General Likes and Preferences," consisted of 54 items from Strong's (1927) Vocational Interest Blank. Part III, "Your Views About the Ideal Marriage," contained 24 questions pertaining to husband–wife relationships. Part IV, "Parents and Childhood," had 11 items dealing with family background. Three demographic questions about age, sex, and educational level were also included in the survey.

Adams also had the 4000 students complete the Personal Audit and the Personal Inventory I. The Personal Audit was constructed by Adams and Lepley (1945) and contained nine tests, each consisting of 50 items, that measured the relatively independent personality factors of seriousness, firmness, tranquility, frankness, stability, tolerance, steadiness, persistence, and contentment. The Personal Inventory I, developed by Guilford and Martin (1943), consisted of 150 questions that measured three factors: objectivity, agreeableness, and cooperativeness.

Students who had completed a premarital test form, were then followed into marriage. Data were then collected maritally, and in no case were marital data collected when the couple had been married for less than 6 months. As the dependent variable, Adams used a combination of measures that he entitled "Appraisal of Marital Happiness." This measure consisted of Terman's (1938) Psychological Factors in Marital Happiness instrument, which was similar to Burgess and Cottrell's (1939) Index of Marital Adjustment. Where Terman's and Burgess and Cottrell's surveys differed, items from each were included. Furthermore, 13 questions measuring marital happiness that had been developed by Hamilton (1929) were also included. The data were scored into three separate marital adjustment measures: Terman, Hamilton, and Burgess and Cottrell. In addition to the items pertaining to marital adjustment, 20 demographic items regarding education, parental approval of marriage, length of courtship, and so on, were included as well as 13 questions dealing with sexual adjustment.

Adams limited his study to 100 married couples. For the 100 couples, both husband and wife completed and returned the questionnaires. The husbands' average age was 26.4 years, and that of their wives was 24.1 years. The average length of marriage was 2.36 years. The 100 couples had a total of 44 children: 18 boys and 26 girls. However, it was not specified how many of the couples had children.

Results and Implications

The marital adjustment scores of the 100 couples showed that regardless of the scoring technique employed, husbands tended to have higher mean adjustment scores than did wives. None of the 100 husbands in the sample had seriously contemplated divorce, although 3 had seriously contemplated separation. However, of the 100 wives, 12 had seriously considered separation, including 6 who had seriously contemplated divorce.

Adams's study provided correlations between the forms or questionnaires administered *before* marriage and the adjustment or satisfactions scores determined *after* marriage. Based on the results, Terman's "Prediction Scale," which primarily measures personality and background variables, had significant, but not high, positive correlations with the three measures of happiness or adjustment in marriage for both husband and wife (correlations ranging from $r = .24$ to $r = .38$). Correlations for husbands and wives were quite similar in each of the three scales.

The results for the Personal Audit measures showed several significant correlations. Adams reported that men who were tranquil, frank, and steady before marriage were likely to be happier in marriage than those who were irritable, evasive, and emotional. Adams also found that women who were frank, stable, and contented before marriage were more likely to be well-adjusted in marriage than those who were evasive, unstable, worried, or discontented.

Correlations for the Personal Inventory I scales were computed only with the Terman adjustment scale. For the husbands the correlations were as follows: .11 for *objectivity,* .16 for *agreeableness,* .14 for *cooperativeness;* the correlations for the wives were respectively .09, .18, and .21. Adams noted that "while none of the correlations were high, several are found to be significant and possibly helpful in premarital counseling" (p. 189).

Adams also correlated the paired scores on the Personal Audit for the 100 couples. Five of the nine personality factors were reported as "approaching" significance. Adams concludes that these findings suggest that individuals tended to select mates whose personality traits were similar to their own. This was especially the case with the traits of seriousness, stability, tolerance, persistence, and contentment. Another finding was that wives tended to marry men who were less tranquil, less frank, less stable, and more tolerant than they were.

In summary, Adams drew several "tentative" conclusions from the results of his study. First, adjustment or happiness in marriage can be measured reliably. Second, husbands reported slightly higher happiness scores and had contemplated separation or divorce less than did wives. Third, the three tests of marital adjustment were fairly similar, correlating from .72 to .83. Fourth, Terman's "Prediction Scale" (1938) seems to have some value in predicting marital happiness, although correlations were not high. Fifth, men who were tranquil, frank, and stable as described by the Personal Audit (Adams & Lepley, 1945) before marriage appeared somewhat happier in marriage than those found to be irritable, evasive, and emotional. Sixth, women whose "Audit Scores" before marriage indicated frankness, stability, and contentment seemed to be happier in marriage than those who were evasive, unstable, and discontented. Finally, significant resemblances in personality traits were found between husbands and wives, especially with the traits of seriousness, stability, tolerance, persistence, and contentment.

Terman and Oden (1947)

Purpose and Theoretical Perspective

In 1947, Terman and Oden published the book *The Gifted Child Grows Up*. This book reports a portion of the findings from a 25-year longitudinal study of gifted individuals. In broad terms, Terman and Oden (p. 2) described the purpose of this study as setting out to answer the question, "What are the physical, mental, and personality traits that are characteristic of intellectually superior children, and what sort of adult does the typical gifted child become?" While this study investigated a number of different aspects related to the adult lives of gifted individuals, the results that are of interest to our review here were presented in two chapters of the book: Chapter 18 entitled "Marriage, Divorce, Marital Selection, and Offspring" and Chapter 19 entitled "Marital Adjustment." No specific theoretical perspective was used in this study, but like many of the prediction studies of its time, there was a clear focus on background and personality factors.

Participants and Methods

In the 1920s, data were gathered on 1528 (857 male and 671 female) gifted individuals who were living in California. The individuals selected for this study ranged in age from first grade to high school. The "gifted," as identified in this study, were comprised of those who scored in the top 1% of the general school population on one of four national intelligence tests (Stanford-Binet, Terman Group Test, National Intelligence Test, or Army Alpha).

Data were originally collected on the participants' developmental history, school achievement, health and medical information, character, interests, personality, and home ratings. The subjects were primarily Caucasian and of European descent. The subjects' parents were highly educated, having received 4 to 5 years of additional schooling beyond the average person in their generation. The gifted subjects were generally raised in wealthy homes, with their families' median income being twice as high as that of the general population in California.

Many of the subjects were recontacted several years after they were originally selected and surveyed. In 1940, data were gathered on the marital history of 800 of the gifted men and 624 of the gifted women. The mean age at time of marriage was 23.4 years for the women and 25.2 years for the men. In addition to the marital history data, information was also gathered on the marriages of the gifted in two other areas relevant to this review: marital happiness and marital aptitude. The construct *marital aptitude* was defined by Terman and Oden as a measurement of the "personality factors and the factors in childhood and family background that contribute to one's chances of marital success or failure" (p. 252). While this type of measurement strays from this review's focus on marital quality and stability, we include those findings here because Terman and Oden made an effort to show how their measure of aptitude was related to marital happiness. It should be noted, however, that much of the marital aptitude information was gathered retrospectively and then correlated with a concurrent measure of marital happiness. In this regard, the marital aptitude data reported by Terman and Oden are best compared with the findings of the cross-sectional studies found in a later section of this review.

Terman and Oden measured *marital happiness* by asking respondents questions about 15 aspects of marriage. The marital happiness questions focused on common interests, agreement, conflict resolution, recreation, regret of marriage, choice of spouse, contemplation of separation or divorce, admission of unhappiness, spending leisure time with spouse, happiness when alone together, irritation or boredom with spouse, spouse's personality, certainty that no other spouse would have been so satisfactory, a subjective rating of happiness, and a report of the faults of the spouse.

The test used to measure the *marital aptitude* of the gifted subjects consisted of three categories of questions: personality (117 items), childhood and family background (33 items), and background of the marriage (30 items). In order to conceal the purpose of the test (i.e. to measure marital aptitude), all three parts were administered in an eight page questionnaire booklet entitled "Personality and Temperament."

A total of 636 gifted participants and their spouses took the marital happiness and marital aptitude questionnaires at the 1940 follow-up. However, the analyses were based on the first 567 couples (317 gifted men and their wives, and 250 gifted women and their husbands) who completed the test.

Results and Implications

Terman and Oden looked at the predictive value of data gathered in the 1920s to later *marital happiness* measured in 1940. They found that there was no correlation between IQs or the "achievement quotient" of 1922 and later marital happiness. However, some personality measures were shown to be significant predictors. For example, wives of gifted men who were shown to demonstrate "above average masculinity of play interests" tended to have a lower happiness score; however, there was no relationship for husbands in this area. Another finding was that husbands who, in 1922, rated low in "sociability" as indicated in their play interests, averaged lower in marital happiness than did others. Emotional stability also tended to be somewhat associated with higher levels of happiness in marriage for both husbands and wives.

An interests test given in 1923 also seemed to have some predictive value. It found that medium range scores for "social interests," rather than extreme scores (high or low), were related to greater marital happiness of husbands, and that wives who scored high in intellectual interests averaged below other wives in happiness. The ratings on 25 personality traits by parents and teachers in 1922, and similar ratings on 12 traits in 1928, yielded no statistically reliable correlation with the 1940 marital happiness scores. The same was true of the 1922 and 1928 data on nervous symptoms and social adjustment. Terman and Oden also reported that "little or no correlation was found between marital happiness scores and birth order, number of opposite-sex siblings, attachment to siblings, childhood residence, history of sex shock, adolescent 'petting,' amount of religious training, rated adequacy of sex instruction, and many other variables having to do with childhood and family situations" (p. 247).

All three components of Terman and Oden's measure of *marital aptitude* (personality, childhood and background, and background of marriage) were shown to be moderately correlated with the concurrent measure of marital satisfaction. This was found to be particularly true for the personality and background of marriage items (correlations ranging from $r = .43$ to $r = .52$). In fact, when the childhood and family background items were combined with the personality items, there were only minimal increases for both men and women (from $r = .45$ to $r = .48$ for wives and $r = .52$ to $r = .53$ for husbands). From these findings the authors conclude that "the effects of childhood and family background are nearly all contained in the personality items themselves" (p. 258).

Using longitudinal case history data gathered during the 1920s, ratings of "social adjustment," "social maladjustment," and "general adjustment" were shown to be predictive of later marital aptitude measured in 1940. In fact, social adjustment ratings from as far back as 1922 (18 years previous) were shown to have a "fairly significant" correlation with marital aptitude. Terman and Oden conclude that these data on marital aptitude "support the hypothesis that one's marital happiness, is to a considerable extent, determined by all-round happiness of temperament and personality" (p. 258).

Burgess and Wallin (1953)

Purpose and Theoretical Perspective

In 1953, Burgess and Wallin published the results of a large-scale, 5-year longitudinal study in a book entitled *Engagement and Marriage*. In this study, noted as "the most ambitious yet undertaken" (p. 44), the major goal was to see "whether information secured from persons *before* marriage would predict their marital success or failure" (p. 44). Similar to the other prediction studies of the 1940s and 1950s, no theoretical perspective was noted in this study.

Participants and Methods

This study began with 1000 engaged couples recruited largely from students attending colleges and universities in metropolitan Chicago and followed 666 of these couples for the next 3 to 5 years. For this study, Burgess and Wallin used an "extended" definition of *engagement* that not only included formally engaged couples, but also included couples with an informal but definite understanding that they would be married at some future date. The "engagement data" were gathered between 1937 and 1939 (Time 1), and the "marital data" were gathered from 1940 to 1943 (Time 2).

Information about the couples was gathered by three questionnaires and an interview. The first questionnaire, filled out by all 1000 couples, consisted of items measuring variables that had been identified in an earlier study (Burgess & Cottrell, 1939) as predictors of success in marriage. The questionnaire also included items that measured the adjustment of the couples in their engagements, as well as a large number of questions about the subjects' personalities. A short time later, a second questionnaire was filled out by the 226 couples who were seen for interviews. These couples were asked to complete a 14-page questionnaire, referred to as the "engagement interview schedule," at the time they were interviewed. This questionnaire was designed to secure additional information from the couple about their sex experiences, relations to parents, previous emotional involvements, and the dynamics of mate selection and love.

A third questionnaire was filled out by the individuals who distributed the engagement schedules. This form asked these "distributors" to make a number of predictions regarding the marital happiness of the couples based on additionally gathered data such as respondents' socioeconomic status and ratings of personality traits. These prediction data were gathered for approximately 80% of the 1000 couples. No explicit information is given about the status of the "distributors," but it can be inferred that many of them were college students who placed questionnaires as part of a class assignment.

Out of the 1000 originally engaged couples, 150 broke off their engagements, leaving 850 couples who married. From the 850 couples, 33 married and subsequently divorced or separated, and 10 of the marriages experienced the death of either the husband or the wife. Thus, 807 eligible married couples participated in the follow-up portion of the study. Completed questionnaires were received from 666 of the possible 807, resulting in a return rate of approximately 80%.

The data were gathered when the majority of the couples (73.2%) had been married 3 to 5 years. The marriage schedule or questionnaire was 18 pages in length and contained all of the questions that were found to be "predictively significant" in Terman and Oden's (1947) study, as well as items that were designed to measure marital happiness (measured with Terman's [1938] and Burgess and Cottrell's [1939] scales of marital adjustment), sexual aspects of marriage, common interests and activities, and personality items.

In addition to the marriage schedule, data were also obtained from two friends of each couple; the friends filled out forms containing questions about the success of the couple's marriage, as well as the personality characteristics of the couple. In all, 811 of these forms were obtained, which reported on 470 couples, resulting in less than two forms per couple. Interviews were also held with 124 married couples. These couples were among the 226 who were originally interviewed at the time they were engaged. The interviews focused on the problems of marital adjustment, the influence of children on the parents' relationship, and the satisfaction or dissatisfaction of their marriage.

The individuals in the final sample were primarily Caucasian and from lower-middle and upper-middle socioeconomic conditions. Generally, the participants had highly educated parents and were mostly Protestant (52.4% of the men and 57.5% of the women). The average age at marriage for the sample group was 25.7 years for the men and 23.9 years for the women. Previous to marriage, the average time of acquaintance of the couple was 45.0 months. Furthermore, the couples had dated for an average of 31.5 months, and had been engaged, on average, for 13.2 months. At the time of follow-up, 71.1% of the couples had one or more children. In sum, the sample consisted of individuals who were "largely urban, predominately middle-class, and largely of high school or college level of education" (p. 58). When compared with those who did not complete the Time 2 follow-up, the persons in the sample were younger, had more education, and were rated as being more liberal in their social and political views and as more likely to be successful in marriage. The statistical techniques used to analyze the data were partial and multiple correlation.

Results and Implications

Deciphering the results of this study is somewhat difficult, because Burgess and Wallin reported their results together with the results of other studies (i.e., Burgess & Cottrell, 1939; Terman & Oden, 1947). Because of this effort to compile several studies' findings together, there are some portions of their chapters where it is difficult to know if they are referring to the data of this or another study. We have made a detailed effort to pull out the unique findings that this study offered.

The findings of Burgess and Wallin's study suggest that several background items are predictive of later marital success, namely, parent–child interaction, economic behavior, premarital sexual intercourse, development of couple identity, personality traits, and consensus. In conjunction with this, Burgess and Wallin reported that "a young person has better than an average chance of marital success if he has been reared in a home of education and culture where the parents are happily mated, where they have close and affectionate relations with their children, and where discipline is kindly but firm and physical punishment rare" (p. 512). Background factors concerning sex attitudes and behaviors were also found to be correlated with success in marriage. In particular, it was noted that couples who did not engage in premarital sexual intercourse, and who received "wholesome" sex instruction, were more likely to have marital success. Overall, Burgess and Wallin reported a Pearson correlation coefficient of .31 for husbands and .27 for wives between background scores and marital success scores. Therefore, the authors note that the correlations demonstrate that "predictive items secured in engagement are associated with marital success scores obtained three to five years after marriage" (p. 519).

According to this study, another factor predictive of later marital success is the development of "couple companionship" during the engagement history. Couple companionship variables found to be predictive of later marital success included: confiding in one's mate, spending enjoyable leisure time together, being satisfied with the amount of affection, liking one's future in-laws, not disclosing about the relationship to others, having confidence that the future marriage will succeed, and objecting to one's partner having dates with others.

Burgess and Wallin noted several other relevant findings. These included: (1) an above average self-rating of childhood happiness was associated with marital success; (2) the socialization of the person, as measured by his sociability and institutional participation, was associated with marital success; (3) the so-called "economic factor" (i.e., amount of savings, regularity of employment, amount of income) in marital success was almost entirely accounted for by other factors, such as personality, family background, and social participation; (4) certain combinations of personality were favorable just as others are unfavorable to marital success; (5) the effect of contingencies occurring after marriage on marital happiness can probably be largely accounted for by premarital factors; (6) success in engagement was predictive of successful marriage; (7) men's premarital items showed a higher correlation than those of women with marital success; and (8) personality items that were found to be predictive of later marital success were emotional stability, consideration of others, yielding (opposite of dominating), companionable, self-confident, and emotionally dependent. In summarizing their results, Burgess and Wallin noted that "it is apparent that the prediction of success or failure in marriage now rests on a solid scientific basis. Predictive methods have met and passed the acid test of relating predictive data obtained before marriage with criteria of marital success secured after marriage" (p. 557).

Vaillant (1978)

Purpose and Theoretical Perspective

Vaillant's (1978) study entitled, "Natural History of Male Psychological Health: VI. Correlates of Successful Marriage and Fatherhood," was a 35-year follow-up on the relationship between quality of object relations and mental health. This study was conceptually guided by object relations and psychoanalytic theory. In accordance with this theoretical perspective, family of origin and other background variables were of primary interest.

Participants and Methods

This study, which began in the late 1930s, was an interdisciplinary study that sampled 268 men who had been selected from classes at a liberal arts college. During their sophomore year of college, all of these men were studied by an internist, a physiologist, an anthropologist, a psychologist, and a psychiatrist. In addition, a "family worker" made a home visit to each subject's parents. Over the next 30 years, the participants were followed with questionnaires and with a home interview when each respondent was 30 years of age.

This study involved a detailed and complex set of measures. Over the years of the study, observers blind to the other data of the study made independent ratings in 12 areas: childhood environment, social class, adult adjustment, psychiatric illness, maturity of defenses, physical health, object relations, social adjustment, participant's children outcome, drug and alcohol use, and "oral" behavior.

In 1966, 102 of the original 268 subjects were randomly selected for reinterview. From the 102 selected, 2 had dropped out of the study in college and 5 had died. Thus, 95 subjects remained in the study with no further attrition, except in the case of death. At the time of the last follow-up questionnaire in 1975, the average age of the participants was 54 years. In 1954 and 1967, all of the subjects rated their marital stability, marital harmony, and sexual adjustment. Their wives rated the same items in 1967 only. At the time of the 1967 ratings, the average age of the participants was 46 years. Based on these ratings, the subjects were grouped into four categories: (1) happy and stable marriages, (2) "intermediate" marriages, (3) marriages wherein divorce had been seriously considered and sexual relations were reported as being "not as good as wished," and (4) divorced, "without successful remarriage over a period of 10 years or more" (p. 654).

Results and Implications

This study found that experiencing a poor childhood environment did not significantly predict a poor marriage $r = .18$). It appear, that many men were able to overcome an unhappy childhood and have successful, satisfying marriages. Similarly, contrary to psychological theory, marital sexual adjustment seemed relatively independent of childhood environment and of maturity of defenses. Another result of this study was that men who were unhappily married were less likely to be married between the ages of 23 and 29, which suggests a possible curvilinear relationship between age at marriage and later marital satisfaction. It was also found that unhappily married men were less likely to have established independence from their mothers. In fact, of the men who had the poorest adult adjustments, all but two remained unusually dependent on their mothers.

Fowers and Olson (1986)

Purpose and Theoretical Perspective

In 1986, Fowers and Olson published an article entitled "Predicting Marital Success with PREPARE: A Predictive Validity Study". The purpose of the study was to assess the ability of the premarital inventory PREPARE in predicting later marital success. Fowers and Olson explained, "This paper describes a premarital inventory than can be used for preventative work with couples before marriage" (p. 404). They continued by saying that "this study will also provide more empirical data on early marital adjustment.... The empirical evidence, to date, is primarily descriptive and based on small samples. This study may provide the beginning of a more predictive analysis of relationship variables that seem important in the early dissolution of marriages" (p. 404). In larger terms, this study was guided by the theoretical idea that the level of attitude consensus between partners is predictive of marital success. In specific terms, this study was based on the hypothesis that satisfied couples would score significantly higher on the inventory than would dissatisfied couples, or couples who had canceled their upcoming marriages. It was also hypothesized that dissatisfied married couples would not differ significantly from couples who had broken off their engagement or those who had divorced.

The authors saw their work as building on the pioneering work of Burgess and Wallin (1953) and Terman and Oden (1947).

Participants and Methods

Fowers and Olson's study consisted of a 3-year follow-up with 164 couples who took the PREPARE inventory during their engagement. The premarital inventory PREPARE is a 125-item questionnaire designed to identify "relationship strengths" and "work areas" in 11 relationship areas: (1) Realistic Expectations, (2) Personality Issues, (3) Communication, (4) Conflict Resolution, (5) Financial Management, (6) Leisure Activities, (7) Sexual Relationship, (8) Children and Marriage, (9) Family and Friends, (10) Equalitarian Roles, and (11) Religious Orientation (Olson et al., 1986). A "Positive Couple Agreement" (PCA) score, which measures amount of couple consensus, is provided for each category. Besides the attitude scales, PREPARE also contains an Idealistic Distortion scale as well as background information such as age, education, monthly income, the number of months prior to the marriage that the couple took the inventory, parent reaction to the marriage, friend reaction to the marriage, parental marital status, birth position, number of siblings, population of the place of current residence, and population of the place of residence during childhood.

The sample for this study consisted of 164 couples (328 subjects) who had been married from 2 to 3 years, and who had taken PREPARE, while engaged, 3–4 months before marriage. This sample was selected by clergy who had previously administered PREPARE to the engaged couples. The clergy were asked to select 2–5 couples who were satisfied with their marriages and 2–5 couples who were divorced, separated, or dissatisfied with their marriages. The sample was subdivided into four categories based on their answers to a marital satisfaction survey. The four subgroups were: (1) "married-satisfied" (consisting of 59 married couples), (2) "married/dissatisfied" (consisting of 22 married couples), (3) "canceled" (consisting of 52 couples who canceled or delayed their marriages), and (4) "divorced or separated" (consisting of 31 couples). The average age of the husbands was 25.2 years and the wives, 23.2 years. The couples were primarily Caucasian, had attended some college, had a median annual income of $14,400, and were of a Christian religion.

Whereas the PREPARE inventory was used to gather data from the couples while they were engaged, a "couple questionnaire" was used in the follow-up study. This questionnaire consisted of a 10-item "Marital Satisfaction" scale taken from the marital inventory ENRICH (Olson et al., 1986) as well as an "Idealistic Distortion" scale, which was a 5-item version of the 15-item Idealistic Distortion scale included in PREPARE. The follow-up couple questionnaire also included several relevant background items. The background or demographic items consisted of age, sex, number of children, educational level, the number of months the couple had been married, income, the population of their current living area, their parents' marital status, and whether the couple had ever had any relationship counseling.

Results and Implications

The results of this study provide evidence that couple consensus about several relationship areas predicted membership to one of the four subgroups (i.e., married/satisfied, married/dissatisfied, canceled/delayed marriage, or separated/divorced). The predicting factors were realistic expectations, personality issues, communication, conflict resolution, leisure activity, sexuality, family and friends, religion, and the overall average couple positive agreement. However, the results showed that no significant differences between the groups existed in the areas of financial management, children and marriage, and equalitarian roles.

Another finding was that satisfactorily married couples differed from couples who separated or divorced in 10 of the 11 PREPARE categories as well as in the average overall Couple Positive Agreement score. Using discriminant analysis, the authors found that using PREPARE scores (both individual and couple [CPA] scores) from 3 months before marriage could predict with 80–90% accuracy which couples were separated and divorced from those who were happily married 2 to 3 years later. The premarital consensus areas that were most predictive were realistic expectations, personality issues, communication, conflict resolution, leisure activities, financial management, sexuality, family and friends, equalitarian roles, and religion.

Kelly and Conley (1987)

Purpose and Theoretical Perspective

In 1987, Kelly and Conley published a study entitled, "Personality and Compatibility: A Prospective Analysis of Marital Stability and Marital Satisfaction." The purpose of this study was to identify important premarital factors that predicted later marital stability and marital satisfaction. Two major theoretical perspectives were noted as influencing the design and interpretations of this study: "Intrapersonal" perspectives (psychoanalytic and trait theories) and "Interpersonal" (behavioral and social exchange theories). The authors noted that these two perspectives are not "mutually exclusive," due to the fact that "the second (interpersonal) perspective may be a description of the process by which the first (intrapersonal) perspective operates" (p. 27). However, despite noting the importance of both of these types of processes, Kelly and Conley only included measures of personality characteristics in this study. In particular, premarital factors of personality, social background, and attitudes were assessed before marriage and information on the sexual history of the couples was assessed from data gathered retrospectively.

Participants and Methods

This study was longitudinal in design and followed 300 couples over a period of 45 years. The 300 couples were recruited by Kelly between 1935 and 1938 to participate in a study of marital compatibility (Kelly, 1955). All of the couples in the sample were engaged to be married. The mean IQ of the subjects in the sample was 113, and approximately two-thirds had completed at least 1 year of college. Ninety percent of the participants lived in Connecticut or an adjacent state at the beginning of the study. All of the subjects were Caucasian. The majority of the subjects (94%) were between the ages of 20 and 30 when they entered the study and the median age of the subjects in 1980 was 68. A breakdown of the religious affiliation of the subjects shows that 69% were Protestant, 9% were Catholic, 7% were Jewish, and 15% gave no affiliation. Although the sample originally consisted of 300 couples, the pertinent parts of the follow-up analysis were completed by only 249 couples.

Major data were collected on the couples three times. Time 1 was collected between 1935 and 1938, Time 2 was collected between 1954 and 1955, and Time 3 was collected from 1980 to 1981. In 1935–38, the couples were measured and tested in person during an interview. In addition to the interview, five acquaintances of each couple were asked to rate the subjects on the Personality Rating Scale (Kelly, 1940). Also, each year, until 1941, the husband and the wife provided a report on their marital lives.

The data gathered in 1935–38 (Time 1) consisted of information pertaining to each subject's personality, social environment, and attitudes toward marriage. The personality trait ratings of the subjects included neuroticism, social extraversion, impulse control, and agreeableness. Five areas of early social environment were studied: (1) psychosocial instability of the family of origin, (2) emotional closeness of the family of origin, (3) nonconformity to social ideals, (4) religious practice in the family of origin, and (5) level of tension in the family of origin. Attitudes toward married life were measured by responses to 33 items included in a questionnaire entitled, "Views About the Ideal Marriage." The 33 items were part of five scales designed to measure companionate marriage, conventionality, equality of partners, premarital sex, and sexual fidelity.

In 1954–55 (Time 2), additional data were gathered on the sexual histories of the couples as well as the experience of stressful life events. Also in 1954–55, as well as 1980–81(Time 3), data were gathered on additional predictor variables, including: educational attainment of the participants, whether their parents were divorced, whether the participants had children, the status of the participant's principal occupation, and the relative influence of husband and wife in family decision making.

The criterion variables or dependent variables were marital stability, marital satisfaction, and "marital compatibility," a composite variable that combined the two. Marital satisfaction was measured in annual reports from 1935 to 1941(Time 1), using a single item with a seven-point scale ranging from "extraordinarily happy" to "extremely unhappy," and during the 1954–55 (Time 2) and 1980–81 (Time 3) follow-ups with the sum of four questions. In 1980, out of the 249 couples, 199 had remained married throughout the study (or were married at the time of death of one of the spouses) and 50 had divorced. Of the 50 couples who divorced, 39 of them divorced between 1935 and 1954 (classified as "early") and the 11 remaining couples divorced between 1955 and 1980 (classified as "late").

Results and Implications

Marital satisfaction was found to be negatively related to neuroticism in both sexes. Impulse control, measured in 1980 (Time 3), was positively correlated with marital satisfaction in both men and women. One aspect of early social environment, level of tension in family of origin, was predictive of marital satisfaction for men. For women, negative predictors of marital satisfaction were the psychosocial instability of the original family and their preadult nonconformity to social ideals. Emotional closeness of family of origin was a positive predictor of marital satisfaction for women. The number of stressful life events encountered in early adulthood negatively predicted marital satisfaction for both men and women. The only attitudinal factor that positively predicted marital satisfaction for men was favorable attitudes toward conventional order in the family. Sexual histories provided additional predictors of marital satisfaction. Premarital romantic/sexual involvements were negative predictors of marital satisfaction for both genders. Kelly and Conley concluded that "personality characteristics must be taken into account in a comprehensive analysis of marital interaction. Many of the disrupted patterns of communication and behavior exchange that recent researchers have noted in disturbed couples may be seen as the outgrowths of the personality characteristics of the partners" (p. 36).

Filsinger and Thoma (1988)

Purpose and Theoretical Perspective

In an effort to build on earlier longitudinal studies (Markman, 1979, 1981, reviewed in the "ambiguous relationship status" portion of this review), Filsinger and Thoma (1988) followed premarital couples over a 5-year period to investigate if couple interactional processes would predict later relationship adjustment and stability. This study was based on a behaviorist conceptualization of marriage that suggests that "successful marriages" are those "in which the benefits obtained from the relationship outweigh the costs" (p. 785). Filsinger and Thoma explained that "behavioral theory further holds that, over time, positive and negative exchanges lead to the current level of relationship adjustment. The etiology of adjustment, therefore, can be traced to the interaction pattern" (p. 786). Therefore, the purpose of Filsinger and Thoma's study was twofold: first, to identify potential behavioral antecedents of marital adjustment, and second, to assess how those behaviors relate to relationship adjustment and relationship stability.

Participants and Methods

The sample consisted of 21 couples who were observed five times over a 5-year period. The couples, living in a large southwestern city, responded to a newspaper advertisement seeking couples who were seriously contemplating marriage. The average ages of the males and females were 25.2 and 24.3 years, respectively. Approximately half of the males held full-time jobs in the community surrounding a university. The rest of the males, and all of the females were affiliated with the university. All of the subjects were Caucasian and childless. At the time of the 5th-year follow-up, 12 couples had become married and 8 couples had dissolved their relationships.

For their premarital assessment, Filsinger and Thoma used an observational design to rate communication patterns. Couples were asked to engage in a 15-minute discussion about a specific problem in their relationship that they had previously determined to be of "medium" intensity. The coders used the Dyadic Interaction Scoring Code (DISC; Filsinger, 1983) to rate and categorize positive and negative behaviors. Intercoder reliability was assessed for the new codes by using Cohen's (1960) kappa and reliability of the codes ranged from 63% to 75%. In addition to investigating negativity and positivity, this study also investigated "negative reciprocity," "positive reciprocity," and rate of interruptions. Reciprocity refers to one's immediate response when his/her partner makes a positive or negative statement. According to Filsinger and Thoma, "if the other partner immediately follows a negative (comment by his/her partner) with his or her own negative, it is called negative reciprocity. If the response is positive to the initial positive, it is called positive reciprocity" (p. 786, parentheses in original). At times 2 (6 months), 3 (1½ years), 4 (2½ years), and 5 (5 years), the couples were contacted by mail and asked to complete a questionnaire designed to measure dyadic adjustment and stability. Marital adjustment was measured using the Dyadic Adjustment Scale (DAS; Spanier, 1976).

Results and Implications

Two findings pertaining to dyadic adjustment were found. First, female interruptions were found to significantly predict male's dyadic adjustment at 1½ years $r = -.67, p < .05$), 2½ years $r = -.56, p < .01$), and 5 years $r = -.71, p < .01$); but not at 6 months $r = .30$). In other words, couples in which the female interrupted the male had lower levels of dyadic adjustment later in their relationship. Second, positive reciprocity by the male predicted female dyadic adjustment at 5 years $r = .50, p < .05$).

In comparing stable and unstable couples, this study found that marital instability measured at 1½, 2½, and 5-year follow-ups, was predicted by premarital indicators of negative reciprocity, positive reciprocity, and level of female interruptions. This differed from marital adjustment, which was found to only be consistently predicted by female interruptions measured premaritally. The authors concluded that these findings suggest that "the seed of later troubles may be associated with relationships in which a tit-for-tat style of interaction is characteristic" (p. 793).

Larsen and Olson (1989)

Purpose and Theoretical Perspective

In 1989, Larsen and Olson reported the results from a study that was designed to replicate the Fowers and Olson (1986) study. Similar to the previous project, the purpose of this study was to evaluate the predictive utility of the premarital inventory PREPARE. Also in accordance with the previous study, consensus of attitudes was the focus of analysis.

Participants and Methods

The sample consisted of 179 married couples who had taken PREPARE as engaged couples in 1982. All of the couples in the sample had been married for at least 2 years. PREPARE was administered to the premarital couples by their clergy or a premarital counselor, 4 months prior to their marriage. The subjects' average length of acquaintance previous to marriage was 32 months. The sample was primarily Caucasian (98%), and affiliated with a Christian church (95%). The mean age at marriage was 24 years for the men and 22 years for the women.

All of the married couples reported having at least one child, with an average of 1.71 children. In general, the sample of the 1989 study was quite similar to the 1986 study (reviewed above) in demographics such as age, length of acquaintance, education, and income.

Whereas PREPARE was administered premaritally, marital satisfaction was measured using the relationship assessment inventory ENRICH. The married couples were divided into two groups based on their ENRICH score. The upper third of the couples constituted the married/satisfied group (n = 49), while the lower third of the couples comprised the married/dissatisfied group (n = 57). The PREPARE counselors provided marital status information that was used to identify 36 couples who had divorced or separated, and another 37 couples who had canceled their marriages some time after taking PREPARE.

Results and Implications

This study concurred with Fowers and Olson (1986) in that they both indicated the importance of the scales measuring Realistic Expectations, Personality Issues, Conflict Resolution, Communication, Leisure Activities, Family and Friends, and Religious Orientation in differentiating between the married/satisfied and the married/dissatisfied groups. Both the 1986 and the 1989 studies did not find any predictive validity for the Financial Management or the Children and Parenting scales.

Smith, Vivian, and O'Leary (1990)

Purpose and Theoretical Perspective

In 1990, Smith et al. published a study entitled "Longitudinal Prediction of Marital Discord From Premarital Expressions of Affect." Using "social learning and systemic" theories that hold that "marital satisfaction is founded on good communication" (p. 790), this study set out to evaluate the association between affective or emotionally expressive features of premarital communication and marital relationship satisfaction. The authors stated that their study furthered the work of identifying longitudinal predictors of marital satisfaction for three reasons: (1) their use of observationally-coded marital communication samples, (2) their inclusion of all participants in the sample rather than selecting from the extreme tails of the marital satisfaction distribution, and (3) because of their use of a comprehensive dimensional measure of communicated affect.

Participants and Methods

The sample consisted of 91 couples who were a subset of those participating in the Stony Brook longitudinal study of spousal aggression. The sample originally consisted of 393 couples from which 127 couples were randomly selected to be interviewed 6 weeks before their marriage. From the 127 couples who were interviewed, audiotaped problem-solving discussions were produced for 91 couples. All of the subjects were Caucasian and had never been previously married. In 1983, the time of their premarital assessment, the couples averaged 25.17 years of age and 15.71 years of education. The men's average annual income was $19,203.08 and the women's was $13,647.94.

Along with the interview, couples were also asked to engage in a 10-minute discussion on a relationship issue about which they both disagreed. The interviewer left the room during these discussions, leaving the couples alone to discuss the issue during which they were audio-taped. These discussion sessions were then observationally coded using a system designed to measure the affective processes (e.g., pleased, sad, calm) rather than the actual content of the interaction. Confirmatory factor analysis was used to analyze these affective processes and create groupings or factors. This process resulted in three factors: "Negativity," "Positivity," and "Disengagement." *Positivity* was evidenced by friendliness, kindness, being relaxed and at ease, happiness, calmness, cheerfulness, lightheartedness, affectionate, tenderness, attentiveness, and interest. Items that factored into *negativity* were dissatisfied, upset, distressed, annoyed, anxious, disgusted, angry, aggressive, downhearted, aroused, tormented, bewildered, sad, fearful, hostile, sorry, startled, and surprised. *Disengagement* was described by being quiet, sluggish, silent, weary, tired, energetic, excited, sheepish, nervous, and quiescent.

Following the premarital assessment (Time 1), the couples were assessed again at 6, 18, and 30 months after their marriage. At each time the couples were asked to complete the Short Marital Adjustment Test (SMAT; Locke & Wallace, 1959), a 15-item inventory consisting of 8 items on level of agreement of certain issues and 7 items tapping general marital happiness, leisure time preferences, regrets about marriage, willingness to confide in spouse, and the typical outcome of marital disagreements.

Results and Implications

The results of this study showed that marital satisfaction increased from one time period to the next. Interestingly, the SMAT scores were lowest for the premarital couples. Another finding was that *premarital* negativity was correlated with *concurrent* relationship satisfaction; however, neither positivity nor disengagement correlated significantly with the remaining relationship satisfaction variance.

Unlike the premarital assessment stage, negativity at the 6-month post-marriage follow-up was no longer correlated with SMAT scores. At 18 months, premarital SMAT scores significantly predicted marital satisfaction, and disengagement emerged as a significant predictor beyond premarital SMAT $r = -.27, p < .05$). From these findings, the authors concluded that "because this effect is negative in direction, increases in marital satisfaction were associated with *increases* in engagement" (p. 795).

At 30 months after marriage, premarital relationship satisfaction continued to predict later marital satisfaction, although the strength of this effect was diminishing. As was the case at 18 months, at 30 months, disengagement was the only variable that predicted marital satisfaction $r = -.33, p < .01$). Smith et al. explained that "at 18-and 30- month follow-up assessments, premaritally assessed Disengagement was negatively related to marital satisfaction. The more satisfied couples at 18- and 30- month follow-ups were those who at premarriage could be characterized as communicating about problems in a nonquiet, non-sluggish, nonsilent, energetic, and excited manner" (p. 796). In a later review of these findings, Smith et al. (1991) concluded that while negative communication proves to be "truly negative" in current marital functioning, "it would be a misnomer to attach this label when discussing these variables in a causal or predictive sense" (p. 17).

Holman, Larson, and Harmer (1994)

Purpose and Theoretical Perspective

In 1994, Holman et al. reported the results of a study, the purpose of which was to "describe the development of a comprehensive (multi-item/multi-concept) premarital assessment instrument, the PREParation for Marriage Questionnaire, or PREP-M" (Holman et al., 1989, p. 46) and to "evaluate the ability of the questionnaire to predict marital satisfaction and stability one year after marriage" (p. 46). The conceptual thinking underlying the PREP-M questionnaire was pre-dominately drawn from the social exchange and symbolic interactionist perspectives. Two hypotheses were tested in this study: (1) "that the higher the premarital PREP-M scores, the higher the marital satisfaction and marital stability of those individuals who had married" and (2) "that those who were married and most satisfied or were married and most stable would have significantly higher mean scores on the PREP-M than those who were married with lower satisfaction, married with lower stability, or who had canceled or delayed marriage" (p. 47).

Participants and Methods

The study consisted of 103 engaged couples, or 206 individuals who took the PREP-M in late 1989 or early 1990. The majority of the participants grew up in the western United States (68%) and were predominately Caucasian (95%). The participants ranged in education from completion of high school to graduate work, with the majority having completed some college (72%). The participants had a mean age of 22.0 years, and ranged in age from 17 to 48 years. Most of the participants were students (69%), with some professionals (12%) and service employees (8%). The respondents identified their religious affiliation predominately as Latter-day Saint (Mormon) (80%), with 9% identifying themselves as Protestant, and another 5% as Catholic.

The PREP-M is a multivariate questionnaire that measures partners' responses in five content areas: "Couple Unity in Values, Attitudes, and Beliefs" (8 scales, 38 items), "Personal Readiness" (9 scales, 36 items), "Partner Readiness" (8 scales, 30 items), "Couple Readiness" (5 scales, 30 items), and "Background and Home Environment" (6 scales, 44 items). Each of these scales, except for the Partner Readiness scale, is used to compute a total PREP-M score for each respondent.

Of the 103 couples who took the PREP-M premaritally, at the 1-year follow-up, 91couples had married and 18 individuals had either canceled or delayed their marriage. Six individuals could not be contacted. Questionnaires were sent to all of the married couples and 85 couples returned their completed questionnaires, resulting in a 93% response rate.

The criterion variables in this study were marital stability and marital satisfaction. Marital stability was measured by responses to three items: (1) "if the respondent had ever thought the marriage was in trouble," (2) "if getting a divorce had ever crossed his/her mind," and (3) "if the spouses had ever suggested divorce to each other" (p. 48). Marital satisfaction was examined by respondents' ratings on their satisfaction in 32 areas of the marital relationship from the Marital Comparison Level Index (MCL; Sabatelli, 1984). Respondents selected answers using a five-point Likert scale ranging from "very dissatisfied" to "very satisfied."

Results and Implications

The results confirmed the study's hypotheses. First, higher PREP-M scores were associated with higher subsequent marital satisfaction and marital stability scores. Correlations were computed of total PREP-M and PREP-M scales with marital satisfaction and marital stability. All of the 44 correlations, with the exception of one, were in the hypothesized direction, and 26 of the correlations were significant at the .05 level. Another finding was that husbands' PREP-M scores appeared to be more highly correlated with their later marital satisfaction and stability than the wives' (with marital satisfaction; husbands $r = .44$, $p <$

.01; wives $r = .23; p < .01$). The results also suggest that PREP-M scores predict later marital satisfaction and stability for both members of the couple. Furthermore, PREP-M scores were related more to marital satisfaction than to marital stability.

The findings also confirmed the study's second hypothesis in that the individuals in satisfying and stable marriages had higher mean scores on the PREP-M than did those in the least satisfied/stable marriages, or those who had canceled or delayed their marriage. Analysis of variance was used to compare the means of husbands and wives in five groups: married satisfied, married stable, married dissatisfied, married unstable, and canceled/delayed. It was found that PREP-M scores distinguished between those who were most satisfied and stable in their marriages and those who were least satisfied and stable in their marriages 1 year after their marriage. In fact, the married satisfied means were a full standard deviation above the means for the married dissatisfied and the canceled/delayed groups. The finding was basically the same in the area of marital stability. The canceled/delayed group had the lowest premarital score of any group, indicating that their choice not to marry was probably wise.

Fowers, Montel, and Olson (1996)

Purpose and Theoretical Perspective

In a recent study, Fowers et al. investigated the validity of a premarital typology in predicting later marital satisfaction and stability. The premarital couple types used in this study were developed by Fowers and Olson (1992) in earlier cross-sectional work, but had yet to be tested for their predictive value in terms of later marital quality. In particular, the authors noted that "the most appropriate test of a typology of premarital couples would involve a prospective examination of the marital outcomes of the four couple types. It was expected that couples in the four types would have distinct outcomes over the first 2 to 3 years of marriage" (p. 106). While this study did not use an explicit theoretical perspective, it is similar to these researchers' earlier studies (Fowers & Olson, 1986; Larsen & Olson, 1989) in that it used a multivariate approach and focused on levels of couple agreement.

Participants and Methods

In 1992, Fowers and Olson developed a typology of premarital couples based on the premarital inventory PREPARE with a sample of over 5000 engaged couples. As noted previously, the PREPARE inventory has 11 scales that assess a variety of areas of premarital relationship quality. Using couple's agreement scores on these scales, Fowers and Olson (1992) found four types of premarital couples, which they termed "Vitalized," "Harmonious," "Traditional," and "Conflicted." *Vitalized couples* were found to have a high overall premarital relationship satisfaction and expressed a very high level of comfort with their ability to discuss feelings and resolve problems together. The couples reported high levels of consensus in other areas of their relationship (e.g., affection, financial matters) and saw religion as important to their marriages. *Harmonious couples* were defined as having a moderate level of overall relationship quality and were relatively satisfied with communication and problem-solving processes in their relationship. However, these couples differed from vitalized couples in that they had less realistic expectations for marriage, less consensus on parenting and child issues, and indicated that religion was not an important part of their relationships. *Traditional couples* had a PREPARE profile that suggested moderate dissatisfaction with interactional areas of their relationship (i.e., communication and conflict resolution) and their partners' personal habits. However, these couples had strong consensus in areas that involved decision making and future planning. Traditional couples also tended to have a realistic view of marriage and saw religion as very important in their marriages. *Conflicted couples* showed distress on all of the PREPARE scales. They reported dissatisfaction with their partners' personality and habits and had problems in their ability to communicate and resolve problems. Problems also existed for these couples in areas of leisure activities, their sexual relationship, and relating to one another's families and friends.

In this current study, Fowers et al. (1996) designed a two-stage longitudinal study to test the predictive value of their premarital couple typology. The sample for this study included 393 couples (786 individuals) who were part of the authors' two previous predictive studies using PREPARE (Fowers & Olson, 1986; Larsen & Olson, 1989). The two distinct samples from these previous studies were combined for the analyses conducted in this study. Participants completed PREPARE with a clergy member or counselor 3–4 months before their marriage. They were followed up 2–3 years later. At the time they took the PREPARE inventory, the average age for the men was 25.1 years and for the women was 23.2 years. The sample was primarily Caucasian (95%) and all belonged to a Christian religion.

As noted previously, PREPARE is a 125-item inventory designed to identify relationship strength and work areas in 11 relationship areas. At follow-up, participants completed the ENRICH Marital Satisfaction (EMS) scale. This measure is a 15-item scale that includes a 10-item Likert format measure of global marital satisfaction and a 5-item idealistic distortion scale that was used as a correction for the tendency to overreport marital satisfaction.

Counselors and clergy who administered PREPARE were contacted to solicit their assistance in obtaining the sample for the follow-up. In all, 564 couples who were married at the time of the follow-up were asked to complete the follow-up questionnaire and 237 returned useable responses, which resulted in a 42% response rate. PREPARE users also identified 89 couples who had canceled their marriage plans and another 67 couples were identified who were separated or divorced at the follow-up. Combined with the 237 married couples, the total sample comprised 393 couples. As noted in the review of the previous studies (Fowers & Olson, 1986; Larsen & Olson, 1989), scores on the EMS scale were used to divide the married couples into married/satisfied and married/dissatisfied groups.

Results and Implications

Using a *k* means cluster analysis algorithm, the authors found that the sample for this current study fit their typology of premarital couples. Specifically, 114 couples were identified as Conflicted couples (29%), 90 as Traditional couples (23%), 97 as Harmonious couples (25%), and 92 as Vitalized couples (23%). With these couple types several analyses were conducted. As anticipated, Conflicted couples were most likely to have canceled their marriage plans, followed by Traditional, Harmonious, and Vitalized couples. Similarly, the Conflicted couple type had the greatest proportion of separated and divorced couples. In fact, nearly half (48%) of the couples in this outcome group were Conflicted couples. Of note, Traditional couples were found to be the least likely to have separated or divorced, with a lower likelihood than Harmonious or Vitalized types.

Other analyses found that the likelihood of being in the satisfactorily married outcome group was quite variable across the four types and that, at the individual level of analysis, marital satisfaction was highest among individuals in Vitalized couples, followed by spouses in Harmonious, Traditional, and Conflicted couples. The author's concluded that "the results of this study offer clear support for the external validity of the premarital typology developed by Fowers and Olson (1992)" and that "the four couple types differed in their marital outcomes in a predicted manner" (p. 113).

Holman, Linford, Brooks, Olsen, Rhoades, and Carroll (Chapter 8, this volume)

As noted in Table 8.1 of the current volume, four multivariate studies have been done by Thomas B. Holman and his associates during the last several years. Each of these four studies is detailed in this book for the first time. Since each of these studies received detailed attention in Chapter 8, the reader is referred there for a full review of the methods and results of these studies.

Longitudinal Studies where the Relationship Status Is Ambiguous

It is possible that the studies reviewed in this section fit in the preceding section in that data were collected on couples before they married. However, these studies did not specify the participants' marital status (i.e., whether married, engaged, seriously dating, or cohabiting) at the time of the follow-up(s). Therefore, these studies are about premarital couples and their later relationship satisfaction, probably later marital satisfaction, although it is unclear from the research reports whether all of the couples had married or not.

Markman (1979, 1981)

Purpose and Theoretical Perspective

Here we review two published studies simultaneously, because the second study was merely a report of an additional follow-up done with the same sample. Markman (1979, 1981) is largely credited with initiating the first longitudinal research designed specifically to investigate the power of premarital communication patterns in predicting marital satisfaction. The hypothesis under examination in this study was to test the assertion of behavioral models of marriage that unrewarding couple interaction precedes marital distress. The purpose of this study was twofold: first, to test the hypothesis by using a longitudinal design, and second, to increase understanding of the development of marital distress.

Participants and Methods

There were four stages in the design of this study: initial interview and laboratory sessions (Time 1), 1-year follow-up (Time 2), 2½-year follow-up (Time 3), and 5½-year follow-up (Time 4). The study originally began with 26 premarital couples; however, due to couple breakup and missing data, results were drawn from 14 couples at Times 2 and 3, and only 9 couples at Time 4. The participants of the study originally consisted of 26 couples, some of whom were students who received credit, and others who responded to a newspaper advertisement. The participants' average age was 20.3 years, and they had been acquainted with their partners an average of 32.2 months.

In this study, couples were asked briefly to discuss five tasks, plus the major problem area in their relationship that they had previously determined. While they talked, each couple used a "talk table" (Gottman et al.,1976) to rate the intended impact (intent) and actual impact (impact) of their statements on a five-point scale ranging from "supernegative" (1) to "superpositive" (5). The "impact ratings" were designed to create a measure of perceived positivity of the interaction from the listener's perspective, while the "intent ratings" were designed to measure the intended positivity from the speaker's perspective.

Results and Implications

The results of this study indicated that while perceived positivity/negativity of communication when discussing a current problem area was not associated with relationship satisfaction at follow-up 1 year later, it was highly correlated with the level of marital satisfaction reported at follow-up after 2½ years $r = 0.67, p < .01, N = 14$) and 5½ years $r = .59, p < .05, N = 9$). In other words, the more positively couples rated their premarital communication, the more satisfied they were with their marital relationship 2½ and 5½ years later. From these findings, Markman (1981) concluded that "communication and problem-solving deficits are etiologically related to the development and maintenance of marital distress" (p. 761).

In a later report, Markman (1984) presented the data from the "intended impact" or speaker's ratings. For the males' intent ratings, there was no significant relationship with Time 1 (Premarital) or Time 2 (1-year follow-up) couple relationship satisfaction. However, there was a significant relationship with Time 3 (2½-year follow-up) relationship satisfaction $r = .55, p < .01$). This relationship was still positive at Time 4 (5-year follow-up), but was no longer significant $r = .39$). The female intended positivity ratings followed a similar pattern, but the Time 3 correlation failed to reach the .05 level of significance. Markman concluded that "the more positive the males intended their communication to be at Time 1, the more satisfied the couple was at Time 3 (2½ years later)" (p. 261).

In this later report of his earlier longitudinal data, Markman (1984) also reported the predictive power of the intended impact in terms of the relative frequency of each button (superpositive, positive, negative, supernegative) pressed. These findings showed that the best predictor of Time 3 (2½-year follow-up) relationship satisfaction was the relative frequency of use of the negative buttons. This finding held true for both male negative intent $r = -.73, p < .001$) and female negative intent $r = -.62, p < .005$).

Markman, Duncan, Storaasli, and Howes (1987)

Purpose and Theoretical Perspective

In 1987, Markman and his colleagues reported the results of a study designed to build on his earlier work (Markman, 1979, 1981, 1984). Similar to the previous studies, the purpose of this study was to test whether or not

dysfunctional communication precedes and possibly causes marital dissatisfaction. However, this study differed from Markman's previous work in that it
also included an intervention component. A portion of the sample participated in
the Premarital Relationships Enhancement Program (PREP) and a major purpose
of this study was to test the effectiveness of this program by comparing the
couples who participated in the intervention with those who did not. This study
also differed from the earlier ones in that it also focused on personality factors
and individual psychological adjustment and their potential connection to later
relationship functioning.

Participants and Methods

Markman and his associates hoped to expand the generalizabilty of their
previous findings by using a larger ($N =$ 135 couples), more heterogeneous
sample in this study. The participants' average ages were 23.3 and 24.1 years for
the females and males, respectively. The majority of the couples were engaged
(65%) and were predominately Caucasian and middle-class. The average time of
acquaintance was 2½ years, and 41% of the couples were cohabiting.   The
couples were recruited through community wide publicity (newspaper and radio)
that requested those who were planning to marry to participate in a study of
relationship development.   The study consisted of five phases: preassessment
(Time 1), intervention, postassessment (Time 2), 1½-year follow-up (Time 3),
and 3-year follow-up (Time 4).

In the preassessment phase, couples participated in two laboratory sessions
during which they were interviewed, completed questionnaires, and completed
two interactional tasks. Following the second preassessment session, couples
assigned to the intervention group were invited to participate in a preventive
intervention program. The program was offered to 85 of the 135 couples; 33
(39%) completed the program, 43 (51%) declined the program, and 9 (11%)
partially completed the program. The authors report that the goal of the PREP
intervention program is to modify or enhance dimensions of couples'
relationships (i.e., communication and problem-solving skills) that have been
linked to effective marital functioning. The program is "future-oriented" and
involves five meetings that last about 3 hours each.

Approximately 8 weeks after the preassessment phase, all of the couples
participated in a postassessment session. Similar to the preassessment session,
couples again completed questionnaires and engaged in another series of
problem-solving interactions. About 1½ years later, couples participated in the
first follow-up session. This session was similar to the postassessment session.
Finally, 1½ years after the first follow-up (3 years after preassessment), couples
participated in a second similarly structured follow-up session.

Results and Implications

The results provided evidence that, taken together, all of the predictor variables accounted for approximately 45% of the variance in Time 3, and 34% in Time 4 relationship quality. A finding that contrasted with Markman's earlier studies was that communication ratings were found to be an increasingly strong predictor of future relationship satisfaction. The results also suggested that Time 1 psychological adjustment scores accounted for 20% of the variance in relationship quality at Time 4. More specifically, males' psychological stability had a greater effect on relationship satisfaction than did the females'. Males' subscale scores on psychological stability at Time 1 negatively predicted relationship satisfaction at Time 4. The subscale of depression showed a moderate and significant negative relationship for both men and women in concurrent as well as future relationship satisfaction. In fact, for males, depression was more strongly related to relationship satisfaction than any other psychological adjustment subscale. Another finding was that relationship satisfaction appeared to predict later psychological adjustment for males, whereas level of premarital relationship seemed to be a better predictor for females.

Wamboldt and Reiss (1989)

Purpose and Theoretical Perspective

In 1989, Wamboldt and Reiss published a study entitled "Defining a Family Heritage and a New Relationship Identity: Two Central Tasks in the Making of a Marriage." This article is notable because it contains both an extensive review of 12 longitudinal premarital prediction studies and presents research findings that are grounded in a unique theoretical perspective, compared with others in this area of study. The results of this article's literature review are presented at the end of this appendix with the other reviews that have been done of premarital prediction research. In general terms, Wamboldt and Reiss set out to "track down the etiology of marital success and failure" (p. 321). They set out to do this by interpreting their results according to two prominent models within family theory: a socialization model and a social constructivist/developmental model. The primary goal of this study was to investigate possible linkages between family background and couple interactional processes as they relate to later marital quality.

Participants and Methods

This study employed a two-stage, longitudinal design to follow couples from premarital engagement (Time 1) to a year follow-up session (Time 2). The study consisted of 6 premarital couples who considered themselves "seriously attached or engaged." The average ages of the participants were 25.2 years for females and 25.3 years for males. The mean number of years of completed education was 15.1 for males and 16.2 for females. The majority of the individuals in the sample were Caucasian (75%). Fourteen of the subjects were Protestant, 7 Catholic, 5 Jewish, and 6 reported no religious preference.

Both interviews and questionnaires were used to gather data about several potential predictors of marital satisfaction, including: background characteristics, family-of-origin relationship characteristics, couple consensus about interpersonal relationships, and consensus concerning their families of origin. Unlike other studies measuring couple communication processes, this study investigated couple interaction *indirectly* through measuring couple consensus and agreement about relationships.

Results and Implications

One of the findings of this study was that family-of-origin environment predicted relationship satisfaction for the couples, with some gender differences. For example, high expressiveness in females' family of origin led to later marital satisfaction for the female $r = .76$, $p < .001$). In addition, it was found that higher conflict in the woman's family of origin led to decreased marital satisfaction for the man $r = -.69$, $p < .01$). The results also provide evidence that the man's family of origin influences later marital satisfaction. Relationship satisfaction decreased for both partners if the man experienced low expressiveness and high control in his family while growing up. Wamboldt and Reiss explained that "greater expressiveness in both partners' families of origin predicted greater relationship satisfaction for women, while greater conflict, especially in the women's origin families, predicted poorer relationship satisfaction for males" (p. 326).

The agreement variables used to index early consensus-building processes also proved to be predictive of later marital satisfaction. Once again, gender differences were found. Women who have greater agreement with their partners about general relationship ground rules reported higher levels of relationship satisfaction $r = .75$, $p < .001$), while men who reported greater agreement with their partners concerning the environment of her family of origin reported greater relationship satisfaction $r = .68$, $p < .01$). Interestingly, greater consensus concerning the males' families of origin predicted lesser relationship satisfaction in the couples' concurrent relationship. In reviewing the intercorre-lations of these variables, Wamboldt and Reiss conclude that "the females' families of origin are especially important during early marital development" (p. 327).

In discussing their results, the authors concluded that their study gives partial support for the socialization perspective that holds that "socialization of good communication practices is a primary mode of family-of-origin influence on later marital success/failure" (p. 329). However, they also concluded that because the constructivist/developmental model provides a "clear explanation about the mediation of the effects between past family environment and agreement concerning the origin families" (p. 331), it surpasses the socialization model in its explanation of the etiology of marital success and failure.

Longitudinal Studies in which Premarital Data Were Collected Retrospectively

In this section longitudinal studies are reviewed in which the premarital data were collected retrospectively, after the couples were married.

Bentler and Newcomb (1978)

Purpose and Theoretical Perspective

A study conducted by Bentler and Newcomb (1978) focused on the influence of personality traits and background characteristics on marital satisfaction and stability. This study was primarily guided by psychological and trait theories and set out to test the hypotheses that the level of similarity partners have on personality traits and background items would be predictive of later marital success.

Participants and Methods

For this study, newly married couples completed questionnaires that measured personality and background, and 4 years later, the same couples completed a marital adjustment inventory (Marital Adjustment Scale; Locke & Wallace, 1959). The original sample consisted of 162 newly married couples and 77 (53 intact; 24 separated/divorced) of these couples were reached for the follow-up study. The couples resided in Los Angeles, were primarily Caucasian, and their religious choices were split between "none" and Protestant. The mean average age of the males was 27 years and that of the females was 24 years. The mean educational attainment was "some college," ranging from eighth grade to doctoral level for the men and eighth grade to master's level for the women. The mean length of acquaintance before marriage was 2 years, and 12% were never engaged; for those who were engaged the mean length of engagement was 5 months.

Results and Implications

In general terms, this study found some support for the idea that similarity of personality traits between marital partners, assessed at the beginning of marriage, is evidenced to a greater degree in marriages that turn out successfully than for marriages that terminate in separation or divorce. The authors reported that "correlational similarity between marital partners, based on personality traits measured at the beginning of a marriage was substantially higher for couples who remained together after 4 years than couples who decided to end their marriage within that period of time. This pattern was also found for background or demographic variables" (p. 1065).

This study also found that females with higher marital adjustment were more clothes-conscious, more objective, more stable, less ambitious, less interested in art, and less intelligent than those with lower marital adjustment. Personality variables were found to be much more predictive of marital adjustment than were the background variables. Furthermore, the majority of significant predictor variables were from the women's data, providing evidence that women's variables influence marital success more than men's.

Kelly, Huston, and Cate (1985)

Purpose and Theoretical Perspective

In an article entitled, "Premarital Relationship Correlates of the Erosion of Satisfaction in Marriage," Kelly et al. (1985) detailed the results of a longitudinal study designed to examine "the connection between the way in which partners relate to and feel about each other before marriage and their feelings after they have been married" (p. 167). More specifically, the authors noted that they sought to "examine several dimensions that have been found to describe and differentiate premarital relationships and their changes as partners become more committed to marriage" (p. 169). Specifically, this study focused on "the connection between love, maintenance, conflict and ambivalence" (p. 169) in premarital relationships and later marital satisfaction and adjustment. Although no theoretical perspective is explicitly noted in this study, it is evident that the authors drew much of their focus from previous empirical work (i.e., Braiker & Kelly, 1979; Markman, 1979, 1981).

Participants and Methods

In previous research, Kelly and her colleagues (Braiker & Kelly, 1979) conducted extensive retrospective interviews with 50 newlywed couples about the courtship period of their relationships. In particular, couples were asked to provide detailed reports of their relationship histories and were asked to break their courtship down into three phases—casual dating, serious dating, and commitment to marriage. After locating each of these phases on a time line, couples were asked to fill out the Braiker and Kelly (1979) scales, using each of the phases as a frame of reference. From these data, Kelly and her colleagues (Braiker & Kelly, 1979) found four relationship dimensions that they believe to be important indicators of change in relationships during courtship and early marriage. Specifically, these four dimensions were: (1) *love* for the partner, (2) *conflict* and negativity, (3) *ambivalence* about whether to continue the relationship, and (4) *maintenance activities* such as self-disclosure, efforts to solve problems, and attempts by partners to change themselves or their partners. From these results, the authors "reasoned that these particular dimensions might be predictive of the ways in which marital relationships evolve out of courtship" (p. 169).

Building on this previous work, Kelly et al. (1985) used a two-stage design to investigate how these four relationship dimensions, as reported for three periods of premarital relationships (casual dating, serious dating, commitment to marriage), are connected with later marital satisfaction and adjustment. Two years following the original study (Braiker & Kelly, 1979), couples were sent follow-up questionnaires containing the Braiker and Kelly Relationship Questionnaire and the Dyadic Adjustment Scale (DAS, Spanier, 1976).

Of the 50 couples who participated in the first phase of data collection, 21 of the couples completed and returned the follow-up questionnaire. All of these couples had been originally contacted through marriage license records from Centre County, Pennsylvania. In comparison with the couples who did not respond to the request for follow-up data, the sample for this study was higher in the self-reported dimensions thought to be favorable indicators of marital success (i.e., love and maintenance) and somewhat lower on those viewed as negative (i.e., conflict, ambivalence). No information was reported about the ages, length of marriage, the socioeconomic situations, or racial composition of the sample.

Results and Implications

This study found that couples who experienced conflict premaritally continued to fight after marriage. Similarly, the higher the level of conflict premaritally, especially when the couple was committed to marrying, the lower were the "love" and the satisfaction of the wife at the follow-up. For the husband, premarital conflict was also found to lower his marital satisfaction 2½ years later. The level of premarital love and ambivalence were basically unrelated to later marital experience. Unlike love and ambivalence, the characteristics of conflict and maintenance were predictors of subjective and interpersonal qualities of marriage.

Another finding was that the presence of premarital conflict did not influence the couples feelings about each other prior to marriage. This was probably related to the fact that, premaritally, the couples not only experienced conflict but also engaged in maintenance activities such as problem solving. However, after marriage it appears that the conflict continued, but the maintenance activities decreased. Also, high levels of relationship maintenance were associated with love in early as well as in later stages of the relationship.

Cross-sectional Retrospective Studies with Marital Quality Outcomes

As we mentioned at the first of this review, there are some cross-sectional studies that have been done that are relevant to the subject matter at hand. Although these studies are retrospective, and not longitudinal in design, they provide meaningful and important results that we feel may assist future investigations in the premarital/marital prediction arena. The studies are arranged chronologically and are reviewed in a shortened format. Also of note, because of the cross-sectional design of these studies, they were not included in the table in Table 8.1.

Burgess and Cottrell (1939)

The research initiated by Ernest W. Burgess and Leonard S. Cottrell in the early 1930s was the first explicitly designed to "test the feasibility of predicting success or failure in marriage" (Burgess & Wallin, 1953, p. 36). In their book that summarizes this research, entitled *Predicting Success or Failure in Marriage*, Burgess and Cottrell (1939) attempted to identify premarital background items that predict later marital adjustment scores of couples. Using a sample of 526 couples, the authors correlated each background item for the husband and wife with their current marital adjustment score.

The following conclusions were made based on the results of the study. First, the greater the educational level (especially for the wife) at the time of marriage, the greater were the chances that the marital adjustment score was high. Second, individuals (especially the husband) who had membership in social groups were found to have greater potential for higher marital adjustment. Third, happy marriages of the participants' parents were positively correlated with happiness of the marriage of their children. Fourth, close relationships with mother and father and a lack of conflict in the family of origin were also positively correlated with the child's adjustment in marriage. Fifth, participating in religious activity such as duration and frequency of attending Sunday school and church was significantly associated with marital adjustment. Finally, number and gender of friends, participation in social organizations, and residence in neighborhoods of single-family dwellings were also found to be related to greater marital adjustment.

Roscoe and Benaske (1985)

In 1985, Roscoe and Benaske (1985) published an article on courtship violence and later spouse abuse. The subjects were 82 married women who were clients at domestic violence centers across the state of Michigan. The findings indicated that of the 82 women, 29% had been physically maltreated as children in their family of origin. Additionally, married women who sought assistance at the domestic violence centers had experienced a similar pattern of violence in their dating histories. Furthermore, the forms and frequencies of violence the women experienced in marriage corresponded closely to that which they experienced in dating. Finally, the study concluded that many (30%) of the premarital couples for whom physical abuse occurred actually continued in their relationship and married, and 53% of the victims remained in the relationship with the perpetrator. From these findings, the authors concluded that there are similarities between violence in dating and marital relationships and that "to understand domestic violence it may be more advantageous to study courtship violence than violence in the family of origin" (p. 424).

Grover, Russell, Schumm, and Paff-Bergen (1985)

In a study entitled "Mate Selection Processes and Marital Satisfaction," Grover, Russell, Schumm, and Paff-Bergen (1985) focused on the length of time couples dated prior to marriage and its possible correlation with later marital satisfaction. Specifically, two hypotheses were analyzed: (1) that length of time spent dating, prior to engagement, would positively correlate with marital satisfaction, and (2) that couples who "survived" a breakup during their dating history would report higher levels of marital satisfaction.

The study found that couples who had dated for more than 2 years prior to their engagement scored consistently high on marital satisfaction, whereas couples who dated less than 2 years experienced a wide range of scores in marital satisfaction from very high to very low. Support for the second hypothesis was not found in that the data did not support the idea that couples who experience a breakup in their premarital relationship experience higher marital satisfaction later on.

Wilcoxon and Hovestadt (1985)

Wilcoxon and Hovestadt (1985) conducted a study focusing on the relationship between family-of-origin experiences and marital adjustment. Their study was based on the premise that couples who share similar family-of-origin experiences are more likely to report greater marital adjustment. Using a sample of 20 couples, this study compared participants' reports of family-of-origin experiences with concurrent levels of relationship adjustment as measured by the Dyadic Adjustment Scale (Spanier, 1976). The findings of this study suggested that the degree of similarity in family-of-origin experiences in couples is strongly correlated with marital satisfaction. This finding especially held true for couples who were in the early years of marriage. In other words, the more family-of-origin similarity, the less struggle couples experienced in the form of "yours or mine" in reference to modeling their respective families of origin and subsequently the more couples reported greater marital satisfaction and longevity.

Couillard (1990)

Couillard (1990) studied the connection of levels of emotional health in the family of origin on differences in marital adjustment. The results indicated that husbands and wives reported more marital adjustment when both partners came from families with medium or high levels of emotional health. Furthermore, similarity in levels of emotional health in family of origin proved to be advantageous for couples except those wherein both partners came from families with low levels of emotional health. Additionally, wives with the greatest marital adjustment reportedly came from families with high levels of emotional health, regardless of the level of emotional health of the family of origin of the husbands. Moreover, wives who were the least adjusted in their marriages came from families of origin with low levels of emotional health, again independent of the husbands' family-of-origin emotional health, be it high or low. However, it appears from the findings that husbands' marital adjustment was affected from the wives' family-of-origin emotional health, such that the lower the wives' family-of-origin emotional health scores, the lower the husbands' marital adjustment.

Whyte (1990)

In Whyte's (1990) book, *Dating, Mating, and Marriage,* several predictors of marital quality were analyzed. Whyte found that marrying young, degree of conflict in family of origin, black respondent, wife liberal attitude, and wife managing her earnings negatively influenced marital quality. Whyte also found premarital love feelings, shared habits and traits, shared family values, shared leisure activities, frequency of joint social life, and ties to husband's kin, positively related to marital quality.

Reviews of Research

This section summarizes the reviews of research that have been completed in the area of predictors of marital quality and stability in the last 20 years. Due to the attention these reviews received elsewhere in this book, our review of them here is purposefully brief. Our purpose in listing them here is to make the reader aware of them and to note their particular "categorization of variables" as they pertain to marital prediction research.

Lewis and Spanier (1979)

In a chapter in the landmark edited text, *Contemporary Theories About the Family* (Burr, Hill, Nye, & Reiss, 1979), Lewis and Spanier identified 25 propositions concerning the relationship between premarital factors and marital quality. These propositions were then categorized into five main areas: (1) homogamy, (2)resources, (3) parental models, (4) support from significant others, and (5) independent first-order propositions (conventionality, premarital sexual behavior, premarital pregnancy, and internal/external pressures). The 25 propositions listed drew heavily from the work of Burr (1973) and were listed in an attempt to detail the process of "inductive theory building to better understand the complex interrelationship between a host of variables which are purported to be related to the quality and stability of marriage" (p. 268).

Wamboldt and Reiss (1989)

As noted earlier in the review, Wamboldt and Reiss (1989) published an article designed to investigate "the roles of family of origin environmental characteristics and couple building process within the development of marital relationships" (p. 317). In preparation for their study, the authors conducted a thorough review of 12 longitudinal studies of marital success/failure and categorized their review under three main headings: background factors, personality characteristics, and interactional processes. From their review, Wamboldt and Reiss concluded that couple interactional processes have been found to be the best predictors of later marital outcome (explaining 35 to 65% of the variance), while background factors have been found to explain between 15 and 30% and personality characteristics between 25 and 50% of the variance in later marital success and failure.

Cate and Lloyd (1992)

In their book entitled *Courtship,* Cate and Lloyd (1992) presented another review of the literature of premarital predictors of later marital quality. In a format similar to that of Wamboldt and Reiss (1989), the authors organized their review of significant variables into areas of background factors, personality factors, and dyadic characteristics.

Larson and Holman (1994)

In 1994, Larson and Holman published a comprehensive review of the literature in an article entitled "Premarital Predictors of Marital Quality and Stability." Similar to other reviews, this article organized the existing research into three main headings: (1) Background and Contextual Factors, (2) Individual Traits and Behavior, and (3) Couple Interactional Processes. However, this review differed from previous reviews in two ways. First, the authors subsumed all of the factors under the rubric of an explicit theoretical framework—the ecological (ecosystemic) framework. Second, Larson and Holman incorporated application into their review by providing recommendations for future research and implications for family life education and premarital counseling. In this text, Holman and his associates (Chapter 1 of this volume) have expanded this categorization of variables by adding a fourth major category, "Current Social Contexts," as a separate conceptual domain.

Karney and Bradbury (1995)

These scholars reviewed 115 longitudinal studies of marriage development. Included in these 115 studies were all the premarital to marital longitudinal studies we reviewed in this book.. Using behaviorial theory, stress theory, and attachment theory they suggest three factors that effect marital quality. These are (1) enduring vulnerabilities (to include socioeconomic factors, family background, and personality), (2) stressful events (to include life events and circumstances), and (3) adaptive processes (to include behavioral exchanges, and ability to resolve conflict and transitions).

References

Abbott, P. (1981). *The family on trial: Special relationships in modern political thought.* University Park, PA: Pennsylvania State University Press.

Acitelli, L. K., Douvan, E., & Veroff, J. (1993). Perceptions of conflict in the first year of marriage: How important are similarity and understanding? *Journal of Social and Personal Relationships, 10,* 5–19.

Acock, A. C. & Demo, D. H. (1994). *Family diversity and well-being.* Thousand Oaks, CA: Sage.

Adams, B. N. (1979). Mate selection in the United States: A theoretical summarization. In W. R. Burr, R. Hill, F. I. Nye, & I. L. Reiss (Eds.) *Contemporary theories about the family* (Vol. 1, pp. 259–267). New York: Free Press.

Adams, C. R. (1946). The prediction of adjustment in marriage. *Educational and Psychological Measurement, 6,* 185–193.

Adams, C. R., & Lepley, W. M. (1945). *The Personal Audit.* Form LL. Chicago: Science Research Associates.

Adler, M. J. (Ed.), (1952). *Great books of the western world: The great ideas* (Vol. 2). Chicago: Encyclopedia Britannica, Inc.

Albrecht, S. L., Bahr, H. M., & Goodman, K. L. (1983). *Divorce and remarriage: Problems, adaptations, and adjustments.* Westport, CT: Greenwood Press.

Allan, G. (1993). Social structure and relationships. In S. Duck (Ed.), *Social context and relationships* (pp. 1–25). Newbury Park, CA: Sage.

Amato, P. R. (1994) Father–child relations, mother–child relations, and offspring psychological well-being in early adulthood. *Journal of Marriage and the Family, 56,* 1031–1042.

Amato, P. R. (1996). Explaining the intergenerational transmission of divorce. *Journal of Marriage and the Family, 58,* 628–640.

Amato, P. R. & Keith, B. (1991). Parental divorce and adult well-being: A meta-analysis. *Journal of Marriage and the Family, 53,* 43–58.

Andersen, P. A. (1993). Cognitive Schemata in Personal Relationships. In S. Duck (Ed.), *Individuals in relationships* (pp. 1–29). Newbury Park, CA: Sage Publications.

Antill, J. K. (1983). Sex role complimentarity versus similarity in married couples. *Journal of Personality and Social Psychology, 45,* 145–155.

Attridge, M., Berscheid, E., & Simpson, J. A. (1995). Predicting relationship stability from both partners versus one. *Journal of Personality and Social Psychology, 69 (2),* 254–268.

Auhagen, A. E. & Hinde, R. A. (1997). Individual characteristics and personal relationships. *Personal Relationships, 4,* 63–84.

Bahr, S. J., & Galligan, R. J. (1984). Teenage marriage and marital instability. *Youth and Society, 15,* 387–400.

Bartholomew, K. (1993). From childhood to adult relationships: Attachment theory and research. In S. Duck (Ed.) *Learning about relationships* (pp. 30–62). Thousand Oaks, CA: Sage.

Baucom, D. H., & Epstein, N. (1990). *Cognitive-behavioral marital therapy.* New York: Brunner/Mazel.

Beach, S. R. H. & O'Leary, K. D. (1993). Dysphoria and marital discord: Are dysphoric individuals at risk for marital maladjustment? *Journal of Marital and Family Therapy, 19,* 355–368.

Beck, A. T. (1996) *Beck Depression Inventory II.* San Antonio: Psychological Corporation.

Beck, A., Rush, A., Shaw, B., & Emery, G. (1979). *Cognitive therapy of depression.* New York: Guilford Press.

Bedrosian, R. C. & Bozicas, G. D. (1994). *Treating family of origin problems: A cognitive approach.* New York: Guilford.

Bellah, R. N., Madsen, R., Sullivan, W. M., Swidler, A., & Tipton, S. M. (1985). *Habits of the heart: Individualism and commitment in American life.* Berkeley, CA: University of California Press.

Bellah, R. N., Madsen, R., Sullivan, W. M., Swidler, A., & Tipton, S. M. (1991). *The good society.* New York: Vintage Books.

Belsky J., & Pensky, E. (1988). Development history, personality and family relationships: Toward an emergent family system. In R. A. Hinde, & J. Stevenson-Hinde (Eds.), *Relationships within families* (pp. 193–217). Oxford: Clarendon Press.

Bennet, L. A., Wolin, S. J., & McAvity, K. J. (1988). Family identity, ritual, and myth: A cultural perspective on life cycle transitions. In C. J. Falicov (Ed.), *Family transitions* (pp. 211–234). New York: Guilford.

Bennet, L. A., Wolin, S. J., Reiss, D., & Teitelbaum, M. A. (1987). Couples at risk for transmission of alcoholism: Protective influences. *Family Process, 26,* 111–129.

Bennett, N. G., Blanc, A. K., & Bloom, D. E. (1988). Commitment and the modern union: Assessing the link between premarital cohabitation and subsequent marital stability. *American Sociological Review, 53,* 127–138.

Benson, M., Larson, J. H., Wilson, S. M., & Demo, D. (1995). Family of origin influences on late adolescent romantic relationships. In D. Demo & A. Ambert (Eds.), *Parents and adolescents in changing families* (pp. 161–169). Minneapolis, MN: National Council on Family Relations.

Bentler, P. M., & Newcomb, M. D. (1978). Longitudinal study of success and failure. *Journal of Consulting and Clinical Psychology, 46,* 1053–1070.

Bernreuter, R. G. (1931). *The Personality Inventory.* Stanford University: Stanford University Press.

Berry, W. (1983). *Standing by words.* San Francisco, CA: North Point Press.

Billy, J. O. G., Landale, N. S., & McLaughlin, S. D. (1986). The effect of marital status at first birth on marital dissolution among adolescent mothers. *Demography, 23,* 329–349.

Birchler, G. R., Weiss, R. L., & Vincent, J. P. (1975). Multimethod analysis of social reinforcement exchange between maritally distressed and non-distressed spouse and stranger dyad. *Journal of Personality and Social Psychology, 31,* 349–360.

Birtchnell, J., & Kennard, J. (1984). Early and current factors associated with poor quality marriages. *Social Psychiatry, 19,* 31–40.

Blevins, W. (1993). *Your family, your self.* Oakland, CA: New Harbinger.
Bloomfield, H. (1983). *Making peace with your parents.* New York: Ballatine Books.

Booth, A., & Edwards, J. (1985). Age at marriage and marital instability. *Journal of Marriage and the Family, 47,* 67–75.

Booth, A. & Johnson, D. R. (1988). Premarital cohabitation and marital success. *Journal of Family Issues, 9,* 225–272.

Booth, A., Johnson, D. R., & Edwards, J. N. (1983). Measuring marital instability. *Journal of Marriage and the Family, 45,* 387–394.

Booth, A., Johnson, D. R., White, L. K., & Edwards, J. N. (1986). Divorce and marital instability over the life course. *Journal of Family Issues, 7,* 421–442.

Bowen, M. (1978). *Family therapy in clinical practice.* New York: Aronson.

Bowerman, C. E. (1964). Prediction studies. In H. T. Christensen (Ed.), *Handbook of marriage and the family* (pp. 215–246). Chicago: Rand McNally.

Bowlby, J. (1977). The making and breaking of affectional bonds: I. Aetiology and psychopathology in light of attachment theory. *British journal of psychiatry, 130,* 201–210.

Bowlby, J. (1988). *A secure base: Parent–child attachment and healthy human development.* New York: Basic Books.

Bradbury, T. N. (1995). Assessing the four fundamental domains of marriage. *Family Relations, 44,* 459–468.

Bradbury, T. N., & Fincham, F. D. (1991). A contextual model for advancing the study of marital interaction. In G. J. O. Fletcher & F. D. Fincham (Eds.), *Cognition in close relationship* (pp. 127–147). Hillsdale, NJ: Erlbaum.

Braiker, H. & Kelly, H. H. (1979). Conflict in the development of close relationships. In R. L. Burgess & T. L. Huston (Eds.). *Social exchange in developing relationships* (pp. 135–168). New York: Academic Press.

Brennan, K. A., Shaver, P. R., & Tobey, A. E. (1991). Attachment styles, gender, and parental problem drinking. *Journal of Social and Personal Relationships, 8,* 451–466.

Bretherton, I. (1993). Theoretical contributions from developmental psychology. In P. G. Boss, W. J. Doherty, R. LaRossa, W. R. Schumm, & S. K. Steinmetz (Eds.), *Sourcebook of family theories and methods* (pp. 275–297). New York: Plenum Press.

Bretherton, I. (1996). Internal working models of attachment relationships as related to resilient coping. In G. G. Noam & K. W. Fischer (Eds.), *Development and vulnerability in close relationships* (pp. 3–27). Mahwah, NJ: Lawrence Erlbaum Associates.

Bronfenbrenner, U. (1979). The ecology of human development. Cambridge, MA: Harvard University Press.

Brooks, K. R. (1988). *The influence of premarital factors of homogamy, actual similarity, love, perceived similarity, and quality of communication on marital satisfaction.* Unpublished doctoral dissertation, Brigham Young University, Provo.

Brothers, J. (1997). Why we love who we love. *Reader's Digest, 150,* March, 161–166.

Bubolz, M. M., & Sontag, M. S. (1993). Human ecology theory. In P. G. Boss, W. J. Doherty, W. R. Schumm, & S. K. Steinmetz (Eds.), *Sourcebook of family theories and methods* (pp. 419–448). New York: Plenum.

Burgess, E. W. & Cottrell, L. S. (1939). *Predicting success or failure in marriage.* New York: Prentice-Hall Inc.

Burgess, E. W., Locke, H. J., & Thomes, M. M. (1971). *The family: From traditional to companionship.* New York: Van Nostrand-Reinhold.

Burgess, E. W. & Wallin, P. (1953). *Engagement and marriage.* New York: Lippincott.

Burns, D. D. (1980). *Feeling good: The new mood therapy.* New York: Signet.

Burr, W. R. (1973). *Theory construction and the sociology of the family.* New York: Wiley.

Burr, W. R. (1976). *Successful marriage: A principles approach.* Homewoor, IL: The Dorsey Press.

Burr, W. R., Hill, R., Nye, F. I., & Reiss, I. L. (1979). *Contemporary theories about the family* (Vol 1, pp. 268–294). New York: Free Press.

Burr, W. R., Jensen, M. R., & Brady, L. G. (1977). A principles approach in family life education. *The Family Coordinator, 26 (3),* 225–234.

Burr, W. R., Klein, S. R. (1994). *Reexamining family stress.* Thousand Oaks, CA: Sage.

Burr, W. R., Leigh, G. K., Day, R., & Constantine, J. (1979). Symbolic interaction and the family. In W. R. Burr, R. Hill, F. I. Nye, & I. L. Reiss (Eds.), *Contemporary theories about the family* (Vol. 2, pp. 42–111). New York: Free Press.

Burr, W. R., Mead, D. E., & Rollins, B. C. (1973). A model for the application of research findings by the educator and counselor: Research to theory to practice. *The Family Coordinator, 22 (3),* 285–290.

Burr, W. R., Yorgason, B. G., & Baker, T. R. (1979). *Marital inventories for LDS couples.* Provo, UT: Brigham Young University.

Butcher, J. N., Dahlstrom, W. G., Graham, J. R., Tellegen, A., & Kaemmer, B. (1989). *Minnesota Multiphase Personality Inventory-2: Manual for administration and scoring.* Minneapolis: University of Minnesota.

Byrne, D. (1997). An overview (and underview) of research and theory within the attraction paradigm. *Journal of Social and Personal Relationships, 14,* 3, 417–431.

Canary, D. J. & Emmers-Sommer, T. M. (1997). *Sex and gender differences in personal relationships.* New York: Guilford.

Cate, R. M., Huston, T. L., & Nesselroade, J. R. (1986). Premarital relationships: Toward the identification of alternative pathways to marriage. *Journal of Social and Clinical Psychology, 4,* 3–22.

Cate, R. M., & Lloyd, S. A. (1992). *Courtship.* California: Sage Publications, Inc.

Cohen, J. (1960). A coefficient of agreement for nominal scales. *Educational and Psycological Measurement, 20,* 37–46.

Collins, N. L. & Read, S. J. (1990). Adult attachment, working models, and relationship quality in dating couples. *Journal of Personality and Social Psychology, 58,* 644–663.

Costa, P. T., & McCrae, R. R. (1992). *Revised NEO Personality Inventory.* Odessa, FL.: Pyschological Assessment Resources (1-800-331-8378).

Couillard, G. (1990). *Differences in marital adjustment among couples with similar and dissimilar levels of emotional health in their family of origin.* Unpublished doctoral dissertation, Brigham Young University, Provo, UT.

Cromwell, R. E., Olson, D. H. L. & Fournier, D. G. (1976). Diagnosis and evaluation in marital and family counseling. In D. H. Olson (Ed.), *Treating relationships* (pp. 517–564). Lake Mills, LA: Graphic Publishing.

Derogatis, L. (1983). *Symptom checklist 90-R: Administration, scoring and procedures manual.* Towson, MD: Clinical Psychometric Research.

Dillman, D. A. (1978). *Mail and telephone surveys: The total method.* New York: John Wiley & Sons.

Dindia, K. (1994). The intrapersonal-interpersonal dialectical process of self-disclosure. In S. Duck (Ed.), *Dynamics of relationships* (pp. 27–57). Thousand Oaks, CA: Sage Publications.

Doherty, W. J. & Baptiste, D. A. (1993). Theories from family therapy. In P. G. Boss, W. J. Doherty, R. Larossa, W. R. Schumm, & S. K. Steinmetz (Eds.), *Sourcebook of family theories and methods: A contextual approach* (pp. 505–524). New York: Plenum Press.

Doherty, W. J., & Campbell, T. L. (1988). *Families and health.* Newbury Park, CA: Sage.

Doxey, C. (1994). *Creating couple identity in the transition to marriage.* Unpublished doctoral dissertation, Brigham Young University, Provo, UT.

Duck, S. (Ed.). (1993). *Social context and relationships.* Newbury Park, CA: Sage.

Duck, S. (1994). *Meaningful relationships.* Thousand Oaks, CA: Sage.

Easterbrook, M. A., & Embe, R. N. (1988). Marital and parent–child relationships: The role of affect in the family system. In R. A. Hinde & J. Stevenson-Hinde (Eds.), *Relationships within families* (pp. 83–103). Oxford: Clarendon Press.

Eidelson, R. J., & Epstein, N. (1982). Cognition and relationship maladjustment: Development of a measure of relationship beliefs. *Journal of Consulting and Clinical Psychology, 50,* 715–720.

Ell, K., & Northen, H. (1990). *Families and health care.* New York: Aldine de Gruyter.

Elshtain, J. B. (Ed.). (1982). *The family in political thought.* Amherst, MA: The University of Massachusetts Press.

Elshtain, J. B. (1990). Conclusion: III. The family in a time of trouble. In D. Blankenhorn, S. Bayme, and J. B. Elshtain (Eds.), *Rebuilding the nest: A new commitment to the American family* (pp. 258–261). Milwaukee, WI: Family Service America.

Epstein, N. (1992). Cognitive therapy with couples. *American Journal of Family Therapy, 10,* 5–16.

Etzioni, A. (1993). *The spirit of community, rights, responsibilities, and the communitarian agenda.* New York: Crown Publishers, Inc.

Etzioni, A. (1996). *The new golden role.* New York: Basic Books.

Falk, R. F. & Miller, N. B. (1992). A soft models approach to family transitions. In P. A. Cowan and E. M. Hetherington (Eds.), *Family transitions* (pp. 273–301). Hillsdale, NJ: Lawrence Erlbaum Associates.

Feeney, J. A., & Noller, P. (1990). Attachment style as a predictor of adult romantic relationships. *Journal of Personality and Social Psychology, 58,* 281–291.

Felmlee, D., Sprecher, S., & Bassin, E. (1990). The dissolution of intimate relationships: A hazard model. *Social Psychology Quarterly, 53, 1,* 13–30.

Filsinger, E. E. (1983). Choices A machine-aided marital observation technique: The Dyadic Interaction Scoring Code. *Journal of Marriage and the Family, 45,* 623–632.

Filsinger, E. E., & Thoma, S. J. (1988). Behavioral antecedents of relationship stability and adjustment: A 5-year longitudinal study. *Journal of Marriage and the Family, 50,* 785–795.

Fischer, K. W., & Ayoub, C. (1996). Analyzing development of working models of close relationships: Illustration with a case of vulnerability and violence. In G. G. Noam & K. W. Fischer (Eds.), *Development and vulnerability in close relationships* (pp. 135–172). Mahwah, NJ: Lawrence Erlbaum Associates.

Fitts, W. H. & Warren, W. L. (1996). *Tennessee Self-Concept Scale (2nd ed.).* Los Angeles, CA: Western Psychological Services.

Fornell, C. & Bookstein, F. L. (1982). A comparative analysis of two structural equation models: LISREL and PLS applied to market data. In C. Fornell (ed.) *A second generation of multivariate analysis* (pp. 289–324). New York: Praeger.

Fowers, B. J., Montel, K. H., & Olsen, D. H. (1996). Predicting marital success for premarital couple types based on PREPARE. *Journal of Marital and Family Therapy, 22,* 103–119.

Fowers, B. J., & Olson, D. H. (1986). Predicting marital success with PREPARE: A predictive validity study. *Journal of Marital and Family Therapy, 12,* 403–413.

Fowers, B. J., & Olson, D. H. (1992). Four types of premarital couples: An empirical typology based on PREPARE. *Journal of Family Psychology, 6,* 10–21.

Framo, J. L. (1976). Family-of-origin as a resource for adults in marital and family therapy. You can and should go home again. *Family Process, 15,* 193–210

Framo, J. L. (1981). The integration of marital therapy with sessions with family of origin. In A. S. Gurman & D. P. Kniskern (Eds.), *Handbook of family therapy.* (pp. 133–158). New York: Brunner/Mazel, Inc.

Framo, J. L. (1992). Family-of-origin therapy: An intergenerational approach. New York: Brunner/Mazel.

Franz, C. E., McClelland, D. C., & Weinberger, J. (1991). Childhood antecedents of conventional social accomplishment in midlife adults: A 36-year prospective study. *Journal of Personality and Social Psychology, 60,* 586–595.

Freud, S. (1940/1949). *An outline of psycho-analysis* (J. Strachey, Ed. and Trans.). New York: Norton.

Ganong, L. H., & Coleman, M. (1989). Preparing for remarriage: Anticipating the issues, seeking solutions. *Family Relations, 38,* 28–33.

Garbarino, J. (1982). *Children and families in the social environment.* New York: Aldine Publishing Company.

Giddens, A. (1991). *Modernity and self-identity.* Cambridge, UK: Polity Press.

Ginsberg, B. G. (1997). *Relationship enhancement family therapy.* New York: John Wiley & Sons.

Glenn, N. D., & Kramer, K. B. (1987). The marriages and divorces of the children of divorce. *Journal of Marriage and the Family, 49,* 811–825.

Glenn, N. D., & Supancic, M. (1984). The social and demographic correlates of divorce and separation in the United States: An update and reconsideration. *Journal of Marriage and the Family, 46,* 563–575.

Gottman, J. M. (1994a). *What predicts divorce?* Lawrence Erlbaum Associates, Publishers, Hillsdale, New Jersey: Lawrence Erlbaum Associates.

Gottman, J. M. (1994b). *Why marriages succeed or fail.* New York: Simon & Schuster.

Gottman, J. M., Coan, J., Carrere, S., & Swanson, C. (1998). Predicting marital happiness and stability from newlywed interactions. *Journal of Marriage and the Family, 60,* 5–22.

Gottman, J. M., & Krokoff, L. J. (1989). The relationship between marital interaction and marital satisfaction: A longitudinal view. *Journal of Consulting and Clinical Psychology, 57,* 47–52.

Gottman, J. M., Markman, H. J., & Notarius, C. I. (1977). The topography of marital conflict: A sequential analysis of verbal and nonverbal behavior. *Journal of Marriage and the Family, 39,* 461–477.

Gottman, J. M., Notarius, C. I., Markman, H. J., Bank, S., Yoppi, B., & Rubin, M. E. (1976). Behavior exchange theory and marital decision making. *Journal of Personality and Social Psychology, 34,* 14–34.

Greenberg, E. F., & Nay, W. R. (1982). The intergenerational transmission of marital instability reconsidered. *Journal of Marriage and the Family, 44,* 335–347.

Grover, K. J., Russell, C. S., Schumm, W. R., & Paff-Bergen, L. (1985). Mate selection processes and marital satisfaction. *Family Relations, 34,* 383–386.

Guba, E. G., & Lincoln, Y. S. (1994). Competing paradigms in qualitative research. In N. K. Denzin & Y. S. Lincoln (Eds.), *Handbook of qualitative research* (pp. 105–117). Thousand Oaks, CA: Sage.

Guilford, J. P. & Martin, H. G. *The Personnel Inventory I.* Beverly Hills: Sheridan Supply, 1943.

Hahlweg, K., Markman, H. J., Thurmaier, F., Engl, J., & Eckert, V. (1998). Prevention of marital distress: Results of a German prospective longitudinal study. *Journal of Family Psychology, 12,* 543–556.

Hamilton, G. V. (1929). *A research in marriage.* New York: A. & C. Boni.

Hazan, C., & Shaver, P. R. (1987). Romantic love conceptualized as an attachment process. *Journal of Personality and Social Psychology, 52,* 511–524.

Heaton, T. B., Goodman, K. L., & Holman, T. B. (1994). In search of a peculiar people: Are Mormon families really different? In M. Cornwall, T. B. Heaton, L. A. Young (Eds.), *Contemporary Mormonism* (pp. 87–117). Urbana, IL: University of Illinois Press.

Henry, W. A., III. (1990, April 9). Beyond the melting pot. Time, 135, 28–31.

Hill, C. T., Rubin, Z., & Peplau, L. A. (1976). Breakups before marriage: The end of 103 affairs. *Journal of Social Issues, 32 (1),* 147–168.

Hinckley, G. B. (1997). Look to the future. *Ensign, 27, November,* 67–69.

Holman, T. B. (1981). *A path analytic test of a model of early marital quality: The direct and indirect effects of premarital and marital factors.* Unpublished doctoral dissertation, Brigham Young University, Provo, UT.

Holman, T. B. (1996). Commitment making: Mate selection processes among active Mormon American couples. In D. Davies (Ed.), *Mormon identities in transition* (pp. 125–132). London: Cassell.

Holman, T. B., & Burr, W. R. (1980). Beyond the beyond: The growth of family theories in the 1970s. *Journal of Marriage and the Family, 42,* 729–741.

Holman, T. B., Busby, D. M., Doxey, C., Klein, D. M., & Loyer-Carlson, V. (1997). *Relationship Evaluation (RELATE).* Provo, UT: Marriage Study Consortium.

Holman, T. B., Busby, D. M., & Larson, J. H. (1989). *PREParation for marriage* [questionnaire]. Provo, UT: Brigham Young University.

Holman, T. B., Larson, J. H., & Harmer, S. L. (1994). The development and predictive validity of a new premarital assessment instrument: the PREParation for Marriage questionnaire. *Family Relations, 43,* 46–52.

Holman, T. B., & Li, B. D. (1997). Premarital factors influencing perceived readiness for marriage. *Journal of Family Issues, 18,* 124–144.

Holmes, T. H., & Rahe, R. H. (1967). The social readjustment scale. *Journal of Psychosomatic Research, 11,* 203–218.

Hood, A. B. & Johnson, R. W. (1997). *Assessment in counseling: A guide to the use of psychological assessment procedures.* Alexandria, VA: American Counseling Association

Hoopes, M. H. (1987). Multigenerational systems: Basic assumptions. *The American Journal of Family Therapy, 15,* 195–205.

Houseknecht, S. K., & Spanier, G. B. (1980). Marital disruption and higher education among women in the U. S. *Sociological Quarterly, 21,* 375–390.

Jacobson, N., & Addis, M. (1993). Research on couples and couple therapy: What do we know? Where are we going? *Journal of Consulting and Clinical Psychology, 61,* 85–93.

Janus, S. S., & Janus, C. C. (1993). *The Janus report on human sexuality.* New York: Wiley.

Joanning, H., Brewster, J., & Koval, J. (1984). *The Communication Rapid Assessment Scale*: Development of a behavioral index of communication quality. *Journal of Marital & Family Therapy, 10,* 409–417.

Johnson, M. P., & Milardo, R. M. (1984). Network interference in pair relationships: A social psychological recasting of Slater's theory of social regression. *Journal of Marriage and the Family, 46,* 893–899.

Jöreskog, K. G. & Sörbom, D. (1996) *LISREL 8: Structural equation modeling with the simplis command language* [computer software]. Scientific Software International, distributed by Hillsdale, NJ: Lawrence Erlbaum Associates.

Karney, B. R. & Bradbury, T. N. (1995). The longitudinal course of marital quality and stability: A review of theory, methods and research. *Psychological Bulletin, 18, 1,* 3-34.

Keeley, M. P. & Hart, A. J. (1994). Nonverbal behavior in dyadic interactions. In S. Duck (Ed.), *Dynamics of relationships* (pp. 135–162). Thousand Oaks, CA: Sage Publications.

Kelly, C., Huston, T. L., & Cate, R. M. (1985). Premarital relationship correlates of the erosion of satisfaction in marriage. *Journal of Social and Personal Relationships, 2,* 167–178.

Kelly, E. L. (1940). A 36-trait personality rating scale. *Journal of Psychology, 9,* 97–102.

Kelly, E. L. (1955). Consistency of adult personality. *American Psychologist, 10,* 654–681.

Kelly, E. L., & Conley, J. J. (1987). Personality and compatibility: A prospective analysis of marital stability and marital satisfaction. *Journal of Personality and Social Psychology, 58,* 27–40.

Kerckhoff, A. C., & Davis, K. E. (1962). Value consensus and need complementarity in mate selection. *American Sociological Review, 27,* 295–303.

Klein, D. M., & White, J. M. (1996). *Family theories: An introduction.* Thousand Oaks, CA: Sage.

Klein, R. & Milardo, R. M. (1993). Third-party influence on the management of personal relationships. In S. Duck (Ed.), *Social context and relationships* (pp. 55–77). Newbury Park, CA: Sage Publications.

Knapp, S. J. (1997). Knowledge claims in the family field. *Family Perspectives, 30, 4,* 369–428.

Koski, L. R., & Shaver, P. R. (1997). Attachment and relationship satisfaction across the lifespan. In R. J. Sternberg & M. Hojjaat (Eds.), *Satisfaction in close relationships* (pp. 26–55). New York: Guilford.

Krokoff, L. J. (1991). Communications orientation as a moderator between strong negative affect and marital satisfaction. *Behavior Assessment, 13,* 51–65.

Kurdek, L. A. (1991). Marital stability and changes in marital quality in newlywed couples: A test of the contextual model. *Journal of Social and Personal Relationships, 8,* 27–48.

Kurdek, L. A. (1993). Predicting marital dissolution: A 5-year prospective longitudinal study of newlywed couples. *Journal of Personality and Social Psychology, 64,* 221–242.

LaRossa, R. & Reitzes, D. C. (1993). Symbolic interactionism and family studies. In P. G. Boss, W. J. Doherty, R. LaRossa, W. R. Schumm, & S. K. Steinmetz (Eds.), Sourcebook of family theories and methods (p. 135–162). New York: Plenum.

Larsen, A. S., & Olson, D. H. (1989). Predicting marital satisfaction using PREPARE: A replication study. *Journal of Marital and Family Therapy, 15, 3,* 311–322.

Larson, J. H. (1988). The marriage quiz: College students' beliefs in selected myths about marriage. *Family Relations, 37,* 3–11.

Larson, J. H. (1992). "You're my one and only": Premarital counseling for unrealistic beliefs about mate selection. *American Journal of Family Therapy, 20,* 242–253.

Larson, J. H. (1998). *Comprehensive premarital assessment instruments: A user's guide.* Invited Research Update for Practitioners presented at the AAMFT Annual Conference, October, 1998, Dallas, TX.

Larson, J. H. (2000). *Should we stay together? A scientifically proven method for evaluating your relationship and improving its chances for long-term success.* San Francisco: Jossey-Bass.

Larson, J. H., & Holman, T. B. (1994). Premarital predictors of marital quality and stability: An applied literature review. *Family Relations, 43,* 228–237.

Larson, J. H., Harper, J. M., Wampler, K. S., & Sprenkle, D. H. (1995). *College/university supplement to couple communication instructor manual: Teaching couple communication in the classroom.* Littleton, CO: Interpersonal Communication Programs.

Larson, J. H., Holman, T. B., Klein, D. M., Busby, D. M., Stahmann, R. F., & Peterson, D. (1995). A review of comprehensive questionnaires used in premarital education and counseling. *Family Relations, 44,* 245–252.

Levinger, G. (1979). "A social exchange view on the dissolution of pair relationships." Pp 169–193 in Burgess, R. L. & Huston, T. L. (Eds.) *Social exchange in developing relationships* (pp. 169–193). New York: Academic Press.

Levinger, G. (1983). Development and change. In H. H. Kelly, E. Berscheid, A. Christensen, J. H. Harvey, T. L. Huston, G. Levinger, E. McClintock, L. A. Peplau, and D. R. Peterson. *Close relationships* (pp. 315–359). New York: W. H. Freeman.

Lewis, R. A., & Spanier, G. B. (1979). Theorizing about the quality and stability of marriage. In W. R. Burr, R. Hill, F. I. Nye, & I. L. Reiss (Eds.), *Contemporary theories about the family* (Vol. 1, pp. 268–294). New York: Free Press.

Linford, S. T. (1997). *A comprehensive literature review and empirical test of premarital predictors of marital quality.* Unpublished doctoral dissertation, Brigham Young University, Provo, UT.

Locke, H. J., & Wallace, K. M. (1959). Short marital-adjustment and prediction tests: Their reliability and validity. *Marriage and Family Living, 21,* 251–255.

Liu, J. H., Campbell, S. M., & Condie, H. (1995). Ethnocentrism in dating preferences for an American sample: The ingroup bias in social context. *European Journal of Social Psychology, 25,* 95–115.

Mace, D. R. (1983) The marriage enrichment movement. In D. R. Mace (Ed.), *Prevention in family services: Approaches to family wellness* (pp. 98–109). Beverly Hills: Sage.

Madsen, T. G. (1966). *Eternal man.* Salt Lake City, UT: Deseret Book Company.

Markey, B., & Micheletto, M. (1997). *Facilitating Open Couple Communication, Understanding and Study facilitator manual.* Omaha: Archdiocese of Omaha.

Markey, B., Micheletto, M., & Becker, A. (1997). Facilitating Open Couple Communication, Understanding, and Study (FOCCUS). Omaha Nebraska, Family Life Office, Archdiocese of Omaha.

Markman, H. J. (1979). The application of a behavioral model of marriage in predicting relationship satisfaction of couples planning marriage. *Journal of Consulting and Clinical Psychology, 47,* 743–749.

Markman, H. J. (1981). Prediction of marital distress: A 5-year follow up. *Journal of Consulting and Clinical Psychology, 49,* 760–762.

Markman, H. J. (1984). The longitudinal study of couples' interactions: Implications for understanding and predicting the development of marital distress. In K. Hahlweg & N. S. Jacobson (Eds.), *Marital interaction: Analysis and modification* (pp. 253–284). New York: Guilford.

Markman, H. J. (1991). Constructive marital conflict is NOT an oxymoron. *Behavioral Assessment, 13,* 83–96.

Markman, H. J., Duncan, S. S., Storaasli, R. D., & Howes, P. W. (1987). The prediction and prevention of marital distress: A longitudinal investigation. In Hahlweg, K. & Goldstein, M. (1987). *Understanding major mental disorder: The contribution of family interaction research* (pp. 266–289). New York, Family Process Inc.

Markman, H. J., & Notarius, C. I. (1987). Coding Marital and family in interaction: Current status. In T. Jacob (Ed.) *Family interaction and psychopathology: Theories methods, and findings* (pp. 329–390). New York: Plenum Press.

Markman, H. J., Stanley, S., & Blumberg, S. L. (1994). *Fighting for your marriage: Positive steps for preventing divorce and preserving a lasting love.* San Francisco, CA: Jossey-Bass.

Marks, S. R. (1986). *Three corners.* Lexington, MA: Lexington Books.

Martin, T. C., & Bumpass, L. L. (1989). Recent trends in marital disruption. *Demography, 26,* 37–51.

McLanahan, S., & Bumpass, L. (1988). Intergenerational consequences of family disruption. *American Journal of Sociology, 94,* 130–152.

Milardo, R. M. (1986). Personal choice and social constraint in close relationships: Applications of network analysis. In V. J. Derlega & B. A. Winstead (Eds.), *Friendship and social interaction* (pp. 145–166). New York: Springer-Verlag.

Milardo, R. M., & Wellman, B. (1992). The personal is social. *Journal of Social and Personal Relationships, 9,* 339–342.

Miller, J. B. (1993). Learning from early relationship experience. In S. Duck (Ed.), *Learning about relationships* (pp. 1–29). Thousand Oaks, CA: Sage.

Miller, S. & Miller, P. A. (1997). *Core communication: Skills & process.* Littleton, Co: Interpersonal Communication Programs.

Miller, S., Miller, P., Nunnally, E. W., & Wackman, D. B. (1992). *Couple communication instructor manual.* Littleton, CO: Interpersonal Communication Programs.

Miller, S. & Olson, D. H. (1998). *Great start.* Littleton, CO: Interpersonal Communication Programs.

Morgan, S. P., & Rindfuss, R. (1984). Marital disruption: Structural and temporal dimensions. *American Journal of Sociology, 90,* 1055–1077.

Mueller, C. W., & Pope, H. (1977). Marital instability: A study of its transmission between generations. *Journal of Marriage and the Family, 39,* 83–93.

Murstein, B. I. (1986). *Pathways to marriage.* Beverly Hills, CA: Sage.

Napier, A. Y. (1971). The marriage of families: Cross-generational complementarity. *Family Process, 10,* 373–395.

Napier, A. Y., & Whitaker, C. (1978). *The family crucible.* New York: Harper & Row.

Nelson, T. S., Heilbrun, G., & Figley, C. R. (1993). Basic family therapy skills, IV: Transgenerational theories of family therapy. *Journal of Marital and Family Therapy, 19,* 53–366.

Noam, G. G. (1996). Reconceptualizing maturity: The search for deeper meaning. In G. G. Noam & K. W. Fischer (Eds.), *Development and vulnerability in close relationships* (pp. 135–172). Mahwah, NJ: Lawrence Erlbaum Associates.

Noam, G. G., & Fischer, K. W. (1996). Introduction: The foundational role of relationships in human development. In G. G. Noam & K. W. Fischer (Eds.), *Development and vulnerability in close relationships* (pp. ix–xx). Mahwah, NJ: Lawrence Erlbaum Associates.

Olson, D. H. (1996). *PREPARE/ENRICH counselor's manual.* Minneapolis, MN: Life Innovations.

Olson, D. H., Fournier, D. G., & Druckman, J. H. (1986). *Counselor's manual for PREPARE-ENRICH* (rev. ed.). Minneapolis, MN: PREPARE-ENRICH, Inc.

Olson, D. H., Fournier, D. G., & Druckman, J. H. (1996). *PREPARE.* Minneapolis: Life Innovations (1-800-331-1661).

Oggins, J., Veroff, J., and Leber, D. (1993). Perceptions of marital interaction among black and white newlyweds. *Journal of Personality and Social Psychology, 65,* 494–511.

Orden, S. R. & Bradburn, N. M. (1968). Dimensions of marital happiness. *American Journal of Sociology, 73,* 715–731.

Overall, J. E., Henry, B. W., & Woodward, A. (1974). Dependence of marital problems on parental family history. *Journal of Abnormal Psychology, 83,* 446–450.

Papero, D. V. (1995). Bowen family systems and marriage. In N. S. Jacobson & A. S. Gurman (Eds.), *Clinical handbook of couple therapy* (pp. 11–30). New York: Guilford Press.

Parker, G. & Gladstone, G. L. (1996). Parental characteristics as influences on adjustment in adulthood. In G. R. Pierce, B. R. Sarason, & I. G. Sarason (Eds.), *Handbook of social support and the family* (pp. 195–218). New York: Plenum Press.

Parks, M. R., Stan, C. M., & Eggert, L. L. (1983). Romantic involvement and social network involvement. *Social Psychology Quarterly, 46,* 116–131.

Pierce, G. R., Sarason, B. R., Sarason, I. G., Joseph, H. J., & Henderson, C. A. (1996). Conceptualizing and assessing social support in the context of the family. In G. R. Pierce, B. R. Sarason, & I. G. Sarason (Eds.), *Handbook of social support and the family.* New York: Plenum Press.

Planalp, S. & Garvin-Doxas, K. (1994). Using mutual knowledge in conversations: Friends as experts on each other. In S. Duck (Ed.), *Dynamics of relationships* (pp. 1–26). Thousand Oaks, CA: Sage Publications.

Ponterotto, J. G., & Casas, J. M. (1991). Handbook of racial/ethnic minority counseling research. Springfield, IL: Charles C. Thomas.

Pope, H., & Mueller, C. W. (1976). The intergenerational transmission of marital instability: Comparisons by race and sex. *Journal of Social Issues, 32,* 49–66.

Popenoe, D., Elshtain, J. B., Blankenhorn, D. (Ed.). (1996). *Promises to keep: decline and renewal of marriage in America.* Lamham, MD: Rowman & Littlefield Publishers Inc.

Putallaz, M., Costanzo, P. R., & Klein, T. P. (1993). Parental childhood social experiences and their effects on children's relationships. In S. Duck (Ed.), *Learning about relationships* (pp. 63–97). Thousand Oaks, CA: Sage.

Raschke, H. J. (1987). Divorce. In M. B. Sussman, S. K. and Steinmetz (Eds.) *Handbook of marriage and the family* (pp. 468–489). New York: Free Press.

Raush, H. L., Greif, A. C., & Nugent, J. (1979). Communication in Couples and Families. In W. R. Burr, R. Hill, F. I. Nye, & I. L. Reiss (Eds.), *Contemporary issues about the family* (pp. 468–489. Macmillan Publishing Co., Inc. New York.

Renick, M. J., Blumberg, S. L., & Markman, H. J. (1992). The prevention and relationship enhancement program (PREP): An empirically based preventive intervention program for couples. *Family Relations, 41,* 141–147.

Rhoades, C. J. (1994). *A multivariate model of premarital predictors of marital quality and stability.* Unpublished doctoral dissertation, Brigham Young University, Provo, UT.

Rogers, R. H. & White, J. M. (1993). Family development theory. In P. G. Boss, W. J. Doherty, R. Larossa, W. R. Schumm, & S. K. Steinmetz (Eds.), *Sourcebook of family theories and methods: A contextual approach* (pp. 505–524). New York: Plenum Press.

Roscoe, B., & Benaske, N. (1985). Courtship violence experienced by abused wives: Similarities in patterns of abuse. *Family Relations, 34,* 419–424.

Rusbult, C. E. (1983). A longitudinal test of the investment model: The development (and deterioration) of satisfaction and commitment in heterosexual involvements. *Journal of Personality and Social Psychology, 45,* 101–117.

Russell, M. T. (1995). *Sixteen personality factor couples counseling report.* Champaign, IL: Institute for Personality and Ability Testing (217-352-4739).

Rutter, M. (1988). Functions and consequences of relationships: Some psychopathological considerations. In R. A. Hinde & J. Stevenson-Hinde (Eds.), *Relationships within families* (pp. 334–353). Oxford: Clarendon Press.

Sabatelli, R. M. (1984). The marital comparison level index: A measure for assessing outcomes relative to expectations. *Journal of Marriage and the Family, 46,* 651–662.

Sabatelli, R. M., & Shehan, C. L. (1993). Exchange and resource theories. In P. G. Boss, W. J. Doherty, R. LaRossa, W. R. Schumm, & S. K. Steinmetz (Eds.), *Sourcebook of family theories and methods* (pp. 385–411). New York: Plenum Press.

Sacher, J. A., & Fine, M. A. (1996). Predicting relationship status and satisfaction after six months among dating couples. *Journal of Marriage and the Family, 58,* 21–32.

Santrock, J. W., Minnett, A. M., & Campbell, B. D. (1994). *The authoritative guide to self-help books.* New York: Guilford.

Scanzoni, J., Polonko, K., Teachman, J. and Thompson, L. (1989). *The sexual bond.* Thousand Oaks, CA: Sage.

Schumacker, R. E., & Lomax, R. G. (1996). *A beginner's guide to structural equation modeling.* Mahwah, NJ: Lawrence Erlbaum Associates.

Shachar, R. (1991). His and her marital satisfaction: The double standard. *Sex Roles, 25* (7/8), 451–467.

Shaver, P. R., & Clark, C. L. (1996). Forms of adult romantic attachment and their cognitive and emotional underpinnings. In G. G. Noam, & K. W. Fischer (Eds.), *Development and vulnerability in close relationships* (pp. 29–58). Mahwah, NJ: Lawrence Erlbaum Associates.

Shaver, P. R., & Hazan, C. (1993). Adult romantic attachment theory and evidence. *Advances in Personal Relationships, 4,* 29–70.

Sher, T. G. & Weiss, R. L. (1991). Negativity in marital communication: Where's the beef? *Behavioral Assessment, 13,* 1–5.

Simons, R. L., & Associates (1996). *Understanding differences between divorced and intact families.* Thousand Oaks, CA: Sage.

Simpson, J. A. (1987). The dissolution of romantic relationships: Factors involved in relationship stability and emotional distress. *Journal of Personality and Social Psychology, 53, 4,* 683–692.

Skolnick, A. (1981). Married lives: Longitudinal perspectives on marriage. In D. H. Eichorn, J. A. Clausen, N. Haan, M. P. Honzik, & P. H. Mussen (Eds.), *Present and past in middle life* (pp. 269–298). New York: Academic Press.

Slife, B. D., & Williams, R. N. (1995). *What's behind the research?* Thousand Oaks, CA: Sage.

Smith, D. A., Vivian, D., & O'Leary, K. D. (1990). Longitudinal prediction of marital discord from premarital expressions of affect. *Journal of Consulting and Clinical Psychology, 58,* 790–800.

Smith, D. A., Vivian, D. & O'Leary, K. D. (1991). The misnomer proposition: A critical reappraisal of the longitudinal status of "negativity" in marital communication. *Behavioral Assessment, 13,* 7–24.

Spanier, G. B. (1976). Measuring dyadic adjustment: New scales for assessing the quality of marriage and similar dyads. *Journal of Marriage and the Family, 38,* 15–28.

Sprecher, S., & Felmlee, D. (1992). The influence of parents and friends on the quality and stability of romantic relationships: A three-wave longitudinal investigations. *Journal of Marriage and the Family, 54,* 888–900.

Stahmann, R. F., & Hiebert, W. J. (1997). *Premarital and remarital counseling: The professional's handbook.* San Francisco: Jossey-Bass Publishers.

Stanley, S. M., Markman, H. J., St. Peters, M., and Leber, B. D. (1995). Strengthening marriage and preventing divorce: New directions in prevention research. *Family Relations, 44,* 392–401.

Stein, C. H., Bush, E. G., Ross, R. R., & Ward, M. (1992). Mine, yours and ours: A configural analysis of the networks of married couples in relation to marital satisfaction and individual well-being. *Journal of Social and Personal Relationships, 9,* 365–383.

Strauss, A. (1946). The influence of parent-images upon marital choice. *American Sociological Review, 11,* 554–559.

Strong, E. K. (1927). *Vocational Interest Blank.* Stanford University: Stanford University Press.

Sue, D. W. (1991). Foreword. In J. G. Ponterotto, & J. M. Casas (Eds.), Handbook of racial/ethnic minority counseling research (pp. vii–ix). Springfield, IL: Charles C. Thomas.

Surra, C. A. (1990). Research and theory on mate selection and premarital relationships in the 1980s. *Journal of Marriage and the Family, 52,* 844–865.

Sweet, J. A., & Bumpass, L. L. (1988). *American families and households.* New York: Russell Sage Foundation.

Taylor, R. M. & Johnson, L. P. (1984). *Taylor-Johnson Temperament Analysis (TJTA).* Los Angeles, CA: Psychological Publications.

Teachman, J. D. (1983). Early marriage, premarital fertility, and marital dissolution. *Journal of Family Issues, 4,* 105–126.

Terman, L. M. (1938). *Psychological factors in marital happiness.* New York: McGraw-Hill.

Terman, L. M., & Oden, M. H. (1947). *Genetic studies of genius: Vol. 4. The gifted child grows up.* Stanford, CA: Stanford University Press.

Touliatos, J., Perlmutter, B. F., & Straus, M. A. (1990). *Handbook of family measurement techniques.* Newbury Park, CA: Sage.

Trost, J. (1964). Mate selection, marital adjustment, and symbolic environment. *Acta Sociologica, 8,* 27–35.

Vaillant, G. E. (1978). Natural history of male psychological health: VI. Correlates of successful marriage and fatherhood. *American Journal of Psychiatry, 135,* 653–659.

van Tilburg, T. (1997). There is more to the network than relationships. *International Society for the Study of Personal Relationships Bulletin, 13.* 2, 11–13.

Wamboldt, F. S., & Reiss, D. (1989). Defining a family heritage and a new relationship identity: Two central tasks in the making of a marriage. *Family Process, 28,* 317–335.

Warren, N. C. (1992). *Finding the love of your life.* Colorado Springs, CO: Focus on the Family Publishing.

Weiss, R. S. (1996). Continuities and transformations in social relationships from childhood to adulthood. In W. W. Hartup & Z. Rubin (Eds.), *Relationships and development* (pp. 95–110). Hillsdale, NJ: Lawrence Erlbaum Associates.

Weiss, R. L. & Heyman, R. E. (1990). Observation of marital interaction. In F. D. Fincham & T. N. Bradbury (Eds.), The psychology of marriage: Basic issues and applications (pp. 87–117). New York: Guilford Press.

Werner, C. M., Altman, I., Brown, B. B., & Ginat, J. (1993). Celebrations in personal relationships: A transactional/dialectical perspective. In S. Duck (Ed.), *Social context and relationships* (pp. 109–138). Newbury Park, CA: Sage.

White, J. (1987). Premarital cohabitation and marital stability in Canada. *Journal of Marriage and the Family, 49,* 641–647.

White, L. K. (1990). Determinants of divorce: A review of research in the eighties. *Journal of Marriage and the Family, 52,* 904–912.

White, S. G., & Hatcher, C. (1984). Couple complementarity and similarity: A review of the literature. *The American Journal of Family Therapy 12, 1,* 15–25.

Whyte, M. K. (1990). *Dating, mating, and marriage.* New York: Aldine de Gruyter.

Wilcoxson, S. A. (1989). Application of family-of-origin concepts by marital and family therapists: A qualitative study. *Family Therapy, 16,* 207–214.

Wilcoxon, S. A. & Hovestadt, A. J. (1985). Perceived similarity in family-of-origin experiences and dyadic adjustment: A comparison across years of marriage. *Family Therapy, 12,* 165–174

Wineberg, H. (1988). Duration between marriage and first birth and marital stability. *Social Biology, 35,* 91–102.

Wood, J. T. (1993). Engendered relations: Interaction, caring, power, and responsibility in intimacy. In S. Duck (Ed.), *Social context and relationships* (pp. 26–54). Newbury Park, CA: Sage Publications, Inc.

Yingling, L. C., Miller, W. E., McDonald, A. L. & Galewaler, S. T. (1998). GARF Assessment Sourcebook: Using the DSM-IV Global Assessment of Relational Functioning. Washington, D Brunner/Mazel.

Yorgason, B. G., Burr, W. R., Baker, T. R. (1980). *Marital Inventories* [questionnaire]. Provo, UT: Brigham Young University.

Index